Studies in Economic Ethics and Philosophy

Springer-Verlag Berlin Heidelberg GmbH

Peter Koslowski · Christoph Hubig
Peter Fischer
Editors

Business Ethics and the Electronic Economy

With 3 Figures
and 4 Tables

Springer

Alcatel SEL
Stiftung für
Kommunikations-
forschung

Professor Dr. Dr. h. c. Peter Koslowski
Department of Philosophy
Free University Amsterdam
De Boelelaan 1105
1081 HV Amsterdam, The Netherlands
E-mail: Peter.Koslowski@t-online.de
Website: www.fiph.de/koslowski

Editorial Assistant
Anna Maria Hauk M.A.
Wiss. Assistentin
Forschungsinstitut
für Philosophie Hannover
Gerberstraße 26
30169 Hannover, Germany
E-mail: hauk@fiph.de

Professor Dr. Christoph Hubig
Privatdozent Dr. habil. Peter Fischer
University of Stuttgart
Institute of Philosophy
Department of Theory of Science
and Philosophy of Technology
Seidenstraße 36
70174 Stuttgart, Germany
E-mail: peter.g.fischer@po.uni-stuttgart.de
Website: www.uni-stuttgart.de/wt

ISBN 978-3-642-06055-7 ISBN 978-3-662-06189-3 (eBook)
DOI 10.1007/978-3-662-06189-3

Cataloging-in-Publication Data applied for

A catalog record for this book is available from the Library of Congress.

Bibliographic information published by Die Deutsche Bibliothek
Die Deutsche Bibliothek lists this publication in the Deutsche Nationalbibliografie; detailed bibliographic data available in the internet at *http://dnb.ddb.de*

springeronline.com

Originally published by Springer-Verlag Berlin Heidelberg New York in 2004
Softcover reprint of the hardcover 1st edition 2004

Cover design: Erich Kirchner, Heidelberg

SPIN 11012498 42/3130 – 5 4 3 2 1 0 – Printed on acid-free paper

Preface

The internet and the electronic economy are a technological revolution whose secular importance is apparent. The internet eliminates the temporal and spatial constraints on the exchange of information. It changes deeply the world of production and of labour. It transforms the exchange relationships between producers and consumers as well as between the suppliers within the supply-chain. The electronic economy is able to generate more accurate consumer profiles and, therefore, a more powerful and effective marketing directed to the individual consumer. There is no industry that is not undergoing thorough changes caused by the internet.

The volume at hand gives an analysis of the internet revolution. It covers questions reaching form the highly controversial thesis of the end of property rights in the internet caused by the non-rivalry of the "consumption" of information to questions regarding the repercussions of the internet on our understanding of the human person.

Technological changes like the introduction of the electronic economy pose the question of how to handle it and how to manage reasonably its ethical problems and dilemmas. The ethical problems and the business ethics of the electronic economy in the fields of production and labour, of consumption, and in handling trust and the abuse of trust are analysed by the contributions from applied ethics and business ethics.

Several papers of this volume were discussed at the Fourth Annual Conference of the Committee for Economic Ethics of the German Philosophical Association (Deutsche Gesellschaft für Philosophie) "Business Ethics Problems of the Electronic Economy" held at Stuttgart, Germany, on 15 to 17 November 2001, and organised by the Committee in collaboration with the Department of the Theory of Science and of the Philosophy of Technology, University of Stuttgart, within the Alcatel SEL Stiftungskolleg at the University of Stuttgart, Germany. The papers have been revised since then for the inclusion in this volume.

The editors appreciate the support for the printing of this book received from Alcatel.

Turin, Italy, and Stuttgart, Germany, March 2004

Peter Koslowski Christoph Hubig Peter Fischer

Contents

CONTENTS

Part One

Understanding the Internet-Revolution

Chapter 1

The Evolution of the E-Economy: Consequences for Theory Building in Economics and in the Economy

MICHAEL EHRET, MICHAELA HAASE, MARTIN KALUZA

> "But while the purpose of all things is under the dominion of the purpose of all persons, no one person's destiny is ever subordinated to the destiny of any other person. If there were only one man in the world he would be master of all things. Since this is not the case, as long as every man in the world is as just as much a person as anyone else, each equally responsible for the pursuit of his ends and for the fulfilment of his destiny, all these ends and aims have to be mutually *co-ordinated.* Here we have the origin of the reciprocation of rights and duties among persons." (Walras 1954, p. 62, italics as in the original source.)

I. Introduction

The hopes and fears generated by the e-economy are diverse and often contradictory. This holds true as much in the realm of ethics as it does in the field of economics. The expectations concerning ethical prerequisites for the successful spread of the e-economy and its consequences are articulated in decision makers' *folk theories* (in the sense of everyday theories) on the one hand and in academic theories on the other. The academic view is dominated by the assumptions attached to *homo oeconomicus,* the model of an optimizing individual developed by neoclassical economists. Models of optimization are also found in practice, especially in the laboratories of the software industry. However, models of optimization cannot capture sufficiently those features that characterize the e-economy: communication and cooperation. In many cases, this lack of theoretical foundation impedes an adequate evaluation and debate of ethical issues related to the e-economy. Hence, our goal is to present some points of departure for a more thorough understanding of the complex phenomena related to the e-economy.

We will proceed as follows: In the following section we sketch the philosophical context in which we shall investigate ethical issues of the e-economy, focussing on the *prisoner's dilemma.* In the third section, we will discuss the crucial empirical changes that result from the diffusion of the e-economy: that is, the increasing importance of communication, cooperation and knowledge. In the fourth section, we will discuss to what extent the established approaches of economics can capture these phenomena. In the last section, we derive consequences for the development of a common research agenda of economic theory and business ethics.

II. Scenarios of Conflicts in Cooperative Behavior

The impact of the e-economy on ethical issues is open to debate. Phenomena such as unequal access to the internet (*digital divide*) or questions of data protection do not quite constitute new problem areas, as they can be interpreted as variations of problems already known. In contrast, such as the case of genetic engineering, the emergence of new technology has left philosophers with a set of completely new questions – questions concerning the way we see ourselves as human beings that reach beyond the realm of applied ethics. Compared to that, the problems we address that relate to the e-economy are less fundamental.

1. Three Scenarios

We address the question of consequences the e-economy offers for the cooperative behavior of agents. Our point of distinction is the observation that the use of the internet has changed the business processes between supplier and customer in the sense that cooperation will play a more important role. In addition, since business transactions via the internet are marked by a certain insecurity due to their anonymity, it seems natural that trust in the actions of others will be a central issue for agents in the e-economy. In order to give an idea how far the ethical consequences reach, we will start by sketching three examples of possible set-ups for problems of cooperation.

a) Prisoner's Dilemma

In many cases, members of a group will benefit from cooperative behavior among members. However, it could occur to an individual within the group to free-ride and thus reap the benefits of a cooperative agreement while not contributing his own share. If other members of the group behave in the same way, then cooperation will cease to exist. Consequently, benefits that otherwise would have been produced, are not realized.

The basic structure of this problem is the core of the *prisoner's dilemma,* a thought experiment (based on strongly simplified conditions) well known in game theory.[1]

---

1 See LUCE/RAIFFA (1957), pp. 94ff., for a description from a game-theoretic perspective.

Philosophers discuss it at a high level of abstraction. One way to look at the *prisoner's dilemma* is to consider it a problem within the field of ethics. The question then would be, for example: "Why should people cooperate at all, if as free-riders, they could individually take in a larger benefit?" Another view on the dilemma is to discuss it as a problem of rationality: "In not cooperating, each party individually does the right thing, according to the rules of rationality. And yet, in the end both are worse off than if they had cooperated (and acted irrationally)." David Gauthier defends the view that, in cases like the *prisoner's dilemma,* moral questions and questions of rationality will turn out to be the same thing (we will sketch his approach below).[2]

b) Conflicts of Moral Values and Economic Interests (the Decision Maker "Acts on His Own Account")

The *prisoner's dilemma* is structured in such a way that, if they each cooperate, then both agents actually benefit from the mutual cooperation. However, it is easy to think of situations where an agent would not be made better off by cooperative behavior. Assume that a business owner accepts an order A. A few hours later another customer approaches him with another order B. Order B will pay a lot more than A, but the company cannot carry out both order requests. As it happens, the company would earn more with a breach of the first contract than with its fulfilment. One could hold that the owner should still fulfill the contract for order A. Practically speaking, this could be considered a case of applied ethics, but it may also give rise to a more fundamental debate about the fulfilment of contracts and promises.

c) Conflicts of Moral Values and Economic Interests (the Decision Maker "Acts on the Behalf of a Third Party")

Someone who is not the owner of the company he works for, a manager of a joint-stock company, say, is accountable to the owners for the decisions he makes. If he finds himself in a conflict situation such as in scenario (b) then he will have less options to decide compared to the owner who works on his own account, in cases where the share owners have established explicit criteria to guide the actions.[3] We thus assume that more decisions will be taken in favor of economic interests.

---

2 Cf. GAUTHIER (1986).

3 DEGEORGE (1999), pp. 188ff., points out this difference.

2. Ethical Aspects of the E-Economy: The Role of Trust

The ethical question that guides this research is whether the e-economy causes changes within the respective scenarios. To be more precise, we ask whether there will be more or less breaches in cooperation. We do not believe that the rise of new information technology and changing business processes contribute to the final solution of the *prisoner's dilemma.* In this respect, the field in which we are operating is philosophically not as fundamental as others.

The following section is dedicated to the discussion of business relations. We show that in the New Economy, trust has a significantly more important role in business transactions than ever before. This may have consequences for scenarios such as (b) and (c): If it becomes more important to develop trust between business partners, then it can be assumed that at least in some cases where previously economic interests had been given preference over moral considerations, now, more decisions will be taken in accordance with moral considerations – precisely because the moral option is also the economically more attractive option.

We believe that especially in the case of scenario (c) more decisions will lead to morally preferred actions, simply because the gap between business interests and moral claims will close – even if just a little bit and in special cases which remain to be investigated.[4] The occurrence of actual conflicts will thus be reduced – although in principle it will not cease to exist.

3. Strong and Weak Version of the Term "Trust"

Much in our argument depends on how we use the term "trust". We use it in a version which – although not uncommon in economics – may seem rather weak from the point of view of philosophy. In a strong version, trust could mean that, for example, partner A expects with great certainty that partner B will not back out of a cooperative agreement established between the two partners, even though this would bring economic advantages to partner B; if conflict arises between economic and moral interests, B subsumes

4 This might be compared with *consumerism*, which is a case where moral pressure is canalized into business figures. Companies who change their behavior in view of the morally motivated activities of action groups do not necessarily follow the moral arguments, but economic considerations.

his economic interests to moral interests. Otherwise, one could argue, the concept of trust would be void (if I know that the other person will not give moral claims precedence over economic considerations I cannot trust him).

However, our argument is based on a weaker version of "trust." According to our interpretation partner A trusts the arrangement which constitutes the framework for a transaction, and supports the coordination of actions involved in the transaction he desires to carry out with B. For instance, partner A knows that B would suffer sanctions if partner B backed out of the cooperative agreement. In a strict sense, this might not be a case where trust is involved. However, we believe that it is useful to speak of trust in this case – partner A knows that his moral claims (where an agreement should be carried out unless both parties agree upon a cancellation) are supported (though not guaranteed) by the transaction arrangement and a common framework of legal and non-legal conditions. Since contracts cannot cover every single detail of a business transaction, the identity of the cooperative partners plays an important role as well – although contracts remain a significant aspect of the transaction arrangement.

4. Trust and Gauthier's Constrained *Maximizer*

In certain points, our thesis is compatible with the approach offered by David Gauthier[5] in his book *Morals By Agreement.* Gauthier proposes the solution of cooperative dilemmas in two main steps: First, he argues that it is rational for both parties of a potential cooperative agreement to negotiate in the beginning, and eventually come to an agreement. However, that alone will not ensure that the agreements will in fact be fulfilled. According to Gauthier, the fulfilment will be assured by the fact that someone known to have backed out of an agreement will not be accepted as a partner for cooperative agreements by others in the future; in fact, negotiations would never be initiated with the guilty partner. Hence, each agent makes the fundamental decision of whether they desire to be known as (1) one who generally complies with cooperative agreements (in Gauthier's words a *constrained maximizer*) or, (2) one who generally does not comply. This non-compliance is motivated by the belief that a short term payoff will result if they commit a breach in the agreement (*straightforward maximizer*). Gauthier argues that it is rational to be a *constrained maximizer* because this is the only way an

5 Cf. GAUTHIER (1986).

agent will be able to reap the benefits that are produced by a cooperative agreement, that could not be realized on the basis of non-cooperative individual behavior.

In Gauthier's book, the concept of trust appears only once and only in passing. Yet we think there is a parallel to our argument: In Gauthier's world, agents engage in cooperative agreements because of trust. The fact that Gauthier's argument assumes a fundamental decision concerning the person an agent wants to be ensures a far-reaching application: Gauthier's argument has thus the force to be a proposal for the solution of the fundamental *prisoner's dilemma* (scenario (a)).

According to our "weak" thesis – from a philosophical point of view – agents exhibit trust because they believe that a certain transaction arrangement renders it more unlikely that their cooperative partner will back out of the agreement. Within a different framework and less appropriate arrangements, they might be more suspicious. In Gauthier's argument, trust does not depend on actual arrangements. It arises from the fact that, for those involved in a cooperative agreement, the rational decision is to cooperate, i.e., to fulfill their agreements. At this point it becomes clear why we do not defend a strong thesis: The changes following the rise of the e-economy do not justify a reinterpretation of fundamental questions in the area of rationality (the same holds, we assume, for fundamental moral questions).

III. The E-Economy: Empirical Changes – Theoretical Description

1. The Role of Communication and Cooperation in the Evolving E-Economy

Scientific theories, developed in the realm of academic research and "popular" theory used by practitioners, are both derived from the concept of *homo oeconomicus*. This concept is based on the assumption that economic actors have complete knowledge of their preferences as well as complete knowledge of the technological means available for their fulfilment.[6] In the context of models based on the *homo oeconomicus* assumptions, economic decisions are a mere optimization problem, which deciders can solve without

6 Cf. SAMUELSON/NORDHAUS (1989), pp. 446-447, LANCASTER (1987), pp. 55-60.

the help of communication. This kind of decisions could just as well be delegated to a computer.[7]

The use of this model in economics is based on methodological considerations. Whereas the microeconomic models are built on the assumption of the smooth friction-free adjustment of decisions made by producers and consumers, we regularly can observe frictions in reality. Microeconomic models help to gain insights into these frictions by withdrawing certain assumptions in order to analyze the observed frictions. Consequently, as researchers, we can sharpen the understanding of non-equilibrium situations, such as external effects of certain goods, asymmetrical distribution of information or imperfect knowledge. Therefore, criticism lodged against the reality-distant concepts of economics, often articulated by researchers in the field of business administration, doesn't hold true in that respect. To a large degree, economics is not about neglecting reality. It is simply based on a special method of analyzing reality.

So called network effects are popular examples in which microeconomic theory helps to gain an understanding by the focussed elimination of certain assumptions. Network effects take place when the coordination of buying decisions bears a direct or indirect influence on the use of goods.[8] But the results of the theory of network effects put the basic assumptions of the *homo oeconomicus* model into question, which state that economic decisions are made in a strictly isolated maximizing manner. If we agree that in modern markets the coordination of decisions is a basic source of value creation, then approaches are needed that provide insights into the communication element of production, investment and buying decisions.[9]

Researchers face a big challenge caused by the contradictory experiences of different companies in the diffusion of information and communication technologies in the evolving e-economy. Also, companies learned painful lessons in quasi-market experiments. Many of them had to restate the assumption that use of ITC-based concepts can exclusively be generated by optimization models. Since the invention of the transistor ITC concepts encouraged the phantasy of investors, ITC specialists and user companies. As far back as the 1960s, when the race began among big ITC companies like IBM, Xerox, AT&T or Ericson for the development of the "Universal Busi-

7 Cf. LANCASTER (1987), pp. 60-64.

8 Cf. EHRET (2000), pp. 94-98.

9 Cf. KATZ/SHAPIRO (1985) and FARREL/SALONER (1985).

ness System" (UBIS). The basic idea was to integrate all typical functions of an enterprise, such as administration, procurement, manufacturing, sales, and after sales service on the platform of one integrated omputer system. To date, no single company offers a system which applies in all these situations. The Swedish researcher Gunnar Eliasson comments from his analysis of the race for the establishment of the UBIS-system:

> The technocrats of industry and academia, who dominated the early design process, have been corrected by market forces to the tune of billions of dollars.[10]

Eliasson detected the cause of the failure of the ITC-companies as due to ambiguous success criteria for business software applications. The technological model of the engineers was based on the assumption that all information-related activities of a company could be completely and congruently modelled using information systems that include computers and networks.[11] Based on this assumption, all information-related activities of people can be copied and substituted by ITC-technologies. But in the trial and error of establishing ITC-based concepts in business contexts, this assumption is found to be false. Frequently one can find information and communication flows in companies that cannot be imitated using computer codes. Therefore, digitally processed information often bears a need for interpretation and personal decision. ITC companies are facing severe limitations in terms of access to the users concepts and application context. User companies had to learn that ITC technology must be complemented with user concepts in order to gain the originally wanted economic benefits. Here organizational change is the most important activity. At this point, we argue that communication and cooperation of ITC-based companies and users are key drivers for the successful implementation of e-business concepts.

The failed UBIS-experiments have taught at least one lesson: A narrow focus on the technological aspects of innovation precludes, at least in the field of ITC technologies, the desired economic value. Information technologies show their economic potential with the help of an appropriate user context. Here, key issues are the organizational structures, knowledge, and the competencies of the actors.

---

10 ELIASSON (1996), p. 173.

11 Cf. ELIASSON (1996), p. 152.

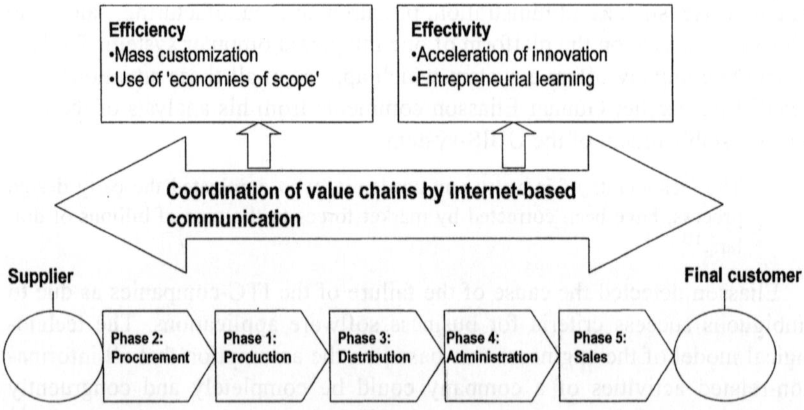

Fig. 1: Stages of the implementation of ITC-based concepts throughout the supply-chain

By integrating the user's perspective, we gain access to interesting starting points for theory building. Economic studies frequently show that companies in the service sector are the driving force in the demand for ITC-based products and services.[12] A supply-side approach faces severe limitations because of their reliance on inherent characteristics of product offerings compared to a user-side approach which can open access to valuable insights in the value generated by ITC-concepts. In this context, ITC-utilization can be explained as a technical instrument used in the fundamental change from industrial to postindustrial methods of value generation. The different developmental stages of the e-economy enable more flexibility in production, and customization of customer service. With the application of digital technologies, economic potential is created in the following three dimensions:

12 See the recent study of the German Federal Ministry of Education and Research, Bundesministerium für Forschung und Bildung (Ed.) (2001), pp. 26-28. Studies by the OECD (cf. PAPACONSTANTINOU [1997]) and the Kiel Institute of World Economics (cf. KLODT/MAURER/SCHIMMELPFENNIG [1997], pp. 78-89) show similar evidence.

- **Efficiency:** The application of ITC concepts results in the realization of economies of scope.[13] Traditional industrial firms trimmed costs by mass production of customized products. ITC-based concepts lead the way to new forms of cost savings. With the help of ITC-technologies, companies can implement standardized processes for the generation and fulfilment of customized offerings. This way of mass producing individual offerings is called mass customization. ITC-enabled concepts enable customer-centered management of standard processes, which can be coordinated through the whole value chain since the establishment of internet standards.[14] Cooperation between customers and suppliers is a basic prerequisite for the realization of these advantages.
- **Effectivity**: The diffusion of internet utilization puts the innovation process of the traditional industrial firm into question. Research and development (R&D) were the central functions of innovation. Even before the start of internet diffusion, both academic researchers and management practitioners articulated doubts of whether this innovation model was capable of developing successful innovations for modern markets. More and more, customers as well as suppliers were recognized as critical sources of innovation.[15] The connection of special interest communities enabled by internet infrastructures opened up new channels of communication between technology developers and users. This is reflected by new network-like organizational types that are involved in the innovation process. Even large industrial companies now follow the example set by venture capitalists in the development of so-called corporate venture trusts.
- **The surpassing of traditional borders between effectivity and efficiency:** The traditional industrial firm had to decide between emphasizing either cost or quality leadership. This was caused by the central role played by economies of scale due to realizing cost reductions in industrial production. The utilization of economies of scope is more than a new strategic option for companies. It enables companies to resolve the traditional conflict between cost reduction and customiza-

---

13 Cf. PINE (1993), pp. 44-50.

14 For the basic explanation, see JACOB (1995), pp. 53-79.

15 HIPPEL showed first empirical evidence with his studies conducted at the Massachussettes Institute for Technology, see HIPPEL (1976) and HIPPEL (1986).

tion. E-economy concepts surpass the traditional borders by connecting companies throughout the entire value chain.

From the utilization perspective, the establishment of e-economy concepts looks more like a technical element of economic change than a mere technological process. The central characteristic of this process is the bypassing of function-based specialization which focused on the optimization of specialized activities like procurement, production, sales or R&D. With the help of internet-based concepts, companies obtain an instrument for the functional integration of management processes. Thereby, the importance of the mere optimization aspect of business decisions looses ground. This aspect of business decisions is closest in proximity to the model of the homo oeconomicus.

2. The Role of Knowledge for the Firm and the Market Process

In the context of the changes for economic decisions makers caused by the establishment of the e-economy, Hayek's criticism of the optimization focus of economic models gains new relevance. While observing the central assumption of complete information used in neoclassical models Hayek states:

> **If** we possess all the relevant information, **if** we can start out from a given system of preferences and **if** we command complete knowledge of available means, the problem which remains is purely on of logic.[16]

If we follow Hayek, then the need for economic activity is generated by the fact that economically relevant knowledge is dispersed throughout the entire society. In this context, enterprises are seen as a social invention for the generation and utilization of economically relevant knowledge. In the process of diffusion of communication and information technologies, the optimization element of economic decisions loses its importance. This optimization element can be automated with the help of e-business solutions. Under these circumstances the question of the economic context of these developments helps to broaden the perspective. Here, the capital theory based concept of the firm, developed by the Austrian school of economics, where Hayek played a central role, shows the way to important insights.[17]

16 HAYEK (1945), p. 519.

17 For an analysis of the diffusion of information technologies from a capital theory perspective, see EHRET (2000), pp. 187-193.

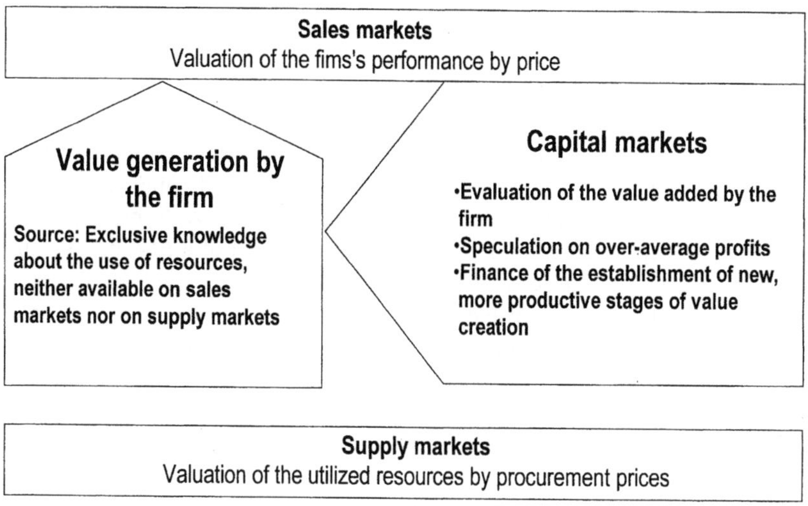

Fig. 2: The firm and the use of knowledge
Source: EHRET (2000), p. 135.

If we follow the knowledge perspective of enterprises developed by the Austrian school of economics, then realized profits are an indicator of the value generated due to exclusive knowledge possessed by the firm, that is not owned by competitors.[18] This is reflected in the valuation of goods in the market process: Prices procured on supply-side markets indicate the value attributed by other participants of the economic process. In a similar way, customers determine the value they place on offerings of the firm. The only way for a company to realize a profit is to find utilization modes for the obtained goods which are not reflected by the actual market prices. In addition, capital markets value transformation processes of the firm and finance the firm in accordance to their expectations.

The diffusion of the internet for business applications accelerates these processes. Electronic market exchanges or auctions provide customers with an easy, cheap tool for evaluating offerings of enterprises. Therefore, firms face increasing pressures to develop exclusive capabilities in their utilization

18 See LEWIN (1998).

of resources. Exclusive knowledge can consist of unarticulated needs, technological development capabilities or implicit, i.e., not articulated knowledge.[19]

Access to this type of knowledge can only be gained by cooperation among other participants of the economic process. A key example is found in the automotive industry. Even before the establishment of the Internet, automobile manufacturers actively cooperated with preferred suppliers.[20] Now, potential suppliers to these automobile manufacturers have to qualify themselves in concept competitions before the development of a new model family takes place. The succeeding participants then take part in joint development teams and are responsible for certain modules in accordance to their core competencies, like chassis or electronics. By participating in such types of projects they not only have to consider the demands of their direct customers – the manufacturers – but also the needs of the end consumer. Thereby, end consumers add a new dimension to the marketing activities of suppliers.[21]

The diffusion of the internet enables such types of inter-enterprise cooperation. This is reflected by the evolvement of the business web concept.[22] These vertical types of initiatives provide a special challenge for the engaged partners, because they imply cooperative roles as well as competitive roles. A basic precondition for the generation of value throughout networks is that the partners must cooperate. But, partners compete for their share of the profit realized by the generated value. Therefore, such types of coopetition will remain fragile unless the partners reach a basic level of trust.

3. Consequences for Building Theories in Economics

After the analysis of e-economy's empirical changes, our preliminary finding is that the development of the e-economy spawns additional pressure on actors' cooperative behavior. If it is right that "interactivity is the key dimension in e-commerce"[23] or that "interactivity is the proper focus of e-com-

19 For an overview, see NONAKA (1994).
20 For recent developments, see BMBF (2001), pp. 69-77.
21 See WOLTERS (1996).
22 Vgl. ZERDICK ET AL. (2001), pp. 180-187.
23 ESSLER/WHITAKER (2001), p. 10.

merce analysis,"[24] then the concept of transaction plays a major role in the analysis of the e-economy. The concept of transaction grasps actors' coordinative behavior within markets as well as within or among organizations. The concept of transaction not only constitutes a relevant unit of analysis,[25] it is also a starting point for social-theoretic and ethical analyses.

The image of an isolated optimizing individual does not incorporate all the demands faced by economic actors, nor does it measure up to the theoretical reflection about their action. That notwithstanding, business economics still argues on the basis of a theory that has not sufficiently integrated the "community context."[26] Partially, differences that oppose geographic and physical dimensions with those of the social sciences also move into the foreground. For example, Essler/Whitaker distinguish between "cyberspace" and "real space." Another example is their contrasting of, inter alia, "informational activities" (pertaining to their sequential models of business transactions) with "physical activities."[27]

However, both "social embeddedness" and "cognitive embeddedness" do matter. According to Schmid[28], customers, who should be convinced by suppliers that a certain product or service embodies the solution to their problems, live in insulated "cognitive rooms" or within "knowledge media" inseparable from their particular social context. It is important not to leave this communicative dimension to the marketing point of view,[29] but to also integrate it into economic models in general.

---

24 ESSLER/WHITAKER (2001), p. 16.

25 Cf. WILLIAMSON (1997).

26 SCHMID (2001), p. 49.

27 ESSLER/WHITAKER (2001), p. 11, characterize cyberspace as "de-territorialized business." "Business transactions" are divided into three phases: "We use the terms poremptive, emptive, and abemptive to denote the activities leading up to, enacting, and leading away from the transaction, respectively" (*ibid.*). Although ESSLER/WHITAKER (2001) subordinate "informational activities" the preparation phase of a transaction, they do not mention the works of information economics about this topic. Information economics begins its development with STIGLER (1961), that is, long time prior to "cyberspace."

28 SCHMID (2001), p. 49.

29 In summarizing that "communication aims at programming brains," SCHMID (2001), p. 49, shortens the task of communication from the marketing point of view. This formulation especially neglects the importance of communication for the organization of the coproduction between customer and supplier. SCHMID

IV. Concepts of Economics and Economy

1. Economics

Economic theories make use of different assumptions about the behavior or actions of economic actors. In our paper, we concentrate on three approaches: the neoclassical theory, the Austrian school, and the new institutional economics (NIE). All three play a major role in the discussion and analysis of the e-economy. The early neoclassical theory focuses less on interpersonal relationships and more on relations between persons and things instead.[30] Thus, it barely provides a starting point for an ethical-economic analysis that utilizes interactive, social action as a central theme.[31] Older neoclassical theory is built upon assumptions about the actions of isolated individuals; while more recent developments in neoclassical theory, like oligopol theory or game theory, incorporates strategic behavior.[32] That notwithstanding, new approaches like game theory maintain strong assumptions about individuals' possession of information or their preference order;[33] or they modify them in a manner that itself gives rise to criticism (like the maximization assumption's transfer to problems concerning information gathering in information economics).

The Austrian school, especially Mises, criticizes the interpretation of rational action in neoclassical economics. The assumption of perfect information ignores problems pertaining to the spread of knowledge; the Austrians regard this as constitutive for an anaylsis of the market process. From the Austrians' point of view, the reduction of economic action to optimization

(2001), p. 48, also maintains this aspect labelled as "reverse engineering:" "Within the new ICT (Information and Communication Technology, the auth.), the environment has become much more communicative in the sense that the client becomes increasingly involved in the design and even in the production process" (*ibid.*).

30 WALRAS (1954), pp. 62ff. Cp. also BIERVERT/WIELAND (1990), p. 12, and KOSLOWSKI (1985), pp. 2ff., who makes use of the formulation "socially disembedded exchange."

31 This also applies to newer approaches inside – as well as outside – of the neoclassical theory, which utilize the price mechanism as a principle of coordination.

32 Though game theory is an important instrument contained in the economists' "box of tools," it is not a self-contained empirical theory.

33 SAVAGE (1954), for criticism cp. SUGDEN (1991).

procedures, and the use of mathematic and statistical methods, is way off the mark set by the central economic problem. That notwithstanding, Mises also refers to models of rational action; he further emphasizes the harmonic accord between individual action and the laws of the market.[34] Hayek dissolves the tension between determinism and freedom with respect to market events by reducing the importance of rational action, processes of thinking, and explicit knowledge, in favor of evolutive mechanisms and implicit knowledge.[35]

Hayek's – and Lachmann's – emphasis on knowledge generation in the market process is still important, and, with respect to the analysis of the e-economy, also current (cp. III.2).[36] It is a crucial task to find out how – explicit as well as implicit – knowledge processes work and how this topic can relate to new developments in the cognitive sciences.[37] The reconsideration

---

34 MISES (1940), p. 1, characterizes economics as a science about a realm that may be described by an "exploration of the regularity in the succession of market phenomena" ("Entdeckung der Gesetzmässigkeit im Ablauf der Markterscheinungen"). In addition to that, for him (*ibid.*, p. 11) "action ... is conscious behavior. We might also say: action is will that is transformed into deed and effects thereby realizing itself, is to behave oneself with respect to means and ends, is the subject's – the human's personality – meaningful answer to the givenness of world and life" ("Handeln ist bewusstes Verhalten. Wir können auch sagen: Handeln ist Wollen, das sich in Tat und Wirken umsetzt und damit verwirklicht, ist ziel- und zweckbewusstes Sichbenehmen, ist sinnhafte Antwort des Subjekts – der menschlichen Persönlichkeit – auf die Gegebenheit der Welt und des Lebens").

35 According to HAYEK (1983), p. 181, it is the order of the whole society ("Ordnung der Großgesellschaft") which gives rise to morality: "it was this big structure that allows [man] to gain knowledge about his environment by an unconscious subdual to morality. ... Not intelligence is the source of order but order is the source of intelligence" ("diese große Struktur war es, die ihm (dem Menschen, d. Verf.) durch Moral, der er sich unwissentlich unterworfen hat, ermöglichte, Wissen zu erwerben, das ihm immer mehr Macht über seine Umgebung gab. ... Nicht die Intelligenz ist die Quelle der Ordnung, sondern die Ordnung ist die Quelle der Intelligenz").

36 Cf. HAYEK (1945) and LACHMANN (1956).

37 LACHMANN (1956), p. 23, discusses this issue in connection with the formation of expectations: "The formation of expectations is nothing but a phase in this continuous process of exchange and transmission of knowledge which effectively integrates a market society." It is the main task of a theory of expectations

of Hayek's postulation that economics should not begin with an equilibrium analysis but rather with an analysis of the way to equilibrium,[38] makes clear that economics has only made little progress in that regard.

In comparison to transactions that are coordinated by the price mechanism, actors need to organize their activities by themselves within a *transaction economy* by making use of transaction arrangements. In this context, we refer to John R. Commons' concept of transaction.[39] Commons made a distinction (besides introducing rationing transactions) between "bargaining transactions" and "managerial transactions." The first-mentioned transaction type designates exchange relationships within markets; the second-mentioned transaction type refers to the coordination of relationships within organizations. By reference to conflict, order, and mutuality, Commons' concept of transaction expresses an explicit social-theoretic underpinning. Bargaining and managerial transactions both offer a starting point for the discussion and analysis of conflicts related to moral aspects of action, on the one hand, and its economic aspects, on the other.

Theoretically, transaction economics is founded on a reversal of the assumption of perfect information[40] *and* on the comprehension of institutions in the analysis. Consequently, for the first time theory acknowledges the actors' social action and, compared to previous approaches, the actors are given much more freedom because the concepts of rational action and optimization of alternatives are no longer treated as being equivalent.[41]

The merits of the concept of a transaction result not only from its social-theoretic underpinning and its offering of an ethical starting point. James S. Coleman argues that, from a methodological point of view and with respect to theories in the social sciences, the transaction is an important unit of analy-

"to describe the structure of the mental acts which constitute the formation of expectations; its second task, to describe the process of interaction of a number of individuals whose conduct is oriented towards each other" (ebd.).

38 Cf. HAYEK (1945).

39 Cf. COMMONS (1931).

40 The information economics is characterized by the sublation of the assumption of perfect knowledge and, based on optimization and rational expectations, by the treatment of information as an economic good. From the information economics, the new institutional economics can be distinguished by the introduction of transaction arrangements and the therewith associated benefits and costs. An important part of transaction costs are then information costs.

41 Cf. DENZAU/NORTH (1994) or DEMSETZ (1996).

sis.[42] It is the link between social action, at the micro level, and the diverse, intended and unintended, consequences of actions, at the macro level. Hence, the concept of transaction represents the methodological as well as textual point of departure for our discussion of the organization of activities within markets and organizations.

In the debate following Commons, Ronald H. Coase's considerations concerning the economic meaning and consequences of property rights have added a social-theoretic dimension to the economic concept of the good that has been influenced by physics up to the present.[43] Within the new institutional economics, the social-theoretic dimensions of the transaction as the unit of analysis are not explicit, however.[44] The treatment of, for example, informal institutions makes this clear: Whereas North emphasizes informal institutions with respect to institutional choice and the formation of institutional arrangements as well, they are banned to the institutional environment by Williamson because, from his point of view, they change only every 100 to 1000 years, thus not being succeptible to economic calculation.[45] Williamson admits the importance of the role that routines play with respect to explanation of behavioral regularities. That notwithstanding, routines can not play a major role in economics because "much of what is interesting about human behavior in general and organizations has reference not to routines but to exceptions."[46]

People act within some situations that gain complexity due to imperfect and asymmetric information, or the prevalence of uncertainty. In addition, actors themselves create and permanently alter the situation by their actions and resultant consequences.[47] Though requirements of actors increase due to bounded rationality, they experience decreased cognitive capacities.[48] To put it in Biervert/Wieland's words,[49] NIE and the Austrian school have over-

---

42 Cf. COLEMAN (1990).

43 Cf. COASE (1960), see also HAASE (2001).

44 WILLIAMSON (2001), p. 12, at least establishes a connection.

45 Cf. NORTH (1990) and WILLIAMSON (1999). With respect to the analysis of organizations, NEE/INGRAM (1998) label informal institutions a "missing link" that, inter alia, makes a negative impact on the analysis of the organizational performance.

46 WILLIAMSON (2001), p. 7.

47 Cf. also LACHMANN (1956), p. 27.

48 Cf. SIMON (1959), WILLIAMSON (1985).

49 BIERVERT/WIELAND (1990), p. 29.

thrown the one-dimensional view of actors' rationality and have begun to become more interested in a multi-dimensional approach to actors' rationality.

The modeling of individual action on the basis of neoclassical optimization has faced a lot of criticism during the past few decades; the criticism especially points to the limited range of applications for models built on optimization. This situation has not changed fundamentally by the development of the e-economy. Neoclassical economics also successfully grasped some of those phenomena, that were previously in opposition to the "pure view," and rendered them useful for deciders within the economy.[50] An alternative approach that could adopt similar integrative and methodic tasks for the theory-building, still remains to be found.[51] Consequently a gap emerges in the process of building social-science theories. On the one hand, an action-theoretical approach is missing; this approach could deal with imperfect information, asymetrically distributed information, limited cognitive processing abilities, and embodies an alternative approach to neoclassical optimization as well. On the other hand, there is no link between individual and social action, which is complementary to the before-mentioned alternative approach. Such a link would provide the basis for the analysis of social systems that are the major unit of analysis for economic theories.[52]

The diverse strands of institutional microeconomics, which are presently subsumed under the concept "NIE," cannot be expelled from this deficit: All of them base on *assumptions* about individual action but not on its *theoretical analysis*. For example, principal-agent theory's formal offspring refers to an information-economic foundation; and the transaction-cost theory to bounded rationality and opportunism, respectively. But now the dynamic strand of institutional theory questions the origin and change of institutions; hence, the perspective is geared towards an analysis of the actors' comprehension and interpretation of reality within the framework of their mental models. Problems related to the acquisition and dissemination of knowledge within the market process, as well as within organizations, returned to the center of analysis.

---

50 We refer to our statement of the phenomenon of net effects in paragraph III.1. With respect to deciders within the e-economy, VARIAN/SHAPIRO (1999) is one of the best textbook presentations of the theory of net effects.

51 Cf. LAVILLE (2000) and REICH (2000).

52 To this is pointed to by WILLIAMSON (1997), who labels the transaction cost economics a "systems approach."

2. Economy

As pointed out in the preceeding paragraphs, in a world characterized by behavioral uncertainty and by the requirement of social action, the neoclassical models' range of application is restricted. Economists are thus interested in the development of alternative models provided with new and enlarged ranges of application.

Additionally, we take into account a metatheoretical criticism on the received view of theories to rethink the too simple-structured relation between theory and evidence.[53] The consideration of actors' action theories offers one opportunity to combine the economic with the meta-theoretical perspective. For theories, new ranges of application can be made accessible by not confronting "the" theory with "the" evidence but by considering the relations between theories accruing from diverse origins and located at different levels of generality.

In the following paragraphs, we discuss the possibility of an ethical complementation of economic and meta-theoretic perspectives. Before proceeding, we will formulate some guiding questions for further research:

First, which action theories do scholars deploy, and on which concepts of rationality are their theories based? Which theories are helpful for the cognizance of actors' mental models?

Second, what is the comparison between social scientists' theories and those influencing actors' action intentions as well as actions within the domain? (i) We begin with the idea that (life-world) actors are guided by discipline-specific, theoretical knowledge, too. This is the case, for example, if students of business economics make use of their learnedness for the formation of organizations and market relationships. The outcomes of experiments with students of economics and other subjects, substantiates this view.[54] (ii) We further assume that knowledge is based on a broad foundation of so-called everyday theories. Everyday theories are a nexus composed of different scientific theories, half- or pseudo-scientific 'theories,' religions, and ideologies, respectively, which are acquired during life. The experiences, the cultural-historic background, the apprehenticeship, the socialization, and the learning processes of actors, respectively, all leave their impression on this theory-architecture.

---

53 Cf., for example, SUPPES (1962) and SUPPE (1977).

54 RÖTHELI (2001) presents an actual example.

The third question concerns whether actors are inclined to obtain exclusive guidance by discipline-specific knowledge or by the assumptions concerning individual action or individual behavior. Obviously, such a connection is taken for granted if it is claimed that the transaction-costs economics'[55] assumption of opportunistic behavior gives rise to the actual execution of opportunistic behavior.[56] Is a change in assumptions of economic theories needed in order to generate an improvement in moral behavior? Would a change from *(bounded) rational man* to *social economic man* unharness moral potential to a higher degree?[57] Or would this change otherwise result in more disappointment in situations that involve 'leaps of faith' and, instead, prevent relationships that would have been executed by an adherence to the assumption of opportunism and supported by an adequate institutional design?

55 Cf. WILLIAMSON (1985).

56 STAEHLE (1975), p. 722, claims that "wrong hypotheses and theories give rise to a reality predicted by this theory itself in terms of self-fulfilling prophecy, and with the help of social techniques which are developed on the basis of the wrong theory" ("falsche Hypothesen und Theorien ... mit Hilfe der auf Grund der falschen Theorie entwickelten Sozialtechnik im Sinne der self-fulfilling prophecy eine Realität (entstehen lässt, d. Verf.), die eben diese Theorie prognostiziert hat"). For a similar treatment see SYDOW (1999), p. 168, who directly refers to transaction cost economics. See also ETZIONI (1988), p. 257, who criticizes the neoclassical rational-action model in a general manner: "The more people accept the neoclassical paradigm as a guide for their behavior, the more their ability to sustain a market economy is undermined."

57 TOMER (2001), p. 288, draws the following image of the Social Economic Man (SEM): "The social part of SEM is other-centered, communal, dependent, and culture-bound. SEM, as social being, combines a strong cooperative, collegial, and caring element along with competitiveness. SEM's character has a higher, idealistic side; he has a conscience, and he acts out of concern for justice, human dignity, duty, loyalty and many other moral and ethical considerations. SEM is a sacred person with inalienable rights. Further, SEM has a need to develop his character in order to realize his higher personal potential. Religiously oriented social economists see SEM as having the capability as achieving perfection in unity with God; whereas more secular social economists see the possibility of social perfection through a cooperative effort to promote the welfare of the entire community."

The fourth question is whether scientists can have access to the actors' cognitive models. Parsons and Schutz's views[58] exemplify different answers to this question: While Schutz argues that the subjective element of action is succeptible to scientific methods,[59] Parsons suggests that there is no insurmountable obstacle in the pursuit of scientific knowledge that is generated in the relationship between actor and scientist. Schutz, who argues on the basis of phenomenology, only accepts the idea of an "understanding" of the subjects, which is located at a prescientific level and thus rests upon a renouncement of the observers' position and his integration – as far as possible – into the subjects' life-world. In principle, we share Parsons' view. That notwithstanding, according to Schutz' perspective, we adopt his idea of introducing representations located at two different levels which may subsequently be compared to each other: an individual actor's representation, on the one hand, and that of a scientist, on the other. The first-mentioned type mirrors the actor's interpretations and theories, the last-mentioned, those of the scientist. Interpretations of the first kind contribute to an improvement in both opportunities and range of applications for economic theories. They further contribute to answering the question of how far contents of economic theories enter into actors' (or groups of actors) everyday theories or action theories, respectively.

The fifth question refers to the distinction between individual and corporate actors. This question is important since, on the one hand, organizations' impact on the economic system exceeds that of individuals in general, and, on the other hand, organizations and individuals cannot be equated with each other. Many other questions of importance, like those of knowledge acquisition and trust acquisition, require a consideration of this distinction, too.

58 Cf. GRATHOFF (1978).

59 Following Schutz, the scientific methods, that are suitable for an analysis of social relationships and social systems, rest on so-called second-order typifications that are built on first-order typifications having their point of origin in life-world actors. The scientific study of social action thus directly bases on the abstraction from unique subjective factors.

V. Consequences for the Relation Between Economics and Business Ethics

The e-economy gives reason to reflect on the existence and consequences of empirical changes in the economy and economics. We sought answers to the e-economy's effects on moral and economic aspects of action as well as for analytical potential as a matter of interest for economists. The answer is the following one: Ethical considerations gain in importance for building theories in both economics and economy; for a concurrance of moral and economic action the leeway increases. Whether the actors' moral intentions also increase, is a completely different question.

According to Lohmann, ethics poses the question of the "right practice" ("richtige Praxis") or for rules that guide the cohabitation of humans.[60] Lohmann stresses problems of coordination and cooperation in this regard which give rise to a common level of analysis between ethics, social theory, and institutional theory. For Koslowski, too, ethics and economics both hold a common interest in the society's optimal coordination.[61] What is considered "right" depends on the reasons given for an action. Economic theories unequivocally favor efficiency[62] in this regard; business economics supplements this with effectiveness. In contrast to that, ethic theories, for example, ask for justice as well as for the acceptance of rules allegedly suited for achieving this end. Efficiency and justice are not generally consonant. In this regard, it is the task of business economics to discern conflicts and to characterize the moral and social dimensions of alternative options.

Effectiveness does not immediately increase the need for moral decision or moral action. Effectiveness provides the basis for integrating decision consequences not only into *products and services* of co-operative production but also into the *processes of their production*. Many customers prefer not only a high-value product or service but also one that is produced by adher-

60 LOHMANN (1997).

61 Cf. KOSLOWSKI (1995).

62 The new institutional economics is interested in a revised form of the efficiency concept that not only – or even not at all – comprises the results of neoclassical maximization but rest on process analyses: "The New Institutional Economics and Public Choice School share the view that efficiency must be judged by the process through which transactions are carried out, not by the results" (PEJOVIC [2001], p. 376).

ence to certain measures such as ecological criteria, labor standards, or children's work. This also affects the formation of relationships between the firm's decision-making body, its employees, and its organizational structure, respectively. These must be shaped in a way that allows employees to act morally.[63] Customer orientation, the strategic presupposition for the management of value-adding processes, evolves into a mediator for values as well as a necessary but insufficient condition for efficiency. For business ethics, both efficiency and effectiveness thus constitute an entrance door into economics and economy. Criticism as advocated by Lutz[64] notwithstanding: economics allows very well a *consideration* of moral and social contexts.

The e-economy relocates the demand for coordination and cooperation within the economy. It enhances the need for relationships between actors who can either trust each other or who can rely on arrangements to shape their relationships. The importance of the prisoner's dilemma notwithstanding, the theory shows when, and under what circumstances dilemmatic situations can be circumvented;[65] evidence shows that cooperative action actually occurs. Business relationships and the support of transactions by institutions play a major role in this regard. Moral action gains in importance for the actors within the ecomony, and hence, for economists, who deal with cooperative action and with conditions that render it both possible and successful.

The discussion of connections between the actors' scientific knowledge and their practical experience is enhanced by connecting moral knowledge and moral action. Many deficits of practical action-consequences result from a lack of both moral knowledge and economic knowledge; specifically, it can be tracked back to the lack of practice in dealing adequately with conflicts. However, if one accepts that economic theories or their assumptions affect the practice of action, then, in principle, this can also apply to ethical theories. This knowledge should especially refer to the handling of conflict situations; that is, it should make explicit the costs of options, that – in the short as well as in the long run – configate with respect to morality, efficiency and effectiveness. We do not plead for a unification of ethical and economic theoretical measures, but we do favor making clear the lines of conflict, action opportunities, and action consequences, respectively, which can become a part of society's democratic discourse. We plead for the maintenance of the

63 Cf. GÖßLING/PRIDDAT (1997).

64 LUTZ (1985), p. 110.

65 Cf., for example, AXELROD (1984) and MARWELL/OLIVER (1993).

distinction between economics and ethics but also for instructions that enable actors to recognize and deal with areas of tension: The Austrian concepts of "ignorance" and "alertness"[66] apply to non-economic cases, too.

The analysis of learning processes that take place when actors interact within markets as well as organizations, is thus important. As pointed out by Hahn (1996), the utilitarians are not alone in neglecting to incorporate learning processes and mental capacities. In order to formulate it within the context of humanistic economics, it is the task of society to enable their members, with the help of education, to freely make up their mind. "Similarly, the concept of free will can be readily clarified within our framework. It has to be seen as the human capacity to choose truth, justice, or beauty over utility."[67]

If the claim held by Farina, Hahn and Vannucci applies, "that economics and ethics are somehow inextricably linked through theories of rational decision-making,"[68] then, with respect to the gap mentioned in paragraph IV.1, the question arises of whether economic and ethical theory building can be unified not only ex post, in order to shed light on their problems from the perspective of the respective other, but whether they both can be further advanced with reciprocative reference. Endogeneous preferences,[69] domain-specific preferences and interdependencies with preferences of other domains,[70] or the assumption of a hierarchical structure of preferences of higher-order preferences,[71] provide examples for this idea. Moral preferences, their origin (cultural background, learning of norms, rationality) and their relations to other-type preferences, are, among other things, a matter of particular interest.

In light of the growing criticism regarding identification of the neoclassical maximization with the model of rational action, there is no reason to move back behind this mark. Moral deliberation presupposes the actors' ability to give reasons for potential or actual actions. The ethical-economic approach is thus guided by an analysis of arguments and situations; it is more closely related to the concept of "reasonableness" than to a rationality con-

66 KIRZNER (1973).
67 LUTZ (1985), p. 107.
68 FARINA/HAHN/VANNUCCI (1996), p. 1.
69 Cf. BOWLES (1998).
70 Cf. HAHN (1996).
71 LUTZ (1985), TOMER (2001).

cept traced back to the person regarding the capacity to maximize the values of variables that express the person's ends.[72]

Preferences and motivations play a major role in the explanation of actions; nonetheless, they cannot do the entire job. By incorporating time and processes, Gauthier has already widened the perspective a little.[73] A fundamental social-theoretical perspective that provides a systematic link between micro and macro theory required for economic theory-building, is still not available. It is for this very reason that *homo oeconomicus* cannot simply be replaced by a more suitable and "realistic" view of humans. Economics and theory of action, on the one hand, and descriptive ethics, on the other, share most of the problems mentioned in this paragraph. With this common background, it makes sense to combine their perspectives in developing the theoretic foundations of cooperative economics.

References

AXELROD, ROBERT M.: *The Evolution of Cooperation*, New York (Basic Books) 1984.

BIERVERT, BERND; WIELAND, JOSEF: "Gegenstandsbereich und Rationalitätsform der Ökonomie und der Ökonomik", in: BERND BIERVERT, KLAUS HELD, JOSEF WIELAND (Hrsg.): *Sozialphilosophische Grundlagen ökonomischen Handelns*, Frankfurt am Main (Suhrkamp) 1990, pp. 7–32.

BOLAND, LAWRENCE A.: *The Foundations of Economic Method*, London et al. (George Allen & Unwin) 1982.

BOWLES, SAMUEL: "Endogeneous Preferences: The Cultural Consequences of Markets and other Economic Institutions", *Journal of Economic Literature*, XXXVI (March 1998), pp. 75–111.

BUNDESMINISTERIUM FÜR BILDUNG UND FORSCHUNG (Hrsg.): *Zur technologischen Leistungsfähigkeit Deutschlands. Zusammenfassender Endbericht 2000. Gutachten im Auftrag des Bundesministeriums für Bildung und Forschung*. Vorgelegt durch: Zentrum für Europäische Wirtschaftsforschung, Mannheim; Niedersäch-

72 BOLAND (1982), SUGDEN (1991).

73 GAUTHIER (1996).

sisches Institut für Wirtschaftsforschung, Hannover; Deutsches Institut für Wirtschaftsforschung, Berlin; Fraunhofer-Institut Systemtechnik und Innovationsforschung, Karlsruhe; Wissenschaftsstatistik im Stifterverband der Deutschen Wissenschaft, Essen; Wissenschaftszentrum Berlin für Sozialforschung, Mannheim, Hannover et al. 2001.

COASE, RONALD H.: "The Problem of Social Cost", *The Journal of Law and Economics*, III (1960), pp. 1–44.

COLEMAN, JAMES S.: *Foundations of Social Theory*, Cambridge (Mass.) and London (UK) (Belknap) 1990.

COMMONS, JOHN R.: "Institutional Economics", *American Economic Review*, 21 (1931), pp. 648-657.

DEGEORGE, RICHARD T.: *Business Ethics*, 5th ed., Upper Saddle River (Prentice Hall) 1999.

DEMSETZ, HAROLD: "Rationality, Evolution, and Acquisitiveness", *Economic Inquiry*, 34 (1996), pp. 484–495.

DENZAU, ARTHUR; NORTH, DOUGLASS C.: "Shared Mental Models: Ideologies and Institutions", *Kyklos*, 47 (1994), pp. 3–31.

EHRET, MICHAEL: *Innovative Kapitalnutzung. Die Entstehung von Business-to-Business-Märkten in der Internet-Ökonomie*, Wiesbaden (Gabler) 2000.

ELIASSON, GUNNAR: *Firm Objectives, Controls and Organisation. The Use of Information and the Transfer of Knowledge within the Firm*, Dordrecht et al. (Kluwer Academic Publishers) 1996.

ESSLER, ULF; WHITACKER, RANDALL: "Re-thinking E-commerce Business Modelling in Terms of Interactivity", *Electronic Markets*, 11 (2001), No. 1, pp. 10–16.

ETZIONI, AMITAI: *The Moral Dimension. Toward a New Economics*, New York (Free Press) 1988.

FARINA, FRANCESCO; HAHN, FRANK; VANNUCCI, STEFANO: "Introduction", in: FRANCESCO FARINA, FRANK HAHN, STEFANO VANNUCCI (Eds.): *Ethics, Rationality, and Economic Behaviour*, Oxford (Clarendon Press) 1996, pp. 1–10.

FARREL, JOSEPH; SALONER, GARTH: "Standardization, Compatibility, and Innovation", *Rand Journal of Economics*, 16 (1985), No. 1, pp. 70-83.

GAUTHIER, DAVID: *Morals By Agreement*, Oxford (Clarendon Press) 1986.

GAUTHIER, DAVID: "Commitment and Choice: An Essay on the Rationality of Plans", in: FRANCESCO FARINA, FRANK HAHN, STEFANO VANNUCCI (Eds.): *Ethics, Rationality, and Economic Behaviour*, Oxford (Clarendon Press) 1996, pp. 217–243.

GÖßLING, TOBIAS; PRIDDAT, BIRGER P.: "Moralische Kommunikation in Organisationen", *Aus Politik und Zeitgeschichte, Beilage zur Wochenzeitung Das Parlament* (1997), pp. 22–30.

GRATHOFF, RICHARD (Ed.): *The Theory of Social Action. The Correspondence of Alfred Schutz and Talcott Parsons*, Bloomington and London (Indiana University Press) 1978.

HAASE, MICHAELA: „Diversität als transaktionsspezifisches Merkmal von Gütern", in: HARALD SPEHL, MARTIN HELD (Eds.): *Vom Wert der Vielfalt*, Sonderheft Nr. 13 (2001) der *Zeitschrift für Angewandte Umweltforschung*, pp. 170-181.

HAHN, FRANK: "Some Economical Reflections on Ethics", in: FRANCESCO FARINA, FRANK HAHN, STEFANO VANNUCCI (Eds.): *Ethics, Rationality, and Economic Behaviour*, Oxford (Clarendon Press) 1996, pp. 13–21.

HAYEK, FRIEDRICH A. VON: „The Use of Knowledge in Society", *The American Economic Review*, XXXV (1945), No. 4, pp. 519-530.

HAYEK, FRIEDRICH AUGUST VON: „Die überschätzte Vernunft", in: RUPERT I. RIEDEL, FRANZ KREUZER (Eds.): *Evolution und Menschenbild*, Hamburg (Hoffmann und Campe) 1983, pp. 164–192.

HIPPEL, ERIC VON: "The Dominant Role of Users in the Scientific Instrument Innovation Process", *Research Policy*, Vol. 5 (1976), No. 3, pp. 212-239.

HIPPEL, ERIC VON: "Lead Users: A Source of Novel Product Concepts", *Management Science*, 32, (1986), No. 7, pp. 791-805.

JACOB, FRANK: *Produktindividualisierung. Ein Ansatz zur innovativen Leistungsgestaltung im Business-to-Business-Bereich*, Wiesbaden (Gabler) 1995.

KATZ, MICHAEL L.; SHAPIRO, CARL: "Network Externalities, Competition, and Compatibility", *American Economic Review*, 75 (1985), No. 3, pp. 424-440.

KELLY, KEVIN: *New Rules for the New Economy. 10 Radical Strategies for a Connected World*, New York (Viking) 1998.

KIRZNER, ISRAEL M.: *Competition and Entrepreneurship*, Chicago und London (University of Chicago Press) 1973.

KLODT, HENNING; MAURER, RAINER; SCHIMMELPFENNIG, AXEL: *Tertiarisierung in der deutschen Wirtschaft*, Tübingen (Mohr) 1997 (= Band 283 der Kieler Studien des Instituts für Weltwirtschaft an der Universität Kiel).

KOSLOWSKI, PETER: "Philosophy and Economics. An Introduction", in: PETER KOSLOWSKI (Ed.): *Economics and Philosophy*, Tübingen (Mohr) 1985, pp. 1-16.

KOSLOWSKI, PETER: "Economics as Ethical Economy in the Tradition of the Historical School", in: PETER KOSLOWSKI (Ed.): *The Theory of Ethical Economy in the Historical School*, Berlin et al. (Springer) 1995, pp. 1–11.

LACHMANN, LUDWIG M.: *Capital and its Structure*, London (G. Bell and Sons) 1956.

LANCASTER, KELVIN J.: *Moderne Mikroökonomie*, Frankfurt am Main/New York (Campus) 1987, 3rd ed. Original: *Introduction to Modern Microeconomics*, Chicago, Illinois (Rand MacNally) 1980.

LAVILLE, FRÉDÉRIC: "Should We Abandon Optimization Theory? The Need for Bounded Rationality", *Journal of Economic Methodology*, 7 (2000), No. 3, pp. 395–426.

LEWIN, PETER: *The Firm, Money and Economic Calculation. Preliminary paper*, Dallas (University of Texas, School of Management) 1998.

LOHMANN, KARL R.: "Was ist eigentlich Wirtschaftsethik? Eine systematische Einführung", *Aus Politik und Zeitgeschichte, Beilage zur Wochenzeitung Das Parlament* (1997), pp. 31–38.

LUCE, R. DUNCAN; RAIFFA, HOWARD: *Games and Decisions*, New York (Wiley) 1957.

LUTZ, MARK A.: "Beyond Economic Man: Humanistic Economics", in: PETER KOSLOWSKI (Ed.): *Economics and Philosophy*, Tübingen (J.C.B. Mohr [Paul Siebeck]) 1985, pp. 91–120.

MARWELL, GERALD; OLIVER, PAMELA: *The Critical Mass in Collective Action: A Micro-Social Theory*, Cambridge (Cambridge University Press) 1993.

MISES, LUDWIG VON: *Nationalökonomie: Theorie des Handelns und des Wirtschaftens*, München (Philosophia Verlag) 2nd ed. 1980 (unveränderter Nachdruck der 1. Auflage, Genf 1940).

NEE, VICTOR; INGRAM, PAUL: "Embeddedness and Beyond: Institutions, Exchange, and Social Structure", in: MARY BRINTON, VICTOR NEE (Eds.): *New Institutionalism in Sociology*, New York (Russell Sage Foundation) 1998, pp. 17–45.

NONAKA, IKUJIRO: "A Dynamic Theory of Organizational Knowledge Creation", *Organization Science*, 5, (February 1994), No. 1, pp. 14-37.

NORTH, DOUGLASS C.: *Institutions, Institutional Change and Economic Performance*, Cambridge (Cambridge University Press) 1990.

PAPACONSTANTINOU, GEORGE: "Technology and Industrial Performance", *The OECD Observer*, 204, (February/March 1997), pp. 6-10.

PEJOVIC, SVETOZAR: "Book review of Ethics, Economics, and Freedom by Timothy Roth", *The Journal of Socio-Economics*, 30 (2001), pp. 375–377.

PINE, JOSEPH B.: *Mass Customization. The New Frontier in Business Cometition*, Boston/Massachusetts (Harvard University Press) 1993.

REICH, WENDELIN: "Heuristics as Plausible Models of Rationality?", *Acta Sociologica*, 43 (2000), No. 3, pp. 251–258.

RÖTHELI, TOBIAS F.: "Acquisition of Costly Information: an Experimental Study", *Journal of Economic Behavior and Organization*, 46 (2001), pp. 193-208.

SAMUELSON, PAUL A.; NORDHAUS, WILLIAM D.: *Economics*, New York, St. Louis, San Francisco etc. (McGraw-Hill) 1989, 13th edition.

SAVAGE, LEONARD J.: *The Foundations of Statistics*, New York (John Wiley) 1954.

SCHMID, BEAT F.: "What is New About the Digital Economy?", *Electronic Markets*, 11 (2001), No. 1, pp. 44–51.

SHAPIRO, CARL; VARIAN, HAL: *Information Rules: A Strategic Guide to the Network Economy*, Boston, Mass (Harvard University Press) 1998.

SIMON, HERBERT A.: "Theories of Decision-Making in Economics and Behavioral Sciences, *The American Economic Review*, XLIX (1959). No. 3, pp. 253-283.

STAEHLE, WOLFGANG: "Die Stellung des Menschen in neueren betriebswirtschaftlichen Theoriesystemen", *Zeitschrift für Betriebswirtschaft*, 45 (1975), pp. 713–724.

STIGLER, GEORGE J.: "The Economics of Information", *The Journal of Political Economy*, LXIX (1961), No. 3, pp. 213–225.

SUGDEN, ROBERT: "Rational Choice: A Survey of Contributions from Economics and Philosophy", *The Economic Journal*, 101 (1991), pp. 751–785.

SUPPE, FREDERICK: *The Structure of Scientific Theories*, Urbana et al. (University of Illinois Press) 1977.

SUPPES, PATRICK: "Models of Data", in: ERNEST NAGEL, PATRICK SUPPES, ALFRED TARSKI (Eds.): *Logic, Methodology, and the Philosophy of Science: Proceedings of the 1960 International Congress*, Stanford (Stanford University Press) 1962, pp. 252-261.

SYDOW, JÖRG: "Quo Vadis Transaktionskostentheorie? – Wege, Irrwege, Auswege", in: THOMAS EDELING, WERNER JANN, DIETER WAGNER (Eds.): *Institutionenökonomie und Neuer Institutionalismus: Überlegungen zur Organisationstheorie*, Opladen (Leske + Budrich) 1999, pp. 165–176.

TOMER, JOHN F.: "Economic Man vs. Heterodox Men: the Concepts of Human Nature in Schools of Economic Thought", *The Journal of Socio-Economics*, 30 (2001), pp. 281–293.

VARIAN, HAL; SHAPIRO, CARL: *Information Rules. A Strategic Guide to the Network Economy*, Boston (Harvard Business School Press) 1999.

WALRAS, LÉON: *Elements of Pure Economics* (1926), Homewood, Ill. (Richard D. Irwin), translated by William Jaffé 1954.

WILLIAMSON, OLIVER E.: *The Economic Institutions of Capitalism – Firms, Markets, Relational Contracting*, New York (The Free Press) 1985.

WILLIAMSON, OLIVER E.: "Hierarchies, Markets and Power in the Economy: an Economic Perspective", in: CLAUDE MENARD (Ed.): *Transaction Cost Economics: Recent Developments*, Cheltenham (UK) and Northampton (MA) (Edward Elgar) 1997, pp. 1-29.

WILLIAMSON, OLIVER E.: "The New Institutional Economics: Taking Stock/Looking Ahead: Adress to the Annual Conference, September 17, 1999", *ISNIE Newsletter* (Fall 1999), pp. 9–20.

WILLIAMSON, OLIVER E.: "Why Law, Economics, and Organization?" *http://www.-haas.berkeley.edu/bpp/oew/papers.html* (version from January 2001).

WOLTERS, HEIKO: „Auswirkungen der Systembeschaffung für die Customer Integration aus Sicht von Zulieferunternehmen der Automobilindustrie", in: MICHAEL KLEINALTENKAMP, SABINE FLIEß, FRANK JACOB (Eds): *Customer Integration - Von der Kundenorientierung zur Kundenintegration*, Wiesbaden (Gabler) 1996, pp. 233-244.

ZERDICK, AXEL; PICOT, ARNOLD; SCHRAPE, KLAUS; ARTOPÉ, ALEXANDER; GOLDHAMMER, KLAUS; LANGE, ULRICH T.; VIERKANT, ECKART; LÓPEZ-ESCOBAR, ESTEBAN; SILVERSTONE, ROGER: *Die Internet-Ökonomie. Strategien für die digitale Wirtschaft*, Berlin et al. (Springer) 1999.

Chapter 2

Optimizing Individual Communication – Reducing Institutional Communication? The Necessity of a New Form of Business Ethics in the E-Economy Era

CHRISTOPH HUBIG

I. The Problem

A superficial look at the development and destiny of many e-economy start-ups might lead one to the impression that this area of the economy's self- and other-evaluation has fallen prey to a fundamental confusion: new, optimized methods of doing business have been mistaken for new ends; the realization of new strategies for developing, producing, distributing, and using goods, processes and services – methods which have been made possible by implementing innovative information technology – are still considered part of the old economic system of ends. That is why it appears to be consequential when the New Economy falls back into the Old Economy, modernized as it may be by the New. From a philosophical point of view, one is quickly led to the conclusion that instrumental reason has failed; further questions inquire, if at all, as to how business ethics can justify the newly utilized instruments within the context of the general strategy of economization. This would bring us to a new subject matter, one requiring an examination under the old axiologies and criteria. The internet thus seems like a system which makes a universalization in the sense of making communication, tools, machines etc. more flexible but which should be assessed by the old values and criteria.

But this overlooks that by utilizing new technology to transmit, transform and save information, not only are particular economic means and processes are optimized – this also creates new structures which can no longer be reached by old categories and concepts. The various forms of e-commerce are not simply methods of optimizing trade with e-technology, but rather an element in an economy which has changed its face in all aspects, from development to production to marketing, up to and including consumer behavior. The new methods of transmitting, transforming, and saving information not only make it possible to substitute old methods by making them more efficient; they also, as does every new technological advance, make forms of structural changes possible which have not yet been realized as well as "promote" an adequate formation of the conditions of their taking effect – a formation making traditional schemata, structures, and forms of organization obsolete, because they hinder the instrumental implementation of the new methods.

The most important tendency in this process, manifested in models, key words and postulations, is the fact that the new possibilities of informational interlinking could result in an increase in individual flexibility of functional transfer functions in every aspect, which itself opens the way for processes of making new structures on the way from self-organization. Individual flexibility can be seen in the broadest sense: It effects the possibility of individualization of developmental processes, of production processes including the supply of raw materials, semi-finished products, supporting services in individual placement, and the delivery of goods for making individual products for individual usage in connection with individual services to secure this usage for individual customer orientation, etc.

One the one hand, the process of individualization includes everyone from the developers to the producers to the customers; the gigantic amounts of information which need to be transferred, structured, organized and set into algorithms are not a problem for new technologies, just as the newly created information about these information processes, including any amount of higher-level transfer- and archiving organization, is easily dealt with. This can currently be seen best in stock-market technology, where derivate business is developed, but also, to name one example from many, in the first pilot projects involving directly controlled customer-specific variations on products traditionally manufactured in mass serial production, itself accompanied by individual marketing. These processes of individualization, it could be said, are continuously expanding, so that products and services can become increasingly "tailor-made": de-massing production, as it were, towards more individualized mass production (Alvin Toffler). If this new flexibility is brought into the market efficiently, this means a further shift from a supply- to a demand-oriented economy: On Demand is a motto placed on products and producers, services and service provider, processes and those involved in the processes. It no longer has its organizational form in companies as a fixed scheme needed to be clarified, advertised for and justified, but rather in the organization of projects involving a form of project management which "performs at the basis", whereby the term "perform" doesn't completely describe the process which, rather, helps these conditions become effective.

It would be, on the other hand, jumping to conclusions if we attempted to equate "demanding" individuals with just those customers who appear primarily as new individuals and not just as demographical segments, clients, or groups: the producers and individuals on the supply side are actually meant – those who compete with and against each other as emancipated demand subjects, for example in relation to individual work rhythms and working hours, each with individual performance potentials and as individuals willing to perform outstanding services. That can lead to an internal and/or an external Darwinism on both sides: this can be observed in project-oriented development and production of goods, processes, and services. The projects compete against each other (externally), and within the project there is internal competition amongst individual project participants towards fulfilling the project goals so that, for example, the question is always open as to which employees of what kind can be afforded.

A corresponding Darwinism is hidden, however, on the demand side as well. Uncoordinated customer wishes are immediately in displacemental competition with one another since the majority of uncoordinated demand *profiles* can also, in the light of management of objectives, displace justified special preferences on the supply side which can no take part in the self-organized profiles. A tendency against "tailor-made products" could also be seen in the technically possible option of structuring the sale of good in the world wide web (www) according to the model of the stock market, with variable prices and ad hoc flexibility according to demand. That would be implementable, however, only for standardized products. Flexibilization and individualization of products as well as the flexibilization and individualization of demand functions can thus work against each other, that is: one would restrict the effectivization of the other's options (*against* Tofflers "de-massing" of production: because of a individualization of the demand *modus*).

In the course of interlinking and of self-organized forms of new structures, the required responsibility and much-emphasized delegation of responsibility to individuals in the form of shallow hierarchies in all areas shows effects which are no longer founded in individual responsibility of each individual person involved. The classic selection mechanisms, filters, and safeguards, accompanied by corresponding justificational discourses (even if these took place in simplified and common form, such as with major marketing or the activities of consumer organizations) appear to lose their effectiveness and their assertive power. The radicalized decentrality present in the web is not controllable by any means; following norms is no longer guaranteed (example: music piracy, p-to-p computing). A de-institutionalization is taking place, by some euphorically praised and housed anticipatorily in new utopias of a radically liberalized market – a market offering access to everyone and for everything (including all information). That, at least, is the parole of the "new" Magna Charta of the Information Age (Alvin Toffler et al.), no longer really new. Others, however, complain that the new formational possibilities available through the information technologies this option offers will help the capitalist economy achieve its final, manifested form, in its most potent radicality, thus dismissing the old European idea of institutionally secured individual autonomy for the release of the primal freedom of arbitrariness. Before these simplified characterizations are differentiated further, I would like to call the basic idea of institutionalization to mind which also inspired thought in classical economic- and business ethics, so that both the potential and the dilemmas of the newer developments can be diagnosed more exactly.

II. Institutional Services

Institutional services are services which make individual action possible. A form of restriction follows as a natural result of such facilitation. The facilitative services attempt, in general, to achieve three things: First, necessary resources in the broadest sense which the individuals could not attain on their own are provided. These can comprise material and financial resources as organized available means of action in a narrow sense of the term, epistemic resources in the form of recognized knowledge assets, temporal resources achieved by no longer needing to complete other actions or institutional lowering of opportunity costs for time exposure. Providing these services must take place within predefined limits, such as temporal and cost limits. Secondly, an orientation service is provided by imparting the myriad of different choices with calculable gratifications and sanctions, the legal aspect with employment-, technology-, environmental- and economic law (including the derived set of rules such as ISO, DIN, guidelines and certificates) to the production aspect with predetermined target yields, the market with its standards of quality coming from the dynamics of supply and demand, up to and including the ethical discourse about the acceptability and justification of corresponding economic goals. Thirdly, action schemes set up in this way make it possible to plan so that other individual actions can be anticipated and that actions can be coordinated even if individual plans of action are not explicitly communicated, so that individual action, for example, can be gauged as cyclical or anticyclical. Institutional determination of action schemes, to which individual action can be brought into relation, makes the emergence of trust possible, and its corresponding consequences: to use Luhmann's terminology, the emergence of *institutional trust* in the validity and general compliance with rules – trust in the stability of recognizing action schemes as a basis for planning – as well as *systemic trust* as a form of trust in the security of certain compensatory services in the case of accidents – a form of trust which can form the basis for the necessary willingness to undertake risks involved with innovative action, making a controlled dynamism of the system's development possible. In view of the restrictive effects necessarily connected to these forms of facilitative services, expressed by the criticism of the clumsiness, inflexibility, and inefficiency of traditional institutionalization, the reduction of institutional schemes is often rashly considered as the actual innovation of a New Economy made feasible through technology complete with its new flexibility and efficiency. In the following, this view will become relativized, although it is not my intention to rehabilitate the old schemes, but rather call for justifiable new schemes capable of compensating the deficits mentioned now. This is connected with the call for further developing an ethics of economy, and, in particular, business ethics.

III. Reducing Institutional Schemes

Reducing institutional schemes in the context of interlinked individual communication and related self-organizational processes in all economic areas leads to new problem zones in a different way. I will summarize these under the following perspectives: a) individualized communication in the narrow sense with the consequence of loss of institutional trust; b) being left alone with errors and loss of trust in the system; c) loss of necessary resources for sustainable action; d) loss of established social structures.

a) Individualized electronic communication, from individual customer-influenced production to individual marketing, from individual communication between company employees in the intranet to the individual communication between teachers and pupils in the areas of knowledge transmission and training/coaching are all released not only from the pressure of public justifiability but are also separated from the security function of publicly realized recognition processes. The primacy of strategic communication can be observed here, leading to awkward consequences, especially the loss of trustworthiness. In the web, we are not only exposed to virtual realities whose level of reality remains unclear and hidden, but also virtual realities which because of their diversity evoke unreality and the distance of a wax museum (narrowing of reality through its expansion). New transaction costs arise because of necessary "trust-building measures" (c.f.). This is not only germane to the authenticity and truthfulness of the communicated contents, but also the security of antecedent individual decisions no longer able to orient themselves on the implicitness of the validity of corresponding *standards*. The consequence is the "self-organized" formation of acceptance fields which are not secured by acceptability discourses, but rather undermine these and become an institutional substitute, a new reference point for individual-strategic action, since those forms of superindividual action and communication require such a reference point in their strategic intention. This is expressed in the key words of addressee- and user profiles, which in Kobsa/Wahlster's classic and treacherously circular definition are those stereotypes comprising the characteristics of those users who fulfill the stereotype. The dilemma of the transformation of individual flexibilization into a new factual inflexibility is visible here in unbeatable clarity (these problems also can be found in research on functional deficits of the intranet which are supposed to make communication more flexible). It also refers to the above-mentioned dichotomy between stereotype formation and individualization in the sense of a "hostile takeover" (Oevermann), clearly visible in e-bookselling, where the customers (organized according to stereotype) are assigned offers and suggestions which serve to strengthen the antecedent pigeonhole.

b) In addition, the reduction of institutional schemes can be noted in areas of damage prevention and –compensation (i.e., the dimension of system trust). Individualized communication hinders the construction or the continuation of an error-sensitive culture, i.e. that area of the so-called *organizational* memory which makes learning from mistakes possible. This presupposes that revealing mistakes and a corresponding public reflection is encouraged with gratification and motivational systems, which can only be institutionally ensured because it is foreign to individually strategic action and communication. A corresponding error-sensitive culture is also the presupposition for risk management able to present and offer specific know how and specific relieving power to act beyond mere individual implementation.

The reduction of institutional schemes also leads to another dilemma in the perspective of innovation optimism, because of the loss of the availability of relevant institutional resources as "background fulfillment" (Arnold Gehlen) for making subordinate actions possible. This starts with problems of the assertion of innovations considered valuable, those having to wait for the uncertain formulation of corresponding acceptance; this continues in the uncertainty of how losses in the resource "training" can be compensated in view of knowledge discounting, insofar as individuals are left to themselves; it is expressed in the loss of institutionally secured repose as a presupposition for creativity, or more generally: the loss of reserves in view of individual action trimmed for efficiency. This loss of reserves with its consequences becomes visible as the other side of optimization processes in production, also in the context of outsourcing and recourse to external services which offer entire system solutions on a flexible and ad hoc manner. This creates a dependence on the actual state of the relevant service capacity of the constituents of an interlinked production.

d) These individualization processes finally penetrate to the field of composing social relationships, social security, and identity construction. The effectivization of development- and production processes made possible by technology, the reduction of leadership hierarchies, by delegating responsibility to projects, and the individuals within projects which are conceived of as individuals themselves in the context of management by objectives – all this leads to a Darwinism of the projects amongst themselves and to a Darwinism of the members of the project team under the criterion of realizing individual project aims. Individualization of working hours and work rhythms made possible by technology coupled with a global project organization for bypassing time zones and self-stylizing individuals as responsible sub-contractors lead to increasing opportunity costs for free time, hardly executable demands on mobility and flexibility at the expense of necessary social structures, and finally to the loss of solidarity relationships in view of diversified teleworking.

These developments, to which I would like to call attention by using the common key words, represent the real challenge to a new ethics of economy to design and justify institutional schemes which could compensate for these deficient developments. Evoking old schemes, including classic social contract architecture or other classic institutional powers based on the utopia of global agreements, is unfruitful since their reference area has changed irreversibly.

IV. Challenges for an Ethics of Economy

This is not the place to fully sketch the foundations of business ethics or the ethics of economy capable of dealing with the above-mentioned problems. It should, however, have become clear that this form of ethics should be conceived as a new institutional ethics which would have to guarantee that the conditions of action capable of being justified from a individual-ethical standpoint would not be compromised. It would have to demonstrate that those institutional schemes of action are justifiable under the dilemmatic structures mentioned above could be avoided. With institutional services of and for communication as a starting point – since the sources for poor developments lie, after all, in the individualization of communicational processes – further institutional services for the provision of necessary resources as well as the formation of pertinent social structures would have to be justified. While there seems to be widespread awareness of the new problematic situation and the necessity for reacting to it in the field of dynamic formation of legal regulations, this awareness is, in my opinion, not yet present in the area of economic ethics. It is this area, however, which takes on a double role: managing the justificational discourse for designing these legal systems on the one hand, and on the other to justify rules for composing non-legal spaces.

The contents of a new institutional ethics should concentrate on the following areas:

How can possibilities of parallel communication be secured as opposed to strategically restricted individual communication? In what way must the establishment of forums for this kind of communication – forums which should permit the testing, correction, reflection, and justification of technically-medially formed communication – be removed from the operative and strategic aims of concrete economic processes and be realized in a specific "unencumbered space"? (A side note: That completed measures of this type, implemented in certain few companies, also have positive effects in the form of attestable economic gratification itself – that they are "worth it" – does not disqualify a relevant ethical justification in the least.)

How can new institutional services be justified while ensuring that the competence of individual action, including institutional trust as well as trust in the system, is not hampered? In other words: planability and sustainability of the ability to coordinate as value of diversity and choice as well as preserving the subjects' identity without incursion effects (legacy values). One would have to prevent forcing individuals as mere seismographs of self-organized processes to reactions whose sufficiency is only demonstrated ex post (like we do when observing the stock market). This would have to entail establishing islands of new institutional entology oder structure within the vast masses of interlinked communication as publicly justified instances of regulation (i.e. for securing privacy: the glass customer is able to be constructed medially on the basis of his wishes to be treated individually).

In view of the way interlinking is being globalized, its basis of participation (taking the participants of discourse into account) can no longer orient itself according to classic structures (political structures, communities of trades) but rather according to the amount of concernment in particular problem areas, as can be seen in the emerging structures of NGO-netizens, but also to a smaller degree in compensatorial www-institutions such as new combines of people affected, exchange markets, "neighborhood"-cooperations, etc. Purely self-organized networks do not have a homogenous shared normative model as institutions do, but simply exchange individual background understanding. This can, however, become the first step towards building trust which can then develop into higher-level institutional trust.

In view of the reactionary tendencies inherent in processes of self-organization, schemes would have to be examined for justifiability which would guarantee sustainability, creativity, and prospective potential. Keeping alternative options for development and space for searching is restricted if areas of consensus are established self-organizationally via technical mediation – somewhat anonymously – which are then perceived as facts of nature or systemic constraints, giving the individual with the choice between assimilation and leaving the system. Various new developments demonstrate that new media are certainly capable of supporting communication processes of an institutional- and public nature. Examples range from the active utilization of the net by alternative groupings and fractions to the possibility of establishing an error-sensitive culture (such as Linux), or from alternative conflict mediation processes to the endeavors of e-government, which envisions new forms of public services and participation and a new transparency in consultancy and decision-making in executive and legislative branches accompanying e-commerce. Such endeavors are, however, threatened by those who, under the abstract motto of increasing efficiency, use the diversification of individuals' lives and "disembeddedness" (Anthony Giddens) to expand their power anonymously by functionalizing flexibility and using the self-strengthening effect of self-organizational processes. This is particularly true when the self-organization is initiated and supported by net-agents whose functional criteria are not known to those affected. The "self" which is being organized here is not a collective self of those who act, but rather a code for processes "without a subject" whose subjectlessness attempts to veil the anonymity of those subjects who place their agents in the net.

Chapter 3

Changes in the Producer-Consumer Relationship in Electronic Commerce – Examples from Book Publishing and Trade[1]

ULRICH RIEHM

I. Introduction

Current developments in the area of information and communication technology immensely stimulate our imagination. So many things have been postulated: a new era of democratisation has begun (Donk/Tops 1992), the conditions for an ideal market are at last realisable (Brynjolfsson/Smith 2000), progressive dematerialisation heralds a sustainable resource-efficient

---

1 I would like to thank my colleagues Carsten Orwat, Bernd Wingert, Knud Böhle and Michael Rader for a review of a draft version of this contribution. Translation by Sylke Wintzer.

economy (Negroponte 1995), limitations of time and space would be overcome (Cairncross 1997), and much more.

With regard to the present topic – changes in the producer-consumer relationship in the "eEconomy" –, the "new power of the customer" has been proclaimed. The customer as "co-producer" would be enabled to design his products by himself. Thanks to the Internet the consumers would gain enormous power, and in the end it would be for them to decide "which way to go". Customers would organise in cartel-like structures and put pressure on the suppliers (Cole/Gromball 2000, Wind/Mahajan 2001).

This discussion is anything but new. For instance, if we look back twenty years, very similar theses were supported. In the following, we will start with such a look back, followed by some considerations on how to determine more precisely the conditions and limits of the changes in the producer-consumer relationships on a general level. Finally, some examples from book publishing and book selling will be analysed to determine whether the thesis of the "new power of the consumers" holds.

II. The Prosumer and the Self-Service Society

In the late seventies and early eighties of the last century two books were published, which drew attention to a new role of the consumers: Jonathan Gershuny's "After Industrial Society? The Emerging Self-service Economy" (1978) and Alvin Toffler's "The Third Wave" (1980). Both authors perceived the phenomena of change in a similar way, and it is somehow surprising how exactly they anticipated the further development, even if their far-reaching conclusions must not necessarily be shared.

Toffler quotes the following examples for the "rise of the prosumer": Self-help groups in the health sector, handycrafts and the „DIY movement", automation at the customer interface, as with the cash dispenser, customized production, e.g. of clothes, which today is discussed as „mass customisation".[2] Toffler sees them as early symptoms of a development in which

2 At that time it was predicted that in twenty years the customer would be able to transmit his or her measurements via home computer and telephone to the clothing company, select the pattern and fabric, and then start the production by an automatic laser cutter. Or a computer-controlled sewing machine was described,

formerly paid work for the market (e.g. professional medical care or craftsmen work) is transformed into unpaid, but self-determined work (by self-help groups in the health sector or "do-it-yourself" workers). The simple consumer develops into a "prosumer". After an era of several thousand years of establishing ever more perfect worldwide markets, the end of marketing, i.e. the "dismarketing" of many goods and services, would have come. The new "trans-market civilisation" neither abandons market structures nor does it fall back into the past, but it is no longer pressurised to further extend and refine market structures (Toffler 1980, pp. 289-293).

Gershuny's argumentation also aims at a transformation of the existing industrial and market-oriented society. His starting point is the critique of the thesis of the service society, as e.g. developed by Daniel Bell. In his approach he considers similar phenomena as Toffler, for instance the „do-it-yourself movement". His central argument against the service economy is that the consumption of services tends to be replaced by goods, in particular by such goods which have a productive function for the consumer, i.e. private means of production. Laundry services are replaced by private work with washing machines, public passenger services by driving in private cars, language tele courses with audio cassettes etc. The service society is thus becoming a self-service society. In the opinion of Gershuny, with this development the utopia of a society becomes apparent – a 'post-economic' society, in which the producers no longer determine consumer needs and consumption (Gershuny 1981, p. 164, p. 167).

III. Conditions and Limits of Co-Production

In this context, the use of the terms 'work' and 'consumption' cannot be analysed systematically. According to the general understanding, work comes prior to consumption; work is a productive activity, while the things produced during work are used up in consumption.

Following the attempt of a "form analysis" of work reflecting the conditions of the "information society" by Priddat (1998), the strict opposition of

---

which would enable even the most "clumsy house husband" to tailor his own shirts (TOFFLER [1980], pp. 280f., p. 283). Today, such examples have actually been realised, even though not on a large scale.

work and consumption becomes questionable. Without collaboration of the driver, the automobile would be an immobile, Priddat (1998, p. 165) writes, disregarding that in this context the collaboration of the driver generally is not aimed at an earned income and that the driver may even enjoy it (but why should work be no pleasure!). Many products require co-production of the customer – the more they are digitised the more this applies: for a modern telephone a telephone list has to be set up and updated, with a video recorder the television channels have to be entered and stored and recording times have to be programmed, the personal computer has to be configured by the customer, software has to be implemented, errors have to be corrected, updates have to be acquired, etc.

In service production a close cooperation between contractor and client has always been inevitable (Hanekop et al. 2001). In case of information products, the work is not finished with the completion of the product, but the consumption of the information involves new work (Priddat 1998, p. 164). Not without reason it is said that information is being "worked through" while consuming.

However, what are the fundamentals for the realisation of this changeover in the producer-consumer relationship, what enables it, and why is it necessary?

If a distribution is made between three levels in this respect, a social, a technical, and an economic one, on the *social level* it is the trend towards an individualisation of lifestyles, which furthers a change in the role of the consumers. The need and demand for customised consumption, which again is an expression of individualised lifestyles, will thus increase. The generally increased standard of living, the reduction of working hours, and also their flexibilisation are conditions of this trend.

At a *technical level,* the new relationships between producers and consumers are based on flexible, program-controlled automation technologies. Priddat sums this up when he describes these technological opportunities as follows: "Anstelle des Einzelstückes als Einzelstück können wir heute Einzelstücke als Serienstücke produzieren" (Instead of producing single items as single items, today we can produce single items as mass products) (Priddat 1998, p. 172). The standardisation of products and product components is the basis of the individualisation potential, an "individualisation" in the framework of these standardised preconditions. While the "flexible automation" of production dates back to the 1960s and 1970s, the global technological networking via telecommunication and Internet has been an additional essential condition since the 1990s. This considerably increases the range and possibilities of influencing control. Finally, an intensive phase of digitisation of formerly physical or tangible products and services can currently be observed (digital music, books, information, consultation, etc.), which will further increase the individualisation potentials.

Economically, we are concerned with rationalisation strategies. The "expensive" labour force provides the incentive for the use of technology and organisational rationalisation. Expensive service work is replaced by more productive automated machine operation; work previously performed by the producer, is now passed on to the consumer (e.g. through self-service).

However, there are *limits* to the trend towards self-service and individualisation. The advantage of individualising a product or service is "offset" by the customer against the *burdens of co-production*.

The respective *market conditions* also enable or limit alterations in the producer-consumer relationship. In saturated markets with strong competition the power of the customers typically increases, and they are more likely to enforce their individualisation demands and reject the burdens of self-service. In case of more monopolistic supply structures, however, the power of the customers is rather low. The book market is a saturated market with relatively strong competition, which offers higher potentials for the "power of the customer" (Banzhaf 2002).

The *product characteristics* themselves also influence the consumers' possibilities of "co-production". According to a common assumption, the complexity of the product (or service) and the degree of customers' participation are inversely related: the more complex the product, the lower the opportunities for self-activity of the customer and the other way round. Based on new information technologies, customers' participation is now becoming more likely even in case of more complex products or services (cf. Hanekop et al. 2001, pp. 76). This shall be illustrated with the example of financial services (see table 1).

The connection postulated above is represented in the four-field scheme of table 1 by the axis from the top left (1) to the bottom right (4). The complex service of asset management confines the self-activity of the customer (in case of a financial layman entrusting a professional with his asset management). The simple activity of cash withdrawal can be done by the customer himself at a cash dispenser.

Table 1: Product characteristics and customer activity – examples from financial services

product characte-ristic	*complex*	1) asset management	2) online banking and broking
	simple	3) postman who delivers money orders	4) cash dispenser
		low	*high*
		self-activity of the customers	

Source: modified according to Hanekop et al. 2001, p. 77

But what happens in the fields (2) and (3)? In the case of the postman who delivers money orders (3) it can be assumed that this species has already died out. Simple services are less and less obtainable without self-activity of the customer. By the way, this is Gershuny's argument against the service society: Especially simple services are replaced by products or by automation and computerisation. Field (3) is being reduced and the respective services move over to field (4) in a *modified* form.

The postulated correlation between the complexity of a product (or service) and the degree of self-activity of the customer is an argument against an entry in the top right field (2) of the table. However, especially computer-based services incorporating product complexity in databases and programs which can be accessed by the customers via simple user interfaces shift this limit to the top right. Increasingly complex products and services are thus becoming objects of the customers' co-production. Online banking or the management of an online securities portfolio are without doubt of higher complexity than cash withdrawal at a dispenser and are performed via Internet quasi in the customer's self-service mode.

As usual, such four-field schemes are instructive for illustrating a connection or trend, but for a detailed analysis they are too simple. One problem is, for example, the delimitation in which the respective service is viewed. Regarding only the operational cash dispenser and the end-user in the case of cash withdrawal disregards the fact that on the side of the suppliers there are also simple as well as more complex types of activities remaining or emerging, which cannot be imposed on the customer, e.g. the simple activity of refilling the dispenser with money or the more demanding activities of maintenance and repair.

A description of the changes in the relationship between producers and customers therefore requires a more comprehensive approach. Besides the respective product characteristics, individual phases on the route from the producer to the consumer have to be distinguished: production, storage (also in the case of digital goods), sale, distribution and consumption. Furthermore, it has to be considered how the communicative and cooperative activity shares as well as the shares of authority and power are shifting in the producer-consumer relationship.

From a producer's point of view, a summarising evaluation can only deal with the question to what extent he will manage to improve his own competitive position and to reduce costs. The consumer is faced with the question of balancing the individualisation potentials in proportion to the new burdens of co-production and self-service.

IV. Examples from Book Publishing and Book Trade

In the following, four examples from book publishing and trading will be presented to discuss changes in the relationship between the producer (here: the author, publisher or his distributor) and the consumer: Online book selling, printing-on-demand books, electronic books and hypertexts. These examples are arranged according to the respective degree of "digitisation".[3] In online book selling only the sales phase is computer-controlled; whereas in the case of hypertext the "digitisation" also includes reception (see table 2).

3 "Digitisation" stands for a comprehensive transition process from analogue to digital storage forms, but also to computer control and telecommunicative or Internet-based interaction.

Table 2: Degrees of digitisation

	production	**storage**	**sale**	**distribution**	**consumption**
online book selling	conventional	conventional	digital	conventional	conventional
printing-on-demand book	digital	digital	digital or conventional [4]	conventional	conventional
electronic book	digital	digital	digital, also conventional	digital, also conventional [5]	digital, also conventional[6]
hypertext	digital	digital	digital, also conventional	digital, also conventional	digital only

1. Online Book Selling

Online book selling currently represents one of the most conspicuous changes in book trade resulting from the Internet.[7] Nevertheless, its share of about 3 percent in the total turnover of the sector in Germany in the year 2001 has still been relatively low. Up to now, only a few suppliers really make profit in this business. It is not surprising, that the expansion phase has been completed for the time being and that an adjustment crisis with bankruptcies, buyouts and mergers is to be observed. The online book trade predominantly deals in printed books. Only the offering of titles by the bookstores and the ordering by the customers are performed "digitally" via computer and Internet. All other phases of the producer-consumer relationship are of conventional nature.

The online book trade is self-service trading on the Internet. In the direct buying situation *communication* is entirely the job of the consumer. In par-

4 The order can also be placed with a stationary bookstore.

5 Conventional distribution with storage on disk or CD-ROM.

6 It can be spoken of a conventional use of electronic books if the books are printed out by the reader, which, however, is not possible in all cases.

7 Cf. RIEHM ET AL. (2001) for details on the following statements.

ticular, the consumer has to satisfy his need for advice by himself with the help of the respective information offer and also has to cope with the entire handling of the transaction, the input of the shipping address, the terms of delivery and payment, etc.

There are two aspects which distinguish online book trading from classic self-service and automated machine trading, where the customer is completely at the mercy of the preconditions of the respective system. Firstly, the communication interface can be individualised: The web interface can be configured e.g. to always first display a special type of new publications or to offer only books of a certain specialist field to search. It can be set up by the consumer to determine that orders from the office are always delivered to a different address than orders from home. It is possible to leave a search profile, the results of which will be transmitted e.g. via e-mail or SMS.

The second aspect refers to the fact that in this computerised communication relation the customer himself "casually", "unintentionally" and largely "unnoticed" produces data, which can be stored, evaluated and fed back to the communication process. With this recursive peculiarity of the electronic procedure a new quality of the self-service interface can be achieved. The customer joins a virtual community of book buyers who e.g. "shout" to him: "We have also bought this book, don't forget that one!".[8]

However, the online book buyer needs specific *competencies:* on the one hand, an interaction competence in working with the shop system and the book database, on the other hand a specialised competence for selecting books. Especially with regard to this specialised competence there are great differences from customer to customer: some of them seem to be completely overtaxed and are therefore glad to take advantage of the advice of the bookseller, whereas others have the competence to evaluate books in a certain specialist field, which cannot be expected from an average bookseller. Online booksellers both try to make up the competence deficits of their customers by an independent editorial offer and to make use of the specialized competence of the customer by integration of their evaluations and reviews.

The *power* of the customer is revealed e.g. in the influence on prices. Under the German retail price maintenance system for books this potential power is of no practical relevance when buying new books. The situation is different on the market for second-hand and antiquarian books, which experi-

8 Cf. LYNCH (2001) regarding this aspect as well as other aspects of the restructuring of the "value added chain" of the book market.

enced a certain boom resulting from the online book trade. At the respective sales platforms (abebooks.de, booklooker.de, etc.) the user can obtain a comprehensive offer for marketable book titles which are easy to sort and select by price, if other criteria (special edition, condition of the book, etc.) are not important. In the USA, where there is no system of fixed prices for books, the customers can use automated book price comparisons on the Internet and select their online bookstore accordingly. This price transparency, as empirical studies have shown, has contributed to the fact that the price level in the American online book trade is generally lower than in the stationary retail book trade. However, this does not mean that the online bookstores with the lowest prices achieve the highest turnover. The market leader, Amazon, is not at all the bookstore with the generally lowest prices. There are other mechanisms which prevent the basically higher price transparency from leading generally to lower prices for the customer (Brynjolfsson/Smith 2000).

2. Printing-on-demand Books

The main characteristic of the production concept "printing-on-demand" is that, initially, the books are only retained in storage in digital form; no edition is printed and held in stock. Only when there is a concrete demand the book will be produced via digital printing press and delivered to the customer, either via a bookseller or directly. An important representative of a special variant of this concept in Germany is the books wholesaler Lingenbrink: since the foundation in 1999, he has put more than 5,500 titles under the name of "Books-on-Demand" on the market, partly new publications, and partly book titles which had been out of print.

Compared with online bookstores the phase of stockkeeping has changed with printing-on-demand – the stock is digital. The initial costs for the publication of a book and the risk of being left with a printed edition has therefore decreased. This leads, as already observed, to a significant extension of the range of books. However, at the same time you might say that for the customer this extension results in a kind of "complication" and "pollution" of the book offer, because books offered in the printing-on-demand process usually do not pass through the quality control of a publisher. The more or less formal and content-related expectations and demands on a publisher's book are undermined.

Printing-on-demand is interesting in terms of the customer's influence on the assortment policy. For publishers, one of the functions of this process is to test book titles on the market. If the title sells it can also be printed in a larger edition using the more cost-effective offset printing. The title "Hagakure: The Book of the Samurai" by Tsunetomo Yamamoto shows the power of the buyers to place a book on the market. At first, no German publisher wanted to include this book (mentioned in Jim Jarmush's film "Ghost Dog: The Way of the Samurai") in his programme, and then it was published on the initiative of a committed reader as a book-on-demand, where it became a real best seller. Meanwhile, the book has also appeared as a normal publication.[9] But this example should not be overestimated. The buyer as the "publisher's programme planner" is no universally applicable model. Normally, the publishers have a good feeling and the respective market knowledge for the printed run of a title.

3. Electronic Books

With electronic books the digitisation includes all phases between production and consumption. The books are no longer printed on paper; the delivery is made via Internet. (At this point, we ignore the variants where electronic books are stored on disks or CD-ROM and distributed via these media, e.g. also in the conventional bookshop.) Electronic books are read with special eBook reading devices (e.g. the Rocket eBook) or at normal PCs using a special eBook reading software (e.g. the Acrobat E-Book Reader or the Microsoft Reader). Some online bookstores sell electronic books, but it would an exaggeration to speak of a market success.

Concerning the producer-consumer relationship, the most important changes with electronic books take place in the production phase. The book file which is sent to the customer via Internet only becomes an electronic book with the appropriate reading software or eBook device of the reader. These "production means" must be available and functional. But also the concrete design of the electronic book delivered quasi as a "blank" can be strongly influenced by the consumer/reader. This refers e.g. to the selection of page and font sizes, colour displays, arrangements or the use of media (e.g. the read aloud function).

This leads to a change in the competence requirements on the customers. Whereas in online book trading the demands on the customers refer to the

---

9 TSUNETOMO YAMAMOTO: *Hagakure. Der Weg des Samurai*, Book on Demand, Euro 10,23; Piper Taschenbuch, Euro 8,64 (Source: Amazon.de 14.11.2001).

orientation, search, evaluation and order phase as well as handling the online shop, with electronic books this technical competence is extended to the production phase and the phase of reception.

A novel aspect of electronic books is that the book software predefines the type of use. Publishers, for instance, are concerned with the fact that electronic books can be copied. The fear of a "Napsterisation" of electronic books is omnipresent in the publishers' discussions. They therefore try to prevent the creation of copies by means of software technology. And this is only one possibility of "spoon-feeding" the users: via book software it is possible to exactly determine whether it can be printed, copied, changed, to what extent, by whom, and in which period of time. Resulting from basically the same process of digitisation which has provided individualisation potentials for the customers, the nightmare of a total control and restriction of use is arising here.

4. Hypertexts

Electronic books are called "books" because they are still largely and sometimes deliberately approximated to the book form. They have pages, a sequential structure typical for books, and the reading software imitates further characteristics of book use (dog-ears, bookmarks, annotations, text marks, etc.).[10] Hypertexts can be understood as special variants of electronic books. They leave the conventional book form and develop a new, independent structure specific to computer-use and often described as non-linear and non-hierarchical. With hypertexts, a particularly advanced linkage of production and utilisation aspects, i.e. a special form of co-production or prosumption, can be observed.

Even with conventional books it is said that every reader reads his "own" book, but with hypertext this "reader control" becomes the most important aspect. Initially, hypertext is nothing but a varied offer of possibilities for the organisation and reception of a text. It is only "generated" in concrete form in its use for and by the consumer (Wingert 1999). Every new reception decision of the reader (generally the pursuit of a "link" from a selection of "links") contributes to the specific and individual generation of a hypertext.

10 For the discussion on electronic books and hypertexts cf. BÖHLE ET AL. (1997).

V. Outlook

Even though a certain scepticism against the promises of the new information and communication technologies is always recommended, it has turned out, that the "new power of the customers" is more than just a chimera. Even with growing product complexity it is possible to increase – on the basis of digital technologies – the influence of the customers in different areas of the producer-consumer relationship: directly at the sales interface, in pricing, in product and assortment policy as well as in the individual product design. However, the mode of customers' participation is not without problems. It requires new competencies, redistributes burdens and leads to some unintended consequences:

- the increase in product variety rises the burden of selection,
- the increase in the individualisation potential of single products results in the burden of their configuration,
- the new software-technical production capacities on the part of the consumers lead to restricting software controls by the publishers.

Returning to the discussion of the 1980s, the following distinction can be drawn (cf. Hanekop et al. 2001, p. 90). The changeover to "unalienated housework" is not the deciding factor. The developments in the publishing and book selling industry considered here are not withdrawn from the commercial market sphere. The "new type of prosumer" (Hanekop et al.) is not the do-it-yourself worker or homeworker but someone who includes features of professional and technically informatised work in his consumption and thus gains influence and power. For the developments in the publishing and book selling industry described above (see also Hanekop et al. for the area of mobile communication), it remains an open question whether the new type of prosumer will be able to pass beyond a peripheral phenomenon for groups with an affinity to technology and spread within mass consumption.

Bibliography

BANZHAF, D.: "Der Markt und die Macht", *Börsenblatt für den Deutschen Buchhandel*, 169 (2002) 8, pp. 8-11.

BÖHLE, K.; RIEHM, U.; WINGERT, B.: *Vom allmählichen Verfertigen elektronischer Bücher. Ein Erfahrungsbericht*, Frankfurt et al. (Campus) 1997 (Publications of the Institute for Technology Assessment and Systems Analysis [ITAS], Vol. 5).

BRYNJOLFSSON, E.; SMITH, M.: "Frictionless commerce? A comparison of Internet and conventional retailers", *Management Science*, 46 (2000) 4, p. 563-585.

CAIRNCROSS, F.: *The death of distance. How the communications revolution is changing our lives*, Boston (Harvard Business School Press) 1997.

COLE, T.; GROMBALL, P.: *Das Kunden-Kartell. Die neue Macht des Kunden im Internet*, München (Hanser) 2000.

DONK, W. B. H. J. VAN DE; TOPS, P. W.: "Informatization and democracy: Orwell or Athens", *Informatization and the Public Sector*, 2 (1992) 3, pp. 169-196.

GERSHUNY, J.: *After industrial society? The emerging self-service economy*, London and Basingstoke (Macmillan Press) 1978 (here cited from the German translation: *Die Ökonomie der nachindustriellen Gesellschaft. Produktion und Verbrauch von Dienstleistungen*, Frankfurt and New York [Campus] 1981).

HANEKOP, H.; TASCH, A.; WITTKE, V.: "'New Economy' und Dienstleistungsqualität: Verschiebungen der Produzenten- und Konsumentenrolle bei digitalen Dienstleistungen", *SOFI Mitteilungen*, No. 29 (2001), pp. 73-91.

LYNCH, C.: "The battle to define the future of the book in the digital world", *First Monday*, 6 (2001) 6 (*http://www.firstmonday.org*).

NEGROPONTE, N.: *Being digital*, New York (Alfred A. Knopf) 1995 (German translation: *Total digital. Die Welt zwischen 0 und 1 oder Die Zukunft der Kommunikation*, München [Bertelsmann] 1995).

PRIDDAT, B. P.: "virtual work / virtual product – Skizze einer Theorie der Arbeit in modernen Umgebungen", in: A. BRILL, M. DE VRIES (Eds.): *Virtuelle Wirtschaft*, Opladen and Wiesbaden (Westdeutscher Verlag) 1998, pp. 158-173.

RIEHM, U.; ORWAT, C.; WINGERT, B.: *Online Buchhandel in Deutschland. Die Buchhandelsbranche vor der Herausforderung des Internet*, Karlsruhe (Forschungszentrum Karlsruhe) 2001.

TOFFLER, A.: *The third wave*, New York (Morrow) 1980 (here cited from the German translation: *Die Zukunftschance. Von der Industriegesellschaft zu einer humaneren Zivilisation*, München [Bertelsmann] 1980).

WIND, J.; MAHAJAN, V.: *Digital marketing. Global strategies from the world's leading expert*, New York, Chichester (Wiley) 2001.

WINGERT, B.: "Der Leser im Hypertext – im Weinberg oder im Steinbruch?", in: B. SUTER, M. BÖHLER (Eds.): *hyperfiction. Hyperliterarisches Lesebuch: Internet und Literatur*, Basel et al. (Stroemfeld) 1999, pp. 159-172.

Chapter 4

The End of Consumption in Information Society

ULI ZAPPE

Dawn of light, lying between a silence and sold sources
JON ANDERSON, *Tales from Topographic Oceans*

I. Participation Instead of Consumption

When used in the context of the so-called "e-economy," the term "consumption" is essentially an oxymoron which only serves to block the view of crucial developments. For the paradigmatic goods of trade in the Internet – information, be it in the form of text, multimedia data, or software – are precisely not consumed when downloaded from the Net. On the Internet, participation in information replaces consumption of finite resources. This, however, makes the traditional rules of exchange obsolete; they all used to be based upon the elementary pattern of distribution of finite, if not scarce, resources (material, as well as time) that change hands or else are consumed for the benefit of the counterpart. The transformation from industrial society to information society is also the transformation from consumer society to participation society.

At the end of the industrial age, a development that has been an integral part of it from the very beginning thus sees both its conclusion and its turning point: the continuous loading of industrial products with more and more information, labeled by sociologists as "scientification of industry." For a good 200 years, the average share of cost of materials and of (per item) production costs in the exchange value has been continually decreasing to the same extent in which the information inherent in the product has been growing: viz the progressively complex expertise of its production and the structure materialized in it, from the designer item to the high-tech device, to the pharmaceutical product whose physical substance often represents but a mere fraction of its exchange value.

Yet, so far, the material share of a product has never been zero and, therefore, in the end always complied with the traditional paradigm of exchange and consumption. The same goes for conventional trade in information which has always been tied to finite resources – be it the substrate storing the information, be it the time of the person imparting it. This has made and still makes sensorily plausible, for instance, that when purchasing a book, one also purchases something physical, something finite. With a computer program costing hundreds of dollars, stored on a data medium being worth not more than a few cents, this gets noticeably more difficult though, which is why the manufacturers initially added sumptuous packaging along with thick manuals. That sufficed to maintain at least the illusion of something physical. With the distribution of data via the Internet, however, this very last remnant ceases. What prevails as a product is pure, substrateless information, potentially omnipresent throughout the entire Net. If costs arise through consumption of finite resources, then it is only for the physical maintenance of the Internet, which – not unlike classical traffic infrastructures – logistically is uncoupled from the respective distribution processes and, consequently, is of no importance for the following basic considerations.

Pure information spreads in a way fundamentally different from that of finite resources: it does not change hands, but expands itself among the recipients and users. In the course of this process, its usability multiplies rather than shifts. The logic of its distribution originates in the academic, not the business community (except for the specific case of strategic information, which will not be discussed here); the broadest possible dissemination would always seem desirable from the standpoint of society as a whole, since the utility of information always increases monotonically (and in the case of reflexive synergies, even exponentially), provided its distribution grows without any additional expense and efforts.

Admittedly, creating information continues to consume finite resources. This has already been a classical dilemma of traditional property rights theories: while, according to common view, it is the property rights granted to authors which motivate their (socially desired) creation of new information despite such consumption of finite resources, these rights will afterwards hamper its (again, socially desired) maximum distribution. So far, confronting this dilemma was de facto circumvented more or less arduously with the help of the construction of "intellectual property" in the early industrial age, which served to project the distribution logic of finite resources onto the specific distribution logic for information. This was a successful strategy as long as information itself was still bound to finite resources and, as such, was finite itself; the substrateless information of the Internet age breaks up this arrangement.

Placed within the coordinate system of classical economics, no *rational* exchange value (cost of labor and materials) can any longer be pre-established for information spread on the Internet. With the cost of labor for generating data remaining constant, independent of the degree of circulation, and with the possibilities of distribution being quasi-infinite within the bounds of world population, the cost of labor per bit of distributed information approaches zero. ("Support," for example, for software that does use the finite resource time, is not taken into consideration here; see also paragraph IV below.) Therefore, with a *nominal* exchange value (price) greater than zero, there is for the first time the potential for a quasi-infinite surplus value for a finite production (and any production is finite).

Presently common neoclassical economics does not bring about results as absurd as this. However, this is so only because it does not manage to perceive justice of distribution from its marginalistic perspective of *relative* optimization processes anyway. Its lack of contradiction merely reveals the fact that behind its quasi-physicalism, there lurks a concept of the market as a pure power play for price definition which does not have a problem with a quasi-infinite surplus value for the winner.

Yet, no-one escapes unscathed with a neoclassical perspective, for the simple reason that the classical perspective still has a far better means of reflecting the lifeworldly legitimization processes which model price as an equivalent for output instead of as winnings in a strategic power play. If this legitimation fails, as in the case of quasi-infinite surplus value, high exclusion costs arise in order to enforce property rights no longer considered legitimate and to shield the goods in question from (de jure) unauthorized access. Transaction cost theory has recently pointed out that neoclassical economics needs to take such costs into account, and that in the case of high exclusion costs, private property rights would become economically pointless (Furubotn/Richter 1998, pp. 98). Hence, with the transaction costs arising from a lack of societal acceptance, the classical perspective re-enters neoclassical economics by the back door.

Whether seen through the eyes of classical or neoclassical theory, the information of the Internet age, a participation good – therefore, an economic good that can only be participated in, but no longer consumed –, does not conform to the paradigm of exchange which has developed along the lines of finite goods and services.

II. Turning Point Strategies

To the extent in which market participants would be able to establish the traditional paradigm of exchange with regard to such new participation goods, they should benefit from the blessings of quasi-infinite surplus value. It is this very strategy that underlies the fabulous rise of the pioneers of information society – Microsoft is the classic example.

In order to be able to harvest the enormous surplus value resulting from treating information (according to the rules of conventional economics) as an economic good tied to finite resources, this treatment needs to be forced upon the market. That was easy to do in the early phases of the development; for the reason alone that the new conditions were just becoming apparent as such, only the old rules were familiar so far and, for the time being, computer programs were indeed tied to comparatively expensive storage media. Nevertheless, a pioneer like Microsoft is an especially good case study for how companies tried (and still try) to take advantage of the opportune moment by using all means to shape information as a consumer good (rather than a participation good) and to stifle any resistance against this strategy:

- The public *source code* upon which a program was based, was immediately closed and minimally modified at a strategically crucial point in such a way that knowledge of the public source code alone no longer made the complete reconstruction of the program's functionality possible. Software thus lost its chief characteristic of being information and became a black-box mechanism, which it originally was not, but which today forms its image as if it were a matter of course. Consequently, for the user this translates into being completely at the mercy of the product which represents the infrastructure of any of the user's work at the computer and, therefore, being at the mercy of the manufacturer and the manufacturer's product strategies.

- It was especially the *data formats* used for the storage of documents that were kept secret. Once important documents are created in such a format, an even greater and more dramatic dependence on the software manufacturer arises. (Fears exist that unreadable documents in a no longer known data format will be one of the severest problems of information society in the long run.) The necessity of document exchange among different individuals solidifies a once established proprietary data format to such an extent, that even dependence of a whole society on the product strategies of one manufacturer can arise. Standards – indispensable for any functional technical infrastructure –, if established as proprietary standards, by necessity lead to the formation of monopolies, which in addition appear to be legitimate due to their standardization function.
- Expensive *licensing and copy protection mechanisms* were integrated into programs, thus deliberately restricting their use and hence their efficiency. (Classic exclusion mechanisms, conversely, aim at utility maximization for the owner while excluding third parties.) In order to legally cushion these absurdities, license terms have been formulated in such a way that the buyer does not acquire ownership of the software anyway, but only a (sometimes temporary) right of use.

Software in itself is pure information. Pure information is not consumed, but flows freely, reduces opacity, and increases autonomy. Software stigmatized by the above features increases opacity, reduces autonomy, cannot flow freely, and may exhaust itself. There is nothing information-like about it any more; the participation good has turned into a consumer good.

In the case of Microsoft, this strategy bore fruit: in just two decades, the start-up in the proverbial garage became the highest capitalized company in the world, surpassing all the giants of industrial society. However, the hereby exemplified practices applied to get there have at least three fatal societal consequences: First, they artificially and purposefully reduce the efficiency of societal labor. Secondly, they necessarily turn the basal infrastructure of the information society into the private property of individual companies. Thirdly, they also block our view of the full range of the structurally new opportunities of the information age, namely that with the concept of information as a consumer good, the Internet is reduced to a consumption-distribution machinery, which in an absurd way, fails to see the economically and societally new potential of the Net, that it is a symmetrical-egalitarian two-way medium, whose uniqueness lies in the unprecedented opportunity of a worldwide 1:1 structure of participation and interaction relations and not in the 1:n structure of the supplier/consumer relation.

This false perspective of the Internet as a new consumer medium is omnipresent in the way the business world handles it: in the asymmetrically designed DSL Internet access facilities that allow the receipt of information many times faster than its sending; in the innumerable attempts (always failing, which is telling) to combine the consumer medium television with the participation medium Internet, which is only superficially supported by the technically long outdated argument of the one already existent and valuable monitor, but in reality based on the false assumption of a substantial similarity of both media; in the vision of the self-refilling Internet refrigerator, which has always symbolically served as the cutting edge of the Internet's accomplishments to come. All this happens against the backdrop of the Internet as a consumer medium. The Internet's true economic innovation, however, points into a wholly different direction.

III. Disintegrating Legitimacy

The practices of dressing pure information as a consumer good with their problematic consequences and the fortunes that companies accumulated thanks to their initially successful establishment, robbed the ideologem of pure information as an exchangeable economic good of the greater part of its legitimacy. Had it already been something of a challenge to determine the rational exchange value of products that mainly consist of information, such as CDs or some pharmaceuticals, the quasi-infinite surplus value so obviously demonstrates from a lifeworldly perspective the absurdity of the economic mechanisms now in power, such that they are no longer accepted by a great many consumers and resistance is beginning to spread. The neoclassical reference to property right theories that could model the economic processes in question consistently does not help either, because it is exactly this property rights legitimacy which allows quasi-infinite surplus value, that has suffered lasting damage. If copy protection mechanisms are constantly "cracked" right after their introduction, then a substantial part of the "hackers" acts more or less explicitly on moral impulses, in order to counterweight the potentially infinite surplus value of information with a potentially infinite distribution, hence making the exchange value at least quasi-rational again (see for example Gilmore 2001).

The fact that the exchange value in its present form is irrational or at least pure economic power play is, incidentally, admitted by the industry itself when it operates with a price discrimination that allows some groups – oftentimes educational institutions and/or private individuals – to obtain one and the same software for a mere fraction of the "commercial" price, at times even free, and in extreme cases, depending on its strategic taste, simply generally gives away a particular software at no charge. For example, in order to sweep their competitor Netscape off the market, Microsoft distributed their web browser *Internet Explorer* free of charge without any restrictions and in versions for non-Microsoft operating systems as well, which did not even bring indirect profit for the company. No manufacturer of consumer goods could ever afford to do this, and if they did, the competition authorities would immediately arrive on the scene and accuse them of dumping – an indicator that the official side, too, does recognize the difference between participation and consumer goods.

Against this background, it hardly appears convincing that the very same companies which fight for market share via such practices, hypocritically now get all worked up about the thus-stigmatized "for-free mentality" on the Internet. This "for free" mentality has nothing to do with "rip-off" by ruthless users and everything to do with an outdated economic paradigm which is beginning to disintegrate, with the companies themselves having contributed to its farewell song.

Relating to society as a whole, the nascent resistance against information as a consumer good is well justified. As mentioned previously, the maximum possible distribution of information (measured by the finite resources) is of paramount interest to a prospering information society. An economic system that severely impedes distribution and, in order to do so, even accepts high exclusion costs along with the corresponding additional use of finite resources, cannot be rational from the point of view of society as a whole. (In many cases it is not rational on a company wide scale, either, if exclusion costs start to abound, and sometimes even the work of the company's own engineers is severely hampered by information restrictions meant to prevent individual employees from acquiring the company's entire expertise.)

Likewise, it cannot be rational that society as a whole, in its basal infrastructure, is dependent upon the locked away ("intellectual") property of individual companies, who thereby are ultimately in a position to manipulate the information flow and thus the backbone of the information society. However, information will necessarily be locked away information as long as it is modeled as a finite consumer good rather than an infinite participation good – an issue that incidentally also features prominently in the debates on genetic engineering which discuss who can and who should "own" the human genome (i.e. its information content).

Finally, it is hard to see why, with the increasing importance of information, academic traditions that were modeled along its lines should be replaced by the altogether heterogeneous laws of the consumer goods market. It is the academic model that is in accordance with information: information is not used up, but grows through (synchronous as well as diachronous) distribution. Whoever generates information will do so, according to Newton's famous dictum, by standing on the shoulders of giants and will add but a mere grain of their own achievements. This alone makes an allocation of private property rights that is supposed to be non-strategic and founded on fact, problematic (as pointed out in part V, the Netscape company is a good example for that). While certainly always possible, a purely strategic allocation, on the other hand, would permanently damage the integrity and hence the efficient societal usability of information in the long run.

It is one of the significant aspects of the budding information society that, at the same time, it equips resistance against these developments with entirely new opportunities. On the one hand, the means of production for the key technology of the information age lie in the hands of each interested individual – as opposed, for example, to an automobile production line. Anyone interested can afford a computer – from a practical perspective, Marx's old utopia of the "socialization" of the means of production has come true in an unforeseen way. On the other hand, the 1:1 structure of the Internet, which the traditional perspective fails to recognize, allows the counterforces to coordinate by distributed organization of their work across the Net, which can bring about alternative forms of labor in societally relevant dimensions.

It is these two points which made it possible for the phenomenon of *Free Software,* a historically new production paradigm, to emerge; one that was exclusively based on intrinsically motivated, mostly unpaid labor of a vast number of individuals involved, who as a rule, knew each other and coordinated their activities only via the Internet. Free software – the most well-known specimen, even if by far not the only one, is the Unix operating system *Linux* – is free (as in free of cost) to be copied and to be used, but furthermore, is also free (as in unrestricted and uncensored) insofar as its source code, and therefore all related data formats, are always open to the public and available to be used and modified by anyone interested. In all respects, thus, it liberates software from the reduction to a consumer good described previously, and turns it into a participation good par excellence. In order to protect this biotope of information society from an environment still dominated by the patterns of industrial society and to consolidate activities in favor of free software, several organizations have been founded, who have created the corresponding license models. Those license models de jure are actually anti-license models de facto, interfaces from industrial to information society, meant to prevent third parties from monopolizing and commercially "protecting" free software with the help of the license mechanisms of industrial society. They are therefore occasionally referred to as *Copyleft.* Historically the first and currently most important organization is the *Free Software Foundation* with their *GNU project*, founded by Richard Stallman (2001) in 1985. (*GNU* is a recursive acronym for *GNU's Not Unix*, which in a playful way, is trying to mirror the never-ending flow of free information.) The license for free software created by the Free Software Foundation is called the *GNU General Public License* (abbreviated *GPL*). Linux is part of the GNU project (hence correctly referred to as *GNU/Linux*).

Work on free software does not regard capital as its goal, but, if anything, merely regards it as a necessary precondition for the required resources. It is powered by and performed for the sake of personal needs and sincere recognition among equals (and therefore equally competent individuals) as well as among users, rather than strategic interest, does not shield itself to the outside world, but relies on the academic customs of the peer review, and puts self-organized participation in joint projects in the place of hierarchic labor organization (compare Freyermuth 2001a and 2001b, also Raymond 2001). The remarkable result of this giant, initially mostly unplanned socio-economic map exercise, is that software evolving from this form of labor is not only free, but as a rule, also of higher quality than its conventionally produced, commercial counterparts. It is exposed to hardly any strategic influences; only the quality of the program code serves as the (intrinsic) criterion; it benefits from the free exchange of thoughts and ideas amongst a maximum number of interested individuals; and anyone with a computer issue can, in principle, remove that issue immediately without passing through a hierarchy.

The market value of free software bears impressive evidence of the fact that it is not an economically just marginally interesting hobbyism phenomenon. Freyermuth (2001a, p. 177) speaks of "investments worth several billion dollars" just for the Linux source code; since Linux is not the only free operating system and, moreover, a lot of free software was created outside of operating systems, the total value may well amount to a two-digit billion sum.

Above all, the very backbone of the information society itself, the Internet, consists of free software in all integral parts of its software technology. This is no accidental concurrence. Not only did free software require the Internet for its success, conversely, the all-encompassing, unrestricted communication network, which comprises the Internet, could only arise via the openness of free software. The Internet and free software have developed with and through each other and are most closely intertwined. The future lurks at the foundation of the commercial attempts at taking first steps in the Internet. E-Commerce is based upon an infrastructure which arose contrary to its logic. All the conventional commercial, proprietary efforts of the 80s and 90s to set up data networks – CompuServe, AOL, MSN, you name them –, failed due to their insistence on "intellectual property" and the isolation policy that goes with it, or were absorbed by the Internet.

Meanwhile, the principles of free software have been applied to other types of information in the Internet, too. Not unlike the GPL, there are, for example, license models for texts such as the *GNU Free Documentation License*. Also, the Usenet (the network of news servers with now more than thirty thousand discussion groups) forms the world's largest and, at the same time, equally free pool of expertise.

It is these developments that support resistance against information as a consumer good and demonstrate most clearly that the construct of "intellectual property" has become obsolete in the information society and, worse, counterproductive. Although "intellectual property" is not much disputed in current everyday politics, this is not true of economic theory. While on the debit side it obviously hampers efficient distribution of existent information, it has been controversial if, in the reverse, on the credit side, only it can create the socially necessary incentives for generating new information. In their introduction to the subject area of "intellectual property," Besen and Raskind (1991, p. 4) list a number of authors who deny this, although they have remained a considerable minority. Under current societal conditions, the idea just comes too easily that it is exclusively the prospect of profitable private property rights that motivates information production in socially required proportions. With the Free Software movement and the related "Internet culture" though, this hypothesis has become more than shaky. The concept of "intellectual property" is up for consideration.

For the concerns of this discussion, it is Georg Wilhelm Friedrich Hegel (1821, §§ 34-104, for the subject at hand, especially §§ 39-46 and §§ 67-69) who elaborates in the most differentiated way on the concept of property. He emphasizes that private property is a condition of the possibility of individual freedom; I become *subject* to the extent in which I shape *nature* through work and thereby in turn transform it into my *object*. In that sense, the determining legitimation of private property would not be valid for *intellectual* property. Hegel, of course, is enough of an apologist of bourgeois society to regard it as constituted by contracts between abstract persons, exclusively characterized as private proprietors. This forces him to provide the free spirit to whom information originally belongs, with the ability to make the same extrinsic and, therefore, transform it into an object, into exchangeable "intellectual property", in order not to exclude poets and philosophers from sociality. Neglecting the theory-edificial motivation and the subsumption under exchangeable goods following from it, the idea that intellectual work, too, can be subject constitutive does sound nice, and in a world of virtual reality is probably inevitable. The crucial point, however, is that under the conditions of industrial alienation, labor cannot fulfill the noble task that Hegel destined for it anyway. Property is reduced to exchange coercion: power relations and bare reproduction.

It is solely this reduced concept of property that is being argued about in today's debates over "intellectual property." But this concept of property has become obsolete in the post-bourgeois sociality of the Net, of the computer as the "quasi-socialized" means of production, of the non-alienated labor organization of free software. It is the *subject constitutive* concept of ownership as intellectual authorship that should not be abandoned. This is not jeopardized though, for information in which others participate does precisely not fade from the creator. On the contrary, the participation good of information

– unlike any consumer good – is suited to combine subject constitution by ownership (in the sense of authorship, not in the sense of property rights) with *simultaneous* recognition via distribution. Accordingly, licenses such as the GPL stress the authorship (which always has to be passed on when copying the information), but do not tie this to any restrictions on distribution. This way, the exchange coercion component of property lapses and hence is no longer an obstacle to strategically undistorted information, thus facilitating a non-strategic self-relationship for the subject constituting itself, that now additionally at the *same time* knows it is elevated in the recognition of others. Participation society makes the reappropriation of labor possible in a historically new shape.

Against this backdrop, "intellectual property" proves to be a historically mediated dispositive. Still without meaning for societal reproduction in feudalism, information became a crucial productive force with the emerging industrialization and at the latest with the scientification of industry. However, since bourgeois society is a society of contracting private proprietors, information, itself still being a finite resource at this point in time anyway, must be adjusted to the regulatory variable of private property. "Intellectual property" is born; the authorship of a work turns into an economic factor. Due to their capital intensity, however, the means of production in industrial society are in the rarest cases in the hands of the producing; thusly alienated labor lets property become a merely formal contractual link, abstract in the bad sense, no longer subject-constituting. Industrial society becomes a consumer society, whose contractual relations are predominantly 1:n relations between suppliers and consumers; the subject degenerates into the consumer. This development is overcome in information society. Once information is pure and free-flowing by itself, the element of coercion inherent in information as a consumer good, its scarcity, becomes badly abstract as a merely imposed exclusion mechanism and, as a consequence, can no longer be enforced; the decentralizable means of production in the hands of those producing information facilitate an intrinsic reappropriation of labor. In the emerging participation society, sociality constitutes itself informally via participative 1:1 relations in the Net. The subject's degeneration to consumer gives way to a constitution through shaped material that, being pure information, can at the same time be distributed, and therefore establish relationships of recognition with others.

Similar to the eve of the industrial age, "intellectual property" in the transition to the information age is once again in the center of a struggle between old and new powers. However, recently abounding debates on copy protection everywhere, hectic activities by industry lobbyists, and bills infringing upon privacy rights, like the DCMA (*Digital Copyright Millennium Act*) may, in retrospect, prove to be unproductive attempts at stopping the wheel of history in the face of its turning.

IV. Alternative Allocation

The fact that dressing information as a consumer good is losing its social acceptance, however, does *not* mean that the (no-longer) consumers would not be willing to compensate, if necessary, for the expenditure of finite resources to create information, as the remarkable example of the British rock band *Marillion* demonstrates. In the 1990s, Marillion had shrunk from star to insider status and, as a consequence, their record company refused to financially support a concert tour of the United States planned in succession to their 1997 album, *This Strange Engine*. When Marillion's keyboarder announced on the Internet that the band had decided to cancel the tour, their supporters spontaneously coordinated via the Net and raised $60,000 in a concerted action. This enabled the band to do their most extensive U.S. tour since the early 90s. Encouraged by this direct interaction with their supporters, Marillion asked all registered fans via email in the summer of 2000 whether they were ready to finance the production of the next CD. As a reaction to that, over 12,000 of them transferred the purchase price for the not yet existing CD to Marillion almost a year in advance, and thus enabled the band to produce the album independently of a record company; Marillion were able to work without artistic restrictions and for the very first time, the result of their work was completely theirs. In May 2001, then, *Anoraknophobia* was launched as the first CD in history to be directly financed by its listeners via the Internet.

Even if the production of Anoraknophobia is as yet a unique case, which moreover took place within a conventional economic environment, there are still some important hints to be found regarding a possible organization of productivity in participation society:

- The disintegration of legitimacy of traditional property rights does *not* mean, as the derogative lamentation about the "for-free mentality" in the Internet suggests, that the "Internet consumers would like to get everything for free," and that the information producers "need to stand in line for the soup kitchen." Rather a new legitimacy is developing: the no-longer consumers are willing to carry the *actual* expenditure of finite resources to create information (the costs of a concert tour, the costs of the production of a CD), even if it "does not pay" as seen from the record company's conventional-economic perspective. They would *not* be willing to accept private property rights that allow for strategic use in order to force a potentially infinite surplus value; Marillion's supporters would not have gotten together via the Internet in order to equip the band with those fabulous fortunes which, according to the cliche of conventional economics, are a prime reason for wanting to become a rock musician. Ironically, this way such participation-societal allocation principles in some respect put the idea into action that it is the contributed performance that needs to be compensated: the very motto that industrial society capitalism carried solely as a banner behind which to hide the bare power play – theoretically elevated by neoclassical economics –, which the race for maximum surplus value actually is.

- To have capital at one's disposal is essentially regarded as the condition for the possibility of production, not as its aim or motivation. It is the beginning, not as it used to be, the end of the process of creative activity. Financial risk/profit calculations like the one inducing Marillion's record company to object to the U.S. tour, play no structural-logical role, since the last link in the chain is the substantial and not the financial profit. This, of course, leads to both the question of allocation mechanisms for the start-up capital, and that of the motivation for the production of information. Answering these questions is of varying difficulty.
- Motivation for production has been intrinsic. In the words of Marillion's lead singer, Steve Hogarth, as printed in a commentary on the production of Anoraknophobia in the booklet accompanying the special edition CD for the supporters of the project, "This is the 21st century and everything is hype – but not this. This is about passion." Intrinsic motivation may indeed suffice for societally relevant productivity, as the Free Software movement shows. The quality of the information produced rises due to the lack of any strategic influence extrinsic to the information ("hype"); for Anoraknophobia, there were no conditions set by a record company to commercialize the music.

- With Anoraknophobia, the allocation of the required start-up capital ensued essentially from the trust of a fan community interacting closely with each other and with the band via the Internet, a community which had admittedly formed at the times of the band's economically conventional success. It is this point from which it is the most difficult to induce a general institutionalizable principle. It is clear that trust plays a key role and possibly must do so as a complementary of intrinsic motivation, supported by the close interaction of those involved via the Net. Such an allocation process provides yet another increase in information quality, in this case through selection: its underlying commitment would not seem likely to mobilize for lukewarm mediocrity which, as experience shows, is precisely the type of information that tends to be particularly successful in a conventionally commercial environment. In that respect, an alternative allocation mechanism has a very clear effect on the contents of socially produced information. The mass phenomenon star cult with its promise of quasi-infinite surplus value is replaced by a more closely intertwined, more discursive community interacting via the Net.

Whether and how these emerging developments will take full institutional shape in a participation society is hard to tell at this early stage. The media giants that appear so untouchable today are likely to disintegrate in favor of decentralized direct production and decentralized direct supply of information via the Internet, locatable with the help of media search engines. The principle of charging for information not by the number of those who participate in it (the basis for a potentially infinite surplus value), but by a singular market value which is tied to the resources consumed, has meanwhile been put into practice successfully by the Free Software movement as *fixed sponsorship*; IBM, for instance, has recently begun to sponsor Linux according to this principle with an amount of a billion. Often, if free software is not created in an academic context, the *service model* is applied. Here the programmers finance themselves by individual services such as support and customer-specific modifications of free software – ergo, precisely in the cases where they put their finite resource time at one individual client's disposal, and in the remaining time work on the generally accessible free software itself; a practice that has been able to flourish under the environmental circumstances of consumer society because the high market value of computer scientists makes a mere part-time job in the traditional sense sufficient for individual reproduction. The most awkward question remains that of societal mechanisms to allocate the required start-up capital, as far as this is still necessary in the times of "socialized" computer means of production; the venture capital boom during the stock market craze of the late 90s was nothing more than a historic predecessor here, taking the form of farce.

It will depend on the development of suitable institutions in a participation society whether information will, in accordance with its own academic character, be able to flow freely and finally fulfill Hegel's vision of a property that constitutes subjectivity rather than protects power.

V. Symptoms of Change

Social change does not occur without tension. From this perspective, the aforementioned, absurd *.com* boom on the global stock markets of the late 90s and the ensuing crash can be read as a symptom of crisis and, therefore, as an indication of the transition from a consumer to a participation society.

In 1981, the personal computer (PC) was born; one year later, the U.S. stock market (and in its wake most global stock markets, too) started to advance significantly after 15 years of stagnation. The strong rise in productivity brought about by computers and automatization allowed the Reserve Banks to gradually lower the interest rates, which had been extremely high at the beginning of the 80s, without the risk of higher inflation – *the* ideal stock market climate. Until 1994, i.e. within 13 years, the stock market quadrupled (going by the U.S. Dow Jones Industrial Index) – an excellent performance from the perspective of that time. It is in this period that Microsoft's growth to a global player came to pass.

Up to that point in time, the Internet, even though it had long been developed, was still unknown to the broad public, since there was no user-friendly access software for PCs. Then Netscape with their web browser of the same name arrived on the scene. The company's founder, Marc Andreessen, was a young Chicago student who had written substantial parts of the software under the wings of the local National Center for Supercomputing Applications (NCSA) of Illinois University, and had first distributed it free (though without the GNU license) and with great success under the name of *Mosaic*. However, when Andreessen recognized the commercial potential of his work, he used the measures described in part II above to transform the free Mosaic of academic origin into the consumer good *Netscape*. Soon the enterprise was celebrated as the "Microsoft of the Internet," and in August 1995, when Netscape saw its IPO, the public company that owned little more than the modified source code of a program written by a student at an academic institution, had become worth two billion U.S. dollars; in the following five months, the stock value tripled. What had taken Microsoft over a decade, Netscape, the first enterprise that wanted to exclusively trade in the pure information of the Internet, seemed to achieve within a matter of months.

Admittedly, in a roundabout way, Microsoft also purchased the Mosaic source code, used it to create the Internet Explorer and thus eventually brought Netscape to its downfall. However, with Netscape's arrival there was no more holding back; for the first time it had become possible to directly experience the meaning of potentially infinite surplus value. The Internet boom broke loose, with the net asset value of companies and their respective stock quotes seemingly unconnected due to the surplus-value promise. Precisely with the launch of the first Netscape version in December 1994, the stock market set out on an undreamed of zoom, tripling once more within only five years.

At the turn of the millennium, when the zoom came to an end and the hangover set in, no-one cared for Netscape anymore. *Napster* was the talk of the town, the very program, that – happily violating "intellectual property" – coordinated an easy, worldwide exchange of all kinds of multimedia information among computer users. The altitude fever of quasi-infinite surplus value had vanished when it became apparent that there was no social acceptance and extremely high exclusion costs were to be expected. Participation society appeared on the horizon and configured the Internet as something other than a giant surplus value accumulation machinery.

As yet, it is unclear how much farther the crisis on the capital markets will progress, and whether it really is a symptom of economic change. However, one thing seems clear: if we really are on our way from an industrial to an information society, if therefore, we are heading for a society in which more people will be occupied with the production, distribution, and reception of information, than with any other activity, then the transition from a consumer to a participation society will be inevitable, too. Just as industrial society finally transformed farming into agricultural industry, participation society will, in this instance, eventually bring industrial production into line with the new conditions. Those societies that are already preparing for this today will be the winners in the future.

Bibliography

BESEN, STANLEY M.; RASKIND, LEO J. (1991): "An Introduction to the Law and Economics of Intellectual Property", *Journal of Economic Perspectives*, 5 (1), pp. 3-27, *http://www.jstor.org*.

FREYERMUTH, GUNDOLF S. (2001a): "Aus der Open-Source-Geschichte lernen, Teil I", *c't*, 20 (2001), pp. 176-183, *http://www.heise.de/ct/01/20/176/*.

FREYERMUTH, GUNDOLF S. (2001b): "Aus der Open-Source-Geschichte lernen, Teil II", *c't*, 21 (2001), pp. 270-277, *http://www.heise.de/ct/01/21/270/*.

FURUBOTN, EIRIK G.; RICHTER, RUDOLF (1998): *Institutions and Economic Theory: the Contribution of the New Institutional Economics*, Ann Arbor (University of Michigan Press).

GILMORE, JOHN (2001): *What's Wrong With Copy Protection*, *http://www.toad.com/gnu/whatswrong.html*.

GNU FREE DOCUMENTATION LICENSE: *http://www.gnu.org/licenses/fdl.txt*.

GNU GENERAL PUBLIC LICENSE: *http://www.gnu.org/licenses/gpl.txt*.

GNU PROJECT: *http://www.gnu.org*.

HEGEL, GEORG WILHELM FRIEDRICH (1821): *Elements of the Philosophy of Right*, ed. Allen W. Wood, trans. H. B. Nisbet, Cambridge (Cambridge University Press) 1991. Original: *Grundlinien der Philosophie des Rechts*, Frankfurt am Main (Suhrkamp) 1970.

RAYMOND, ERIC STEVEN (2001): *The Cathedral and the Bazaar*, Beijing, Cambridge, Farnham, Köln, Paris, Sebastopol, Taipei, Tokyo (O'Reilly), *http://www.tuxedo.org/~esr/writings/cathedral-bazaar/cathedral-bazaar/*.

STALLMAN, RICHARD (2001): *The GNU Project*, *http://www.gnu.org/gnu/thegnuproject.html*.

Note: All URLs given as citations are subject to change. They were last validated on July 1st, 2002.

Chapter 5

Consumer Profiles in E-Commerce: How Companies Form Identities

ANDREAS GREIS

For broad sections of the German population the internet has become an integrated part of everyday life (ARD/ZDF Arbeitsgruppe Multimedia 1999 and 2001). This process can also be seen in other countries. Not only men aged between 20 and 30 with higher education are using the internet. Also more and more women, older people, people with a formally lower education and pupils integrate the internet in their everyday communication.

One would expect that e-commerce should profit from this development. But people are still reluctant to spend money on the internet, especially in Germany (Fuchs 2000). One reason may be the fact, that there are a number of difficult ethical questions which need to be answered. This essay will analyse questions concerning consumer profiles which are generated from the data traces an internet user leaves while surfing in cyberspace. On the basis of these traces one can find out when, how long and how often a person uses which service on the internet. These pieces of information enable assumptions regarding preferences and interests of an user. Such consumer profiles are of great use for advertising companies. Using the information given in the profiles advertising companies can create detailed campaigns directly addressing certain users. Thereby they can increase the campaigns' efficiency.

On the following pages identity theory is taken as an approach to reflect on this process of conceptualizing certain images of people by generating consumer profiles. In a first step the structures of identity development on the internet in general will be described. Afterwards the meaning of identity for ethics will be shown taking into consideration socio-psychological studies. Finally the ethical questions of consumer profiles will be reflected.

I. The Structures of the Internet

The internet include different medial and communicative devices. Analyzing the structure of this media space three dimensions can be distinguished. On the internet people communicate, on the internet people act and both actions are performed under virtual circumstances (Greis 2001, p. 137). The internet's virtuality is made up by the following aspects (Greis 2001, pp. 217f.):

- Displacing: Every single device on the internet (www, chat, email, newsgroup, MUDs) allows telepresence and makes personal presence in communication obsolete. This is also true for other medias. The crucial difference lies in the dimension. Communication on the internet is worldwide, and the number of possible participants is unlimited. Thus the internet has the potential to be a space of communication for the whole global population.
- Disbodying: On internet the flesh becomes word in contrast to the prologue of the gospel of John (the word becomes flesh). Because physical representations ground only on written descriptions, they become free floating and virtual.
- Oscillation between literacy and orality: Communication on the internet is written communication. However, communication on the internet is very similar to oral communication in many respects (e.g. emoticons) (Greis 2001, pp. 47ff.). Written communication is usually characterized by a certain degree of reflection and formality, whereas on the internet people use informal language. The communication reminds very much of a face-to-face conversation. Thus oral utterings become literarized.

- Performation of non-performative speech acts: On internet all descriptions of actions become acts themselves (Döring 1997, p. 270). All acting is speaking. This means that even non-performative speech acts, which describe actions, become performative. This occurs especially in MUDs and chats (e.g. writing "I'm kissing u" means to kiss the other, in case the other person feels like being kissed).
- Instrumentalization of nonverbal expressions: Nonverbal expressions such as gestures and miming make up an important part of face-to-face communication. On the internet these nonverbal expressions are substituted by emoticons, onomatopoeia or other signs. The speaker can instrumentalize these signs for his aims. These substitutions are no more spontaneous, beginning and end are clearly defined. Whereas nonverbal expressions in face-to-face communication can usually be taken as a proof of authenticity, the substitutions in computer-mediated communication (CMC) may be easiliy instrumentalized.

The virtual structures transcend the common borders and dimensions of communication. The inherent virtuality of the internet allows, theologically speaking, transcedence in immanence. The user is enabled to move beyond the borders of time and space, body and language. The virtual structures, however, make traditional garantuees of authenticity obsolete. Neither is there a speaker who can convince by the congruence of verbal and nonverbal expressions in a personal conversation, nor is there a reliable version of a text, such as a book (Greis 2001, pp. 226f.).

II. The Formation of Identity on Internet

In these structures the question on the identity of the user appears, because the media play always an important role in the formation of identity in our society strongly influenced by the media.

- Identity on internet is discussed under three aspects: the loss of identity in an anonymous mass because of de-individuation, the stronger accent on either personal or social identity, or the planned activation of wished identities (Döring 1999, pp. 269ff.).
- Identity formation takes place by four modes: by the takeover of net duties, e.g. chanop or sysop, by active engagement in virtual communities, by modifications of personal traits in order to show someone in

better light, or by the creation of a virtual self in online games or homepages (Döring 2001). The psychologist Nicola Döring distinguishes in this point a mirror motive in order to explorate the own self, and a mask motive to avoid negative reactions or to provoke positive reactions e.g. by gender-swapping (Döring 1999, pp. 269ff.). Concerning this aspect, the "nickname" is very important. These nicknames, chosen by one self, transport the first information about the character behind this name. These moments illustrate the attractions of "encounters" with virtual identities, they mark as well a lack of authenticity.

- On the first view identity on the internet has an emancipative and a restrictive aspect. Constructing his identity the user is free from limits of biographical, physical or social nature. The different settings of identity formation however influence this process (Höflich 1998). Nevertheless the user can search for his real identity and gets a profit of authenticity, but only for himself. Because of the problems discussed above such identities are under suspicion. The markers of authenticity are missing. In contrast to other settings of identity games, e.g. fantasy roleplays there are on the internet no hints to the real identity, like gender or age.
- Nevertheless an identity construction by others plays an important role. But paradoxically in this case the user has no possibility to control or to influence this formation of an identity of his own. This identity is based on data traces left while being online. It depends on the interpretation and combination of these traces. All actions online are saved be it in caches or on proxies, by cookies or other personal tracking systems. Especially advertising companies are interested in these data traces in order to generate consumer profiles. Which sites, how often and how long a site is visited, these data allow a reconstruction of an user. The identity of a surfer is only defined by a combination of his presumed interests. Thus the user cannot control all representations of his own on the internet.

III. Clearings of the Term Identity

After this phenomenological approach first hints regarding the question of the identity of an internet user are clear. Secondly the focus of this contribution, the question of consumer profiles, is identified as one possibility of identity formation on the internet. It is now necessary to keep a view on the term identity itself. Hereby the researches and teachings of George Herbert Mead are as well today basically (Mead 1995). Mead shows:

- Identity is not a result but a process. Identity is based upon retrospective views in order to reflect new experiences and to compare them with more recent experiences. Therefore identity is a process to make one sure about oneself in the retrospective. There are experiences in the past which are connected with one's own identity. The ability to remember identifies experiences with our identity.
- Identities are as well designed. Mead shows that for example plays are possibilities to try oneself's abilities in order to elicit reactions of others. These reactions are hints to the own identity.
- This leads to the next point. Identity depends on the feedback of others. Identity is realized in communities by the reaction of others. Mead introduces the term "generalized other", to describe the sum of all socially possible roles. The individual is able to represent for himself this generalized other and to identify his own roles in this setting. This part of the generalized other concerning a concrete person is called "me" in contrast to the "I" which constitutes the generalized other. "Das Ich als Subjekt ("I") betrachtet sich als Objekt ("me")" (Göbel 1998, p. 117). The "me" organizes the attitudes of other persons which the "I" elicits. Mead describes a circle process. The "I" elicits the "me" and reacts on it. Under an ethical perspective the "me" represents the values of the peer group of a person, while the "I" stands for unpredictable values of an individual, which can expand the values of a peer group.

Thus it is clear, that identity formation takes place in social contexts. Only in a confrontation with others individuation happens (Göbel 1998). Essential competences for identity formation are the ability of role distance and roletakeover, the ability of empathy and identity representation and the tolerance for ambiguities (Krappmann 1972, pp. 132ff.). On the one hand there are intersubjective interactions in a synchronous manner, which allow the self to learn more about itself by the actions and feedbacks of others. On the other hand complementarily, there is the subjective biography in a diachronous manner, which functions as a storage of the dynamics of the identity development (Haker 1998, p. 22). Thus identity includes a retrospective and a prospective dimension. In the retrospective one can recognize himself in his actions as identical or not and gets by this way a basis to design his life in future to be identical to him. The time of life is experienced as a space for designing, and the body is the centre of these experiences (Haker 1998, p. 26). By this, the narrative character of identity becomes clear. Identity is constructed narratively. Narrations integrate the singularitiy and the dynamics of unique situations in the context of an biography (Haker 1998, p. 46).

IV. The Importance of Identity for Ethics

The formation of identity is in two ways linked to ethics. On the one hand personal identity is the prerequisite to speak of an ethical subject, on the other hand ethical reflection is constitutive for the development of identity, because the reconstruction of one's own self from one's biography and from the feedback of others is characterized by evalutions (Benhabib 1995, p. 17). Thus it becomes clear, that "die im Menschen angelegte Moralfähigkeit abhängig ist vom Intensitätsgrad seiner Selbstsuche" (Hunold 1994, p. 44). Ethical questions are therefore inherent the formation of identity. But now the problem occurs, what qualifies an identity as moral.

> Die moralische Identität ist (...) die Identität, die sich selbst und seine Handlungen in der *zeitlichen* Verstrickung verantwortet und entsprechend in seiner Lebens*geschichte* artikuliert. Die moralische Identität ist darüber hinaus diejenige Identität, in der sich die Dialektik von Selbst und Anderem des Selbst in der Weise der *Anerkennung* geltend macht (Haker 1998, p. 162).

This definition has to be explained in different ways. Firstly the decisive criterion for identity evaluation is responsibility. This responsibility can be examined in direction to one self and in direction to others. Thus moral identity is dialectical between disinhibition in the sense of self exposure and inhibition in the sense of acceptance of the others. This tension can be described by the trias of affirmation, instrumentalization and arrangement. The basical affirmation of the own self is followed by the instrumentalization of the own existence to an actual personal need. This instrumentalization has to be arranged as with the multiple further own needs as with the needs of others. (Hunold 1993, pp. 191ff.).

The second important aspect of the definition above is the articulation of the own biography. On the one hand this regards to what Charles Taylor calls the affirmation of normal life (Taylor 1989). Lifestyle gets by this way a central term of ethics (Laubach 1999). On the other hand thus it can be achieved to interprete a universal ethical principle as responsibility in a concrete manner. At last the category of acceptance integrates the social dimension of identity and morality. To be morally identical means to accept one's needs and the needs of the others under the criterion of responsibility in future.

V. Ethical Questions in the Context of the Formation of Consumer Profiles

The virtuality of the internet enables the initiation of identity processes without a social dimension and the organization of identity with no regard to the person itself. That means both ways are deficitary in comparison with the formation of identity described above. In case of the generation of consumer profiles the following points are in my opinion central:

- By the formation of consumer profiles identity is no longer a process but a result. Such a profile is no longer connected with the structure of feedbacks which characterizes the formation of identity between "I" and "me".
- Such a profile has as well no longer a connection to the biography of a user. The identities which the user creates by himself are at least integrated by his body. A consumer profile has no connection to the person. It becomes independent.
- The profiles remain onedimensional and try to fill the missing dimensions by interpretation. As well only that traits are integrated in the profile which can be operationalized.
- The user doesn't know the criterions of the interpretations. He can't understand how this image of himself was generated. As well he doesn't know how he is evaluated.
- It remains uncertain if changes in the structure of his needs are newly integrated in a once generated profile.

In the end it is clear, that especially in the context of e-commerce it is necessary to reflect the problem of identity. The central questions are informational self-determination and participation of a person in the processes of the formation of one's own identity.

Profiles will be generated in the future, but the user has to be clear about the fact, that something happens with his data traces and he has to be informed what happens with his datas.

Literature

ARD/ZDF-ARBEITSGRUPPE MULTIMEDIA: "ARD/ZDF Online-Studie 1999: Wird Online Alltagsmedium?", *Media Perspektiven* (1999), pp. 401-414.

ARD/ZDF-ARBEITSGRUPPE MULTIMEDIA: "ARD/ZDF Online-Studie 2001: Internetnutzung stark zweckgebunden", *Media Perspektiven* (2001), pp. 382-397.

BENHABIB, SEYLA: "Einleitung", in: SEYLA BENHABIB: *Selbst im Kontext. Kommunikative Ethik im Spannungsfeld von Feminismus, Kommunitarismus und Postmoderne*, Frankfurt a.M. (Suhrkamp) 1995, pp. 7-30.

DÖRING, NICOLA: "Kommunikation im Internet: Neun theoretische Ansätze", in: BERNAD BATINIC (Ed.): *Internet für Psychologen*, Göttingen u.a. (Hogrefe) 1997, pp. 298-336.

DÖRING, NICOLA: *Sozialpsychologie des Internet. Die Bedeutung des Internet für Kommunikationsprozesse, Identitäten, soziale Beziehungen und Gruppen*, Göttingen u.a. (Hogrefe) 1999.

DÖRING, NICOLA: "Persönliche Homepages im WWW", *Medien und Kommunikation*, 49 (2001), pp. 325-39.

FUCHS, GERHARD: "e-mail, e-banking, e-commerce – Business für Eliten?", *forum medienethik* (2000), H. 1: *Wissen, Spielen, Unterhalten – Einblicke in multimediale Welten*, pp. 67-71.

GÖBEL, WOLFGANG: "Individualisierung als Identitätsverlust. Problematik und immanentes Ethos des modernen Projekts der Selbstfindung", in: THOMAS LAUBACH (Ed.): *Ethik und Identität*, Tübingen, Basel (Francke) 1998, pp. 115-126.

GREIS, ANDREAS: *Identität, Authentizität und Verantwortung. Die ethischen Herausforderungen der Kommunikation im Internet*, München (kopaed) 2001.

HAKER, HILLE: *Moralische Identität. Literarische Lebensgeschichten als Medien ethischer Reflexion*, Tübingen, Basel (Francke) 1998.

HÖFLICH, JOACHIM R.: "Computerrahmen und die undifferenzierte Wirkungsfrage oder: Warum erst einmal geklärt werden muss, was die Menschen mit dem Computer machen", in: PATRICK RÖSSLER (Ed.): *Online-Kommunikation. Beiträge zu Nutzung und Wirkung*, Opladen (Westdeutscher Verlag) 1998, pp. 47-64.

HUNOLD, GERFRIED W.: "Identitätstheorie. Die sittliche Struktur des Individuellen im Sozialen", in: *Handbuch der christlichen Ethik*, Bd. 1, hrsg. v. Anselm Hertz u.a., Freiburg i.Br. (Herder) 1993 (aktualisierte Neuauflage), pp. 177-194.

HUNOLD, GERFRIED W.: "Zur Moralfähigkeit des Menschen. Selbstkonzept, Selbstwahrnehmung und Selbstbewertung als Verstehenswege der Gewissenskompetenz", *Theologische Quartalschrift*, 174 (1994), pp. 34-45.

KRAPPMANN, LOTHAR: *Soziologische Dimensionen der Identität. Strukturelle Bedingungen für die Teilnahme an Interaktionsprozessen*, Stuttgart ^{2}1972.

LAUBACH, THOMAS: *Lebensführung. Annäherung an einen ethischen Grundbegriff*, Frankfurt a.M. u.a. (Lang) 1999.

MEAD, GEORGE H.: *Geist, Identität und Gesellschaft*, Frankfurt a.M. (Suhrkamp) ^{10}1995.

SCHNEIDER, IRMELA: "Neue Medien in Mediendiskursen. Einige Überlegungen zur Analyse von Netzkommunikation", in: BARBARA BECKER, MICHAEL PATEAU (Eds.): *Virtualisierung des Sozialen. Die Informationsgesellschaft zwischen Fragmentierung und Globalisierung*, Frankfurt a.M. (Campus) 1997, pp. 29-52.

TAYLOR, CHARLES: *Sources of the Self. The Making of Modern Identity*, Cambridge, Mass. (University Press) 1989.

Acknowledgements
I thank Christoph Deeg for his help to translate the first part of this article.

Chapter 6

Virtual Reality as a Problem of the Electronic Economy

PETER KOSLOWSKI

I. Two Concepts of Virtuality

In the discussion on the concept of virtuality two different meanings of virtual are used: 'Virtual' means on the one hand the immediately possible, the being effective in concealment, the powerful but not visible, and on the other hand what is only seemingly existent and possible only in play or in fiction. There are used here quite different meanings of the virtual if virtual is on the one hand what is only seemingly true and on the other hand what is possible in an emphatic sense as the powerful. In the history of ideas, virtual indicates something that is real as potentiality, that is not only potential as potential. It is potentially real as something that is in an intensified way possible. Behind the distinction of being real as a possible and of being possible as a possible lies the observation that possibility and reality are not clearly separated discrete states or description of states or modi of being. Potentiality and reality rather form, as Leibniz demonstrated, a continuum from the possible to the real.

In a similar way, Schelling moved the idea of grades of the possible and virtual to the centre of his theory of the creative and of becoming in the theory of potencies or potentialites in the last version of his philosophy, in his Positive Philosophy.[1] In his theory of potencies, Schelling writes that the potencies are there before there is being. He develops a dialectics of different kinds of potencies and calls that which is able to be that which is closest to being, closest to that which is real. There are different consecutive states of potential being. Among these states of potential being, the potential being that is able to be immediately is the one that is the closest of the three potencies to being. It is almost about to transcend into being whereas there is potential being which is much further away from being. Schelling distinguishes between the above-being, the able-to-be, and the being. The above-being moves through the able-to-be into being. That which is merely existent without all qualifications is at the same time that which is only possible, which is not yet being but above-being and before-being.

The above-being, the merely existent has at the same time a theological meaning in Schelling. Philosophy must think the purely existent. It must start with pure existence. It cannot in contrast to Hegel's theory of dialectics think that the pure nothingness is the beginning of a dialectic of becoming, of the transcendence from nothingness to being. We must start from the above-being, the merely existent without any concretization which then determines itself by way of the different modes of the possible into being.

The idea that there exists something which is immediately before being, the potential or the able-to-be which is of all potencies or potentialities the one that is closest to being is useful not only for metaphysics but also for the cyberspace. In the cyberspace, there are two types of the virtual, two potentialities, first the potentiality or the able-to-be that is of all potentialities the one that is closest to being, and secondly the potential or able-to-be that is only fictitious and far from being. The cyberspace is a space of the above-being, of the possible before being. It is as well a space of the possible as the real which can be transformed at any time from the potential to the real as a space of the above-being that is still far from being able to become real.

---

1 Cf. to Schelling P. KOSLOWSKI: *Philosophien der Offenbarung. Antiker Gnostizismus, Franz von Baader, Schelling*, Paderborn (Ferdinand Schöningh) 2001, 2nd ed. 2003, pp. 650-850.

The cyberspace is therefore not mere potentiality, but it is a specific, well-defined potentiality which can be transformed any time into being. The internet is a blueprint, a sketch of a technology which can be realised at once as reality. This function of the cyberspace as being a space of the economically possible as real or as the economically feasible is of great significance for the virtual firm as Davidow and Malone have shown.[2] The internet opens the possibility to the firm to create a space of the potential which is not only possible in an unspecified way and is not only mere, unspecified potential but can be realised in real production at any time.

From the economic concept of the virtuality of the internet we must distinguish the aesthetical interpretation of the cyberspace. The aesthetic concept of the internet and the cyberspace understands the internet as a space of the possible as the possible, as a space of the simulation of reality in which simulation in play and in fiction is central.

It is necessary to distinguish between the aesthetical and the economic-technological and information-technological interpretation of the internet and of the electronic economy. Both interpretations understand the internet and the cyberspace as a space of the possible or potential. The difference is, however, considerable since the economy and firms are not interested in a general space of the possible, of simulation or of the virtual but in a space which can be transformed into reality at once and whose options are not at random, at will, or infinite, but are well-defined and tailored to the needs of the firm.

Davidow and Malone are right to define the internet as an actual structure of information and relationships that is not so much a medium of simulation but a concrete medium or a medium of concretization. It is therefore necessary to distinguish between the concept of virtuality that is at the foundations of the virtual firm, the ability to have a real systems technology in which the possible is real as the possible on the one hand, and the aesthetical concept of cyberspace in which the possible is possible as the possible.

---

2 WILLIAM H. DAVIDOW, MICHAEL S. MALONE: *The Virtual Corporation: Structuring and Revitalizing the Corporation for the 21th Century*, New York (Harper Collins) 1992.

II. Virtuality as Adaptability in the Business Firm

If one understands the virtual firm as a systems technology it is visible that the virtual world is ambivalent for the freedom of the user. It expands the user's options but it determines them also in detail. The problem can be analysed by recourse to the distinction between action and tool technology, machine technology and systems that Hubig has introduced.[3] The different forms of technology have different consequences for the problem of action, freedom, and justification of technology. The technology of using tools is effective on the level of actions and possesses a high freedom of valuation which is only concretised by giving objectives to the use of the tools as means. It also implies the ability to control the means and the objectives as well as one's own abilities. It implies finally the control of reality by the individual.

In contrast to the technology of using tools, the degree of freedom decreases in the case of the machine and the systems technology at the rate at which the degree of effectiveness increases. In the technology of machines the objectives only are free and available but the connection between means and objectives is fixed by the construction of the machines. In the technology of machines, the goal of the technology is the availability and realisation of possibilities. The technological system and the systems technology fix even the objectives *and* the means of the systematic structure. Objectives and means can only be chosen or rejected as a whole. The systems technology determines the conditions for the use of tools and machines within an extended technological system of objectives-means-connections for the control of comprehensive problem situations. The infranet and internet of the virtual firm, its cyberspace, is a systems technology in which, in its ideal form, all possible options of the decision-maker are already premeditated, structured, and cared for. The decision-maker has only the freedom to realise this or that option that is possible as real not options he might choose beyond those prepared for in the system. Or the decision-maker has the option not to use the

3 CHRISTOPH HUBIG: *Technik- und Wissenschaftsethik: ein Leitfaden*, Berlin, Heidelberg, New York (Springer), 1st ed. 1993, 2nd ed. 1995, pp. 58ff. – Cf. also KLAUS MAINZER: *Computer – neue Flügel des Geistes?*, Berlin, New York (de Gruyter) 1994.

system as a whole at all. The employees in a virtual firm cannot invent new options by themselves. They are given to them in the software.

If one investigates the internet and the electronic economy according to the criteria of forms of technology and their different degrees of freedom it becomes visible that the internet is in a way the most universal system or net of information and relationships into which almost all information and relationships enter to an increasing degree. If with the increasing spread of systems technology the freedom decreases to use this technology as a means or to choose oneself the objectives for which to use this technology, this must apply also to the internet. The functional relationship of the reliance on systems and the decreasing freedom of setting one's own objectives in using this technology and the decreasing freedom not to use it at all is effective also for the internet: The more the internet is in fact the most universal system of information and relationships the less I have the freedom not to participate in the internet. This development is the deeper concern with the digital divide: It consists not primarily in distributional questions whether some people own a computer or not. The digital divide concerns the danger that the exclusion from the internet will more and more imply the exclusion from the central media of communication. If the internet is the most universal system of communication I am outside of the realm of communication if I am not in the internet. The individual has no degree of freedom anymore in the question whether it can use the media internet or not. The individual must use the internet as the most universal and most effective media of communication to be part of social communication at all.[4]

For this reason the internet needs to be free as the most universal and most effective media of communication. The postulate that there should be no censorship in the internet is justified since the internet is not one media but it is *the* media. In the long run the internet will not be one media beside others but the universal media. As this universal media the internet is virtual not as a mere simulation or possible world but it is virtual as an invisible effective reality, as the reality of the possible, and not as the possibility of the possible. The cyberspace is not a virtual possibility but a virtual reality. The virtual firm is the user of this reality of the possible. The production of virtual

4 Cf. PETER GLOTZ: "Die Informationsgesellschaft: Deutsche Rahmenbedingungen, deutsche Hemmungen", *Informatik-Spektrum*, 22 (1999), for a discussion of the "Kulturkritik" on the Cyberspace. Glotz seems, however, to assume that we still have the choice to participate or not in the internet.

products or the production of products with virtual means is the ideal form of a production in so far as it produces immediately and specifically in virtual reality. It must follow, however, the possibilities of the virtual reality as adaptive they might be. Production does not have great degrees of freedom from the media of the virtual possibilities given by the virtual reality of the firm. The production is determined by what is virtually real in the virtual reality. The virtual is the quality of something that can assume the qualities of many things. It is ascribed to a mode that is not real and not possible but the reality of the possible.

The concept of a virtual computer arose at the end of the 1950s in the context of machines that were fast enough that many people could work with them without having the impression that they had to share the computer with others. Davidow and Malone claim that from this time the virtual is also understood as the adaptable or the interactive. Virtual means here over-adapted, highly adapted to the client. For the user the virtual computer was available at any place and any time and was therefore independent of time and space. It formed a virtual reality. Alvin Toffler introduced already in 1980 the idea of the "de-massified production".[5]

The precondition of the de-massification is, according to Toffler, that the development of computers becomes possible which can produce one mega-instruction per second at an acceptable price. The capacity of processing one mega-instruction per second had the price of one million Dollars in 1980. It was assumed in 1980 that the virtual production would become reality if this price of one million Dollars would fall to one hundred Dollars. This price of one hundred Dollars for one mega-instruction per second was reached at about 1992.

If one summarises the theories of the virtual firm one comes to the conclusion that, in the firm, "virtual" means first of all adaptable. Virtuality is formulated in terms of maximal adaptability or adaptedness to reality. In a certain way, the normative character of the real enforces itself in the virtual firm through and despite the concept of the virtual. It enforces the consideration of the real by the very fact that the virtual reality is not possible without the strict consideration of what the customer or consumer really wants. The normative reality of consumer demand is taken into account in the virtual

5 ALVIN TOFFLER: *The Third Wave* (1980), New York (Bantam Books) 1981, pp. 158ff. and 231ff. Toffler speaks of "de-massified media" and "de-massified Society".

firm even more than in the non-virtual firm. The customer demand is not replaced by simulations of this demand. Rather, the specificity of consumer demand is affirmed in a comprehensive way. The economic reality of the market is only perceived rightly by the firm if it is able to take up the needs of the customers in their specificity.

The consideration of the specificity of the fulfilment of consumer needs by the virtual production is, however, not the only problem of managing production. The firm must realise, at the same time, the economies of scale of mass production. The combination of individualisation and mass production is the truly revolutionary result of virtual production. The individualised mass production is the realisation of the synthesis of the opposites of individualisation and mass production.

Davidow and Malone point to the fact that this individualised mass production is most probably the origin of an increased stress in firms, a stress that is caused by the virtual production. The firm has to fulfil two parameters now: On the one hand it must reach high numbers of product units and cannot escape the compulsion to sell in great numbers, and at the same time the firm is forced to produce products that are oriented on the individual consumer. The production task does not become easier by the virtual production but more difficult. The tasks and demands on the employees become rather greater than smaller although the control of virtual production provides the firm with the means to deal with individualized consumer needs.

III. Virtuality as Simulation: The Aesthetic Concept of Virtuality

The economic concept of virtuality in production must be contrasted with the aesthetic concept of virtual reality. The aesthetic interpretation of virtual reality in contrast to the economic one can be found in a recent paper by Welsch. Welsch writes: "Thanks to our use of the medial realities we learn that reality has always been ... a construction."[6] The virtualisation in cyber-

6 W. WELSCH: „Eine Doppelfigur der Gegenwart: Virtualisierung und Revalidierung", in: G. VATTIMO, W. WELSCH (Eds.): *Medien-Welten Wirklichkeiten* (Media-Worlds Realities), München (W. Fink) 1998, pp. 229-248, here p. 241. (Translation P.K.)

space causes a more virtual character of our everyday reality since it increases the virtual element as the fictitious and simulated element in our life. The increase of the virtual leads, according to Welsch, to the insight that reality as such is only a construction. One could reply that the thesis of the death of reality in cyberspace is strongly exaggerated. Particularly for the virtual firm, Welsch's thesis is untenable. The virtualisation of production causes a less virtual or fictional consideration of consumer demand since the reality of individual consumer demand becomes not less but more effective for the way in which goods are produced. Welsch himself qualifies, or even cancels, his own thesis when he says in the same book that a revalidating of reality happens through the virtualisation. He recognises that the thesis of the total dissolution of reality is not satisfying.

The aesthetic concept of virtual reality implies the fictionalisation and simulation of reality. It interprets reality as the result of fictions, of individual and commonly shared fictions. In the aesthetic concept of virtuality, virtual reality implies that reality itself becomes a fiction. Fictions are not understood as a specific form of poetic perception, as the poetic deepening, intensification, and transformation of reality but as that which constitutes reality.

In a further step of reflection, the aesthetic and the economic concept of virtual reality can, however, be synthesized. The contradiction between virtuality as simulation and virtuality as the potential of total adaptation to reality can be overcome if the complementarity of industrial and artistic production is considered. The virtual reality as the space of the possible constitutes a potential complementarity between the arts and business. The arts are a field of experimentation of business in many industries: The arts develop new materials and designs. Virtual worlds precede in the arts their application in the mass production of industry.

On the other hand, the tension between the two cultures of the arts and of industry becomes visible at the two different concepts of virtual reality in industry and aesthetics which Daniel Bell has written about,[7] the tension between the culture of consumption and of the arts in which simulation, play, immediate gratification dominate and the culture of production and business in which, in contrast, adaptation, rationality and deferred gratification prevail. Bell sees the roots of this contrast in modern times and as an unsolvable problem of society.

---

7 DANIEL BELL: *Die kulturellen Widersprüche des Kapitalismus*, Frankfurt a. M. (Campus) 1991.

Against the thesis of the modern character of the contradiction of the two cultures of consumption and production one can reply with Eduard Spranger[8] that the cultures of consumption and of production are always in contrast in human existence and that this contrast of consumption and production cannot be dissolved since both represent necessary sides of human existence.

A further insight can be gained from the ambivalence of the concept of virtual reality. The virtual world of playing with new possible worlds, the opening and the simulation of new possibilities, must also be present in business if it is to create innovation, new products and consumer satisfaction. In an advanced economy both concepts of virtuality have a function. The virtual production in systems of possible reality is in need of the artistic virtuality of the imagination of new real possibilities.

IV. The Ambivalence of the Virtual Character of the Cyberspace and of the Electronic Economy and the Problem of the Disembodiment by Virtual Reality

In the history of ideas, the concept of the virtual has first been developed in theology. It is a deeply theological concept. It has been developed in scholastic theology. In the theological and philosophical discussion, the ambivalence of the virtual as an invisible, yet potent, reality on the one hand and the virtual as mere appearance has been recognised. In this discussion, thinkers saw the necessity to revalidate the real beyond the fictitious and simulated. An interesting case of an intensive discussion about the virtual was the critique of simulation in the christology of the Gnostic theologians. The problem of virtual reality and embodiment becomes here apparent in its relevance. The Gnostics like Valentinus defended the interpretation that Christ had only an apparent body, a simulated or virtual body, as there are also other virtual bodies like those of angels and demons.[9]

---

8 EDUARD SPRANGER: *Kulturphilosophie und Kulturkritik*, ed. by Hans Wenke, Tübingen (Niemeyer) 1969.

9 Demons must have a simulated body according to Valentinus since the can be castigated. If someone has no body he cannot be castigated. If one can castigate demons they must have a body, but their body can only be a virtual body.

The thesis that Christ's incarnation or embodiment was only virtual was criticized as follows: If incarnation is the central event of Christianity it cannot be the appearance of a virtual body as a simulated human body but it must be a real incarnation. Christ's body must, therefore, have been a real body. The Gnostics defended, however, the opinion that Christ has had only a spiritual flash, a *caro spiritalis*. Tertullian in turn replied in two arguments: First, Christ would not have become a real human if his flesh had not been real because humans cannot live separately from their body. Someone who wants to become a human must have a body, otherwise he is not a human. If someone has only a virtual or apparent body he has not become human in reality. His second argument is that the thesis of the virtual reality of Christ's body negates real and empirical humanity: If God had not become a corporeal human he would not have unified himself with humanity, he would have unified himself only with the virtual but not with the actual humanity. This would imply he has not unified himself with humanity at all.

For the philosophical discussion of the cyberspace, it is of interest that docetism, the theory that the body is only apparent or virtual, represented in the second century the heresy of the hatred or at least the contempt for the body and the flesh. In certain forms of the cyberspace and of virtual reality enthusiasm, a certain hatred or at least contempt for the corporeal existence of humans becomes visible. The corporeal existence is subordinated in the cyberworld to the virtual, the spiritual, and technological.

This is demonstrated in the movie film *Matrix*. In *Matrix*, the machines have made humanity their subjects by using the human corporeal existence for the mere production of energy. The humans, however, who live in a merely virtual cyberspace believe that they have a corporeal existence and live a real life in their body. In fact, however, the machines manipulated the humans in such a way that the appliances at the brains of the humans play a virtual reality to them which they mistake for reality. Their experiencing is a virtual reality whereas what is real, the corporeal existence of humans, is used by the machines for a completely different objective, the production of energy for the machines. The humans cannot recognize that the objective of their corporeal and spiritual existence is only the production of energy for others anymore.

The problem of immortality in the internet, or of immortality in a virtual reality, is linked to the phenomenon of the disembodiment of human experience in virtual reality. The new computer technology is obsessed with the idea to create immortality for the humans by the fusion of humans with computers. Bill Joy claims that all the brain data of a human should be stored on a chip and that the human body should be replaced by a computer that will not cost more than 1000 US $ in the year 2025 he predicts.[10] Humans store themselves on a memory chip and achieve immortality on a hard disc – and this at a comparably low amount for which a central European could hardly live decently for one month. Bill Joy quotes Danny Hillis: "I love my body neither more nor less than others but if I can become 200 years old in a body made of silicon I will accept this body."[11] One could ask here: Why so modest? If we will have created a hard disc as our body we will be able to reproduce ourselves in all eternity on computers with the appropriate technology.

One must object that the continuity of the media which consciousness uses for its maintenance is not warranted here. We do not know what happens in the instant of a nanosecond in which my self-consciousness moves from my body to the computer. It is likely that the continuity of the self as a unity of body and soul will be interrupted in this very moment. In modern technology, there is a tendency to devaluate and to aim at overcoming the body.

The technological utopias speak of the project of reconstructing the human and of replacing human organs by machines which secure immortality to humans since they become independent from the ageing of the body.[12] Such a utopia is only possible if one separates thinking, intelligence and consciousness completely from the body and takes consciousness to be a incorporeal unity as it was the case in Descartes' philosophy.[13] Other advanced technologists question, however, exactly this possibility of separating the mind from the body. They emphasize the unity of mind and body in contrast

10 So Bill Joy: „Warum die Technik uns nicht braucht. Die mächtigsten Technologien des 21. Jahrhunderts – Robotik, Gentechnik und Nanotechnologie – machen den Menschen zur gefährdeten Art", *Frankfurter Allgemeine Zeitung*, 6. Juni 2000, pp. 49-50, here p. 50.

11 *Ibid.*, p. 49. (translation P.K.)

12 Cf. Villö Huszai: „Der Kampf um die Vorherrschaft der Intelligenzen. Die technische und literarische Phantasie vom Maschinenmenschen", *Neue Zürcher Zeitung* Nr. 70, 24./25. März 2001, p. 57, and Ray Kurzweil: *The Age of Spiritual Machines: How we will live, work and think in the new age of intelligent machines*, London (Orion Business) 1999.

13 Cf. Ray Kurzweil: „Die Maschinen werden uns davon überzeugen können, daß sie Menschen sind. Nur weil Europa die technologische Revolution verschläft, muß nicht die ganze Welt vor sich hin träumen", *Frankfurter Allgemeine Zeitung* Nr. 153, 5. Juli 2000, p. 51.

to the "technological idealism and spiritualism", that is characteristic of the optimism of the artificial intelligence thinkers.

A computer scientist like Rolf Pfeifer takes the idea to be wrong that intelligence is only a quality of computers and brains: Intelligence is not identical with the brain but a quality of the whole organism.[14] The robotics expert, Rodney A. Brooks, points to the fact that intelligence must be linked to the external world. The body is the connection of intelligence and consciousness in the human with the external world. Consciousness is not only external to the body. Intelligence is in need of the body to be able to interact with the world. Brooks speaks about "embodied intelligence".[15] From the need of the human to be "embodied intelligence", it is likely that humans will prefer in the future to remain so called MOPs, "Mainly Original Substrate Persons"[16] who do not want to store their substrate completely in another media, be it the cyberspace or a hard disc.

The other problem from the point of view of ethics is the price of the project "immortality by machines". Almost-immortality is, as Jaron Lanier remarks, only likely to be feasible for the ultra rich since the substitution of organs by machines is extremely costly. The social inequality caused by extensive organ substitution will be enormous since one can assume that all humans will be ready to invest their whole net wealth for immortality or will be ready to pay almost every price for it. Within the family, this will create considerable problems if parents will invest their whole life income for immortality. The transfer by inheritance between generations is terminated.

V. Virtual Reality as a Concept of Theological Origin

The cyberspace and theology share the conviction that the virtual is a third modus of being between possibility and reality. Virtuality is possibility

---

14 Cited after ANNETTE OHME-REINICKE: „Fortschritt als Provokation", *Neue Zürcher Zeitung*, 24. März 2001.

15 Cf. RODNEY A. BROOKS: „Das Fleisch und die Maschine. Wie die neuen Technologien den Menschen verändern werden", *Frankfurter Allgemeine Zeitung* Nr. 205, 4. September 2000, p. 49, and RODNEY A. BROOKS: *Robot: The Future of Flesh and Machines*, London (Penguin Press Science) 2003.

16 Cf. VILLÖ HUSZAI: „Der Kampf um die Vorherrschaft der Intelligenzen", *loc. cit.*

as reality. Both, the cyberspace and theology, share the conviction that the virtual is not only appearance or only seeming reality. The virtual as being appearance only would not be interesting at all.

The latest edition of a dictionary of theology gives the following examples for virtual reality under the entry "Virtuality".[17] The first exemple are truths that are only virtually and not directly revealed. Virtually revealed truths are those that are not revealed directly but are gained by conclusions from directly revealed truths. Virtual is secondly the virtual distinction in God's unity, the trinity. Trinity is on the one hand a real distinctiveness of persons who are however not really distinct since they are three persons as unity. The distinction of the three divine persons in trinity is therefore only a virtual distinction. Virtual is thirdly God's acting in creation. Theology calls God's action in creation "*virtualiter transeuns*", virtually transcending into the creation.

The concept of the virtual is used here for the solution of a grave theological problem. If God is inalterable, but has created the creation he is different or changed after having created the creation. One says, however, that God is inalterable. If he is inalterable he cannot be a real creator or producer since with the creation something else has come into being and God would be altered after the creation, he would have become a creator which he was not before the creation. The problem is solved in the following way: Since there cannot exist anything that is completely outside of God since this would violate God's unity and perfection, one has to assume that the progression of the creation out of God is only virtually transcending, this progression of the creation from God is only virtually transcending. God's transcendence into creation is only virtual.

The concept of the virtual transcendent can be used for an analogy for the relationship between humans and the cyberspace. Humans are in a virtually transcendent relationship with cyberspace since humans created the space without transcending into it. The reality of the cyberspace lies on the one hand outside of the social space of human relationship since it is invisible and human do not live with their body in this space. On the other hand, the human virtual creation belongs to the social space of humans and modifies the social space by extending its capabilities and possibilities. The cyberspace is a space that lies outside of society and belongs at the same time to the reality

17 W. LÖFFLER, D. MORAT: Article "Virtualität, virtuell", *Lexikon für Theologie und Kirche*, ed. by W. Kasper et al., 3rd ed., Freiburg (Herder) 2001, col. 805.

of society. The cyberspace is only in a virtual, but not in a substantial relationship with the world of humans.

VI. The Centrality of the Financial Functions of the Cyberspace and the Virtual Reality of the Financial Markets

The virtual financial markets of online banking, of online brokerage and online trading are most probably the most important and consequential innovation that has been produced by the internet. The influence of the internet has been felt most strongly in the field of the financial markets since the internet created a completely new capital market[18] that took over the functions of the traditional stock market, particularly the allocation of capital, in a more subtle and more direct way for the following reasons: The internet enables the public to participate in mass speculation. Mass speculation implies that large strata of the population participate in stock market speculation. The internet makes this participation possible. It realizes, by way of online trading, a form of people's capitalism that integrates all groups of the population, and not only the classical owners of capital, into the capital market. If in the United States today one half of the households own wealth in stocks, an enormous change of capital ownership in comparison to the traditional distribution of capital income and labor income is caused by this development. The old "contradiction of capital and labor" is modified by the phenomenon of a people's capitalism in which large strata of the population own and can administer capital via online trading.

By the extension of the number of capital owners and of those speculating in the stock market, an extension of the ability to learn in investment takes place. Far greater circles of the population participate in investment decisions compared to former times. Banks have recognised that, in the last years, investment banking and financial mediation for the capital market have substituted the classical task of loan giving in the banking business.

---

18 See also P. KOSLOWSKI: „Welche Werte prägen den Kapitalmarkt? Zur Ethik der Spekulation", in: TH. BUCHHEIM, R. SCHÖNBERGER, W. SCHWEIDLER (Eds.): *Die Normativität des Wirklichen. Über die Grenze zwischen Sein und Sollen*, Stuttgart (Klett-Cotta) 2002, pp. 286-311, and J. R. BOATRIGHT: *Ethics in Finance*, Malden, Mass./Oxford (Blackwell) 1999.

The emerging people's capitalism will further develop in the future and will increase the capacity to learn in capital investment. The precondition for people's capitalism is the internet, since speculation via online trading and with the help of online brokers has reduced the transaction costs of stock market speculation considerably. There are, however, linked some typical problems of virtualisation with online brokerage and online trading. They are caused by the virtual reality syndrome, the loss of reality by fictionalisation. An example for this developing dangers in online trading is the churning of day traders. Churning describes the fact that online trading seduces day traders to buy and sell shares too often with the result that they end up with very high transaction costs that eat up their capital gains and form an advantage only for the online banks or online brokerage firms to which the day traders pay provision for every transaction. The online day traders end up with losses since, even if their shares make profit, they sell and buy the shares in their portfolio too often. The provision for the trading firms eat up their profits and leave the traders in the end with losses.

Why is the virtual reality of online trading a problem here? The answer is that in online trading the virtual space of action also reduces the corporeal constraints and barriers to such a degree that the trading persons are tempted to trade too often and too easily. Online trading supports the tendency to take fictions for reality also in the financial markets. It is possible to trade anonymously, easily and quickly in the internet whereas one had had to go to the bank or to call a person at the bank in order to sell or buy shares in former days. Since too frequent trading might have enervated the broker or the bank employee, one would have been hindered by the personal interactions with the financial intermediaries to trade too often. In the anonymous online trading centers these barriers have fallen.[19]

Another development of great importance for the financial markets made possible by the internet is the development of online future markets, the markets for future contracts about all kinds of raw materials, currencies, and goods. By the future markets, a new comparably low cost insurance against business cycle price fluctuations has become possible that is not imaginable without the internet. These insurances against future fluctuations of prices

19 RICHARD T. DE GEORGE: *The Ethics of Information Technology and Business*, Oxford (Blackwell) 2003 (= Foundations of Business Ethics, Vol. 3), p. 9, calls the phenomenon of the depersonalization of exchange relationships the "virtual reality syndrome".

can be organized according to groups concerned. Professional groups or industries can insure themselves against price fluctuations on future markets if the transaction costs for futures will decrease due to the lower transaction costs induced by the internet.

Fishermen, for example, have the problem that the prices for fish fluctuate and that considerable problems can arise for the stabilization of their income. They could insure themselves at least partially by way of future contracts about fish and could sell today already the fish of the next year. Futures cause costs, of course. The fishermen will not receive the full price. The other difficulty is that futures can only insure against business cycle fluctuations but not against structural crises if there is, e.g., not enough fish anymore. In the future market a new field of insurance will be opened that has become possible through the internet and in which one will observe further innovations.

One objection frequently raised against the electronic economy is that the share prices for the electronic economy have been virtual in the sense of misleading by their appearance. The internet firms have been reproached that they have created an atmosphere of virtual reality around themselves and in the stock market which has led to valuations of these firms in the share market which do not correspond to economic reality and have become themselves simulated or virtual. Robert Hall of Stanford University has introduced the concept of "e-capital". There is, Hall claims, a surplus in the capital value of electronic economy firms that does not show in the balance sheet of these firms. The electronic economy accumulates a capital which is not accounted for in the normal book-keeping of the assets of electronic economy firms. Many of the internet firms have had price/earnings ratios that have been completely abnormal. How can this be explained since it contradicts normal valuations of shares? The .com firms should have been valuated much lower and their share prices should have fallen earlier. Since this had not been the case there must have been something that has caused this higher valuation of .com firms. Hall calls the price difference between .com and old economy firms the e-capital, a sort of surplus value which the market is not yet able to account for properly.

The question is what happened to this e-capital in the years 2000-2002? It vanished. Nevertheless, Hall points to an important point: The potential of the electronic economy has not been exhausted yet, its use is still in its beginnings. It is visible today that the possibilities of using the electronic economy are enormous. If investors anticipate the future potential it is not irrational to say that these firms may be worth more than the traditional methods of valuation account for.

The second argument for this anticipation of future increases in value is that many services in the internet are not yet sufficiently priced. There is not an economically sufficient exclusion of users that do not pay. At present, the internet economy includes an element of utopia since many of its services are not priced and do not exclude nonpaying users. This utopian element should not be criticized since it creates a space for new ideas about using the internet. From the point of view of the economics and the logic of the evolution of markets, one must assume that this free uses will be eliminated more and more in favor of priced forms of uses since otherwise the enormous investments in the internet cannot pay off.

If one takes into consideration the possibilities that are opened up by the internet it is not justified to describe the internet revolution as a bubble of speculation only. Rather, it makes sense that the investment in a new technology is larger than it appears to be reasonable from the point of view of traditional accountancy. If we draw an analogy from natural evolution we find that also natural evolution knows phenomena of evolutionary overspending. Even in the animal world, more is often invested than seems to be necessary. This investment happens in order that a new path of evolution can be reached. Something similar seems to have happened in the electronic economy. It is too early to decide whether the new virtual reality moved here too much in the direction of virtual reality as mere appearance or whether a new path of economic evolution has been started by the mass speculation of the beginning people's capitalism in internet shares and by means of online trading.

Part Two

Ethical Challenges of the Economic Economy

Chapter 7

Tricksters on the Internet: eCommerce, Data Mining and the Parallel Context

DIETER KLUMPP

I. Introductory Remarks

The Internet brings it to light. Everyone knows it. Everyone does it. Everyone accepts it. Everyone can check it. At the pre-dawn of the Information Society, information is being pushed until the files flicker.

To be more precise: It is massive dealing that is going on, although the word 'dealing' should, perhaps, not be used by a net expert in the headline or in the first three lines, so as not to get intercepted by the next finely-meshed filter system in a completely confusing parallel context. With most other words, the networked scribe can write unfettered, meaning: All the spoken and written word will end up in the parallel, albeit less severe context, anyway. Being 'network unfettered' is nigh total *'freedom of'* but almost never *'freedom from.'*'

'Pushers on the Net' suggests some kind of illegal or illicit trade.[1] However, in the context of network glitz, 'pushing' serves to illustrate the way information recklessly allows itself to be swept away by any wayward context. Often information comes clad in lurid data make-up, and prances with its luscious primary data; habitually, it leads to fertile grounds of knowledge just to be ravished and alienated in that parallel context. Which is perfectly legal – and inevitable. For as long as there are 'human' switches, there is no clearly defined sequence from data via information to knowledge. It is but a type of blurry deduction and not even hindsight – tracing information back from batch to component to element – offers a sharper vision. However, in looking back, the factor 'time' comes in to help determine reasonably the vantage point but not its destination to which it goes in time embraced by synchronicity.

What is this 'parallel-context' (German: "Ander-Kontext") that will from this day forward sail through the Internet launched by a Google search to find its slot according to alphabetical prerogative and somewhere in the vicinity of 'parallel accounts'?[2] What we eventually connotate, cut into bark or leave as writing on the wall – according to our mood and preference - is within a context of our own, which, *invariably and principally,* is different. Context is an everlasting solipsist autist that will not miss a single one of the following six billion contexts. Yet, one could still speak of an effective 'context society,' in which the different contexts can be traced but not modeled in advance.

So much for the introductory remarks that can be understood in different ways, depending on the context. To a freshman, the term 'information' could mean an opening portal from Werner Heisenberg to Stephen Hawking, the term could translate to a graduate as an ironic paraphrase of that well known "perception counts," to a manic-neurotic practitioner as "time lost – and noticed too late" – while to a fickle conference chair it merely prompts erratic checks of his timepiece. That's all there is with "parallel context". To the

---

1 Bert Brecht opined that legally opening a bank was easier than robbing one, both coming to the same thing, though. The Basel II Treaty clearly proves him wrong on the first point because of its rating provisions; on the second point, it is at least conceded that stealing large sums of cyber money hurts up-front investment and only leads to cyber loot.

2 "Internet" is used here – as is commonplace by now – for all kinds of data telecommunications via the "internet protocol" (TCP/IP), hence for FTP, WWW, E-Mail, etc too.

great poets it was simply a question of "as you like it" (Shakespeare) or "beauty is in the eye of the beholder" (Goethe).

II. "Click, Drag'N Paste"

Time and again, an observer is awed by the myriad of fantasy-packed commercial ideas that providers and users on the Internet come up with; no flea market – as wild as it may get at times – could be a match. There, one Euro can buy an item just cents worth – but one has got to rise early, stand in line and carry loads. But most of all, vendor and buyer – despite their anonymity – need to look each other in the eye when one declares to make a loss and when the other claims to have an empty wallet. No such intimacy on the Internet; in fact, no modern media, neither phone nor fax could better camouflage transaction. The Internet does not reveal the flicker in the eye, the trembling voice or the unsteady hand to give away the inexperienced. Possibly, the stock market mania of the year 2000 was unleashed by the belief to get rich in days and clandestinely, without banks or agents, but simply with a mouse click. Today, both couch potato and the mentally agile whiz have an interest in shortening that distance created by the Internet.

After all, the following is true: The Internet merely brings to light what has forever been part of human behavior and that does not, however, work like a simple and easy "Click, Drag'n Paste." A straight use of force, for instance, requires training to overcome the thresholds of inhibition,[3] whatever their origins; an indirect use of force can altogether spring up from peaceful citizens provided they have been conditioned, accordingly. A hurtful word is being hurled faster than a knife; mobbing is easier than sacking, and a tug-of-war can be more sudorific than driving a hard bargain.

3 Given the number of households cudgeling in every which way, there is a supra-culturally enormous contrast in the thresholds of inhibitions between individual use of force and use of force by an authority. In 'isolated' and in 'social' contexts, human beings communicate differently in a significant manner, something which is deemed to have pre-ethic roots.

In a sense, the proliferated Internet can be viewed as a gigantic Milgram experiment.[4] The difference is that the 'experimental group' has not been conditioned by some science authority, but by the obvious "everyone does it," instead. That accusing lamentation, "everyone does it" leads to a reinforcing process of learning – there are historic examples galore – producing the long-term-effect of marginalizing or even stigmatizing those who don't.

"Everyone does it" is 'best practice' for instant cure of initial cognitive dissonance. Long-time married couples know and so do role models caught red-handed; it comforts parket ticket dodgers and expense report artists; it boosts late payers and inspires fair weather politicians. "Everyone does it," as every beginner knows – on the Internet, anyway.

The surprising thing about the Internet's instrumentalization by all is that the computer, as the switching media, cannot introduce rationality to the process. No reasonable person would be willing to take advice from that hybrid calculator-routine-memory-turned device. So, just as one would silence an on-board computer in the car – i.e. that nagging voice telling you to "stop tail-gating at 150 km/h and turn off your high beam" – one would, during some blithe eCommerce exercise, certainly ignore instructions from a software agent such as "shouldn't you verify the existence of the vendor with whom you have just started an online payment process?"[5]. No one and certainly not a computer that is inexorably programmed on codified norms should dare to clamp our index finger just as it is about to mouseclick. Only *freedom from* such tutelage – which we have known ever since HAL took over ship in Stanley Kubrick's *Space Odysee* – allows us *freedom to* engage in our truly human ways, where a simple "Click, Drag'n Paste" turns petty crime into socially conforming behavior because – as we know by now – "everyone does it."

4 A famous and controversial experiment by psychologist Stanley Milgram of Yale University in 1963 tested an average person's willingness (40 American men of different age, profession and education) to obey authority and to execute draconian measures and even inhumane orders (cf. in the net DEAUX/WRIGHTSMAN: Social Psychology).

5 Cf. a D 21 call: "Customers *must above all* be informed about the full name of the company and the identity of the provider, commercial registration, its seat, its electronic and *geographical* provider address. A person responsible and answerable to customers must be named."

For the sake of honesty, a "thou shalt" must be mentioned: In the 'civil charter' of CEPIS, the Council of European Professional Informatics Societies, the following is cast in 'brazen' letters:

> The information one gets should be what one thinks it is (content authentication) and not, for example, a spoof site or part of an international fraud etc. It should never be misleading or misrepresentational in any way. Any commercial arrangement (such as an eCommerce order or a financial transaction) should be verifiable and mutually binding.[6]

There are more examples such as the afore-mentioned, but to cite them would only lead onto the path of good intentions, which is an altogether different story. In the following, a selection of tangible variants of that pushing of data, information and knowledge by the "net-worked, standard society" will give evidence that re-origination of predictable infrastructure frameworks will take a long time coupled with an uncertain, high degree of endeavor.

III. 'Black' Copy Dealing

The most widely known petty crime is dealing 'black' copy of software. In this case, one should mention a *first* group that does not even regard unauthorized copying a crime. As former ICANN director Andy Müller-Maguhn told me, "... other than stealing, copying does not deprive the author just copied of anything, his intellectual property remains intact". Somewhat breathless I retorted that, in the future, authors should receive their original manuscripts as barter instead of payment from their publishers.

A *second* group that focuses on *monetary* rather than *intellectual* property takes it for granted that nothing should be payed, as a matter of principle, to the richest man in the world, Microsoft owner Bill Gates, as he has enough money, already.

Closely related to that group is the *third* that suggests a *technicological* justification for their refusal to pay: Microsoft[7] products were so poor in

6 *www.cepis.org* with additional hyperlinks

7 ... in a similar fashion, so are the services of Deutsche Telekom, German Railways, the Municipal Corporation etc.

quality that "there is a genuine user right to refuse payment." Having an overlap to the third group is a large, *fourth* group that call themselves "congregation" composed of disciples of the Open Source operation systems. That group would never oppose payment to Linux, if Linux were not available already for free copying at any university, as "Open Source" is vernacular for "open to anyone."[8] Moreover, the university network is funded by the taxpayer – which is a fact – and, therefore, belongs to the public.

At this juncture, we are with a *fifth* group that considers software as "shareware" and, therefore, as an integral part of the "public domain." Public domain needs to be understood in the meaning of Swedish or ancient Germanic common law– a view disregarding the historical fact that it was everyone's duty to work on this "domain" for a given period of time so that an emergency food reserve could be harvested for the benefit of all. A few years ago, the traditional Swedish common law that allows free roaming and berry picking for one's own consumption, was fragrantly abused by German tourists who depleted an entire orchard in one night and who brought the produce home on the ferry boat. That particular application of the Swedish common law has no longer been applied, since. The flat rate for a shared medium is going to have the same fate, predictably.

The common web user does not pay heed to complicated ethical or intellectual or other proprietary rights; there are quite pragmatic grounds for using unregistered, commercial software programs and not paying attention to payment demands from providers of public domain software. At purchase of a PC, basic software comes with the computer, usually, and it is perceived as an add-on free of charge. If, let's say, an incomplete office suite were supplied, who would blame the purchaser for "complementing" software with those from friends and neighbors? After all, someone has lined up at ALDI's hours before 8 a.m. and payed those 999 euros. If ALDI hypermarket does not deliver the complete program, it is ALDI's problem. The same applies when a Microsoft office suite is supplied along with the purchase, but then the neighbor enters with his spiel that COREL office suites are more superior and any swap would be financially neutral. Of course, the electronic encyclopedia can be borrowed from the neighbor just like a book was borrowed yesterday.

---

8 No one can say how much time was spent already on the adoption of "several patched" Linux versions. Most OS users never open the source.

The "shareware" assistance programs offered on the web discredit themselves by asking like beggars in the streets for € 10 bank transfers, if the program was to be continued. Obviously, no reasonable person would go to the bank for a withdrawal that small; as far as online banking is concerned, one can say that the credit card number must not be transmitted since the Internet is so unreliable.[9] Besides, € 10 can only buy a cheap product stolen, perhaps, from other software programs. In the eyes of the user, 'shareware' program providers thus cross a thin line between a panhandler and a doorstepping hustler, if the built-in timer cuts off the program after 30 days. Retrieving the program on the web and getting it installed again is time consuming and aggravating.

Subsequently, there is a build-up of a grey zone that keeps growing. Also, the average user is going to resist more vigorously any attempt by program producers to find out which programs have been installed on individual PCs – a procedure widely deemed uncalled for. Clearly, program producers must not rely on a "grey zone" business model. There are professional user companies that work with all-inclusive agreements concluded with software producers, which keeps everyone happy until such time when user companies discover they are to pay additional license fees for the second laptop of one employee.[10]

One concludes: Everyone does it, without exception. Those who do not have a black copy of even the tiniest software on their PC don't use any software or PC, for sure. Trafficking black copy comes with the system. In theory, one could solve the problem by introducing charges whose allocation might cause some serious disruption among the globally operating producers and to outrage among users if, subsequently, fees were imposed. A way out of this dilemma could be the production of "freeware" as a type of hobby configuration and gradually take "shareware" production onto a more stable commercial platform.

Such a platform may not necessarily turn into a launchpad of sheer revenue growth. In an era of electronic government, one needs vast amounts of

9 Even an overwhelming majority of 'heavy users' begin to lose their hitherto boundless faith in the Internet – over the issue of Internet payment.

10 The 1,257 million clicks on *www.bsa.de* last year corroborate the rising sensitivity and high demand for information. The numerous downloads of information brochures or software tools demonstrate the concern of users about inadvertently illegal use of software: cf. *www.bsa.de/presseecke/2001/Bs021-03.html*

'shareware' – often referred to as 'best practice' – that could be installed in software parks, new forms of institutions and working environments, agencies, unions and charities. Similar needs can be discerned in schools and colleges, as well as among the small crafts that simply cannot afford to pay world market prices for software. As an aside: It would be safe to say that employment overcapacities are not to be expected, at this point in time. A civil servant software specialist employed in the public sector yearns to be headhunted by the promised land of private enterprise.

A new and positive development could emerge from new service providers that have solid commercial agreements with software makers and who give payed-for services to users, such as "upgrade on demand" that offers an increment to simple downloading. Not only for German Nerds this seems to involve "too much state" an will be rather a matter of discussion than of business plans.

Overall, pressure is growing to find a solution; be it software as computer programs or content, the courts of law seem to cave in to the notion of 'a technological non-protectionability' of IPRs. The Court of Appeals of the State of California at San Jose ruled that publishing on the Internet software that enables the decoding of DVDs was protected by the constitutional freedom of speech.[11]

IV. Getting Hooked by the "Push"

In 1998, a new 'technology hog' was paraded through the global village: Start-ups discovered "the push" on the web as a surrogate for the ailing business plan that, in any event, was geared towards advertising-driven revenues. Scores of more or less sophisticated ad applets and mastheads with interactive buttons were thrown at the defenseless user pushing him into either message acknowledgments or even purchase orders. The idea was not entirely new but the number of start-ups having adopted that type of business model increased tremendously. The legal model was Amazon that in its portal responded to every keyword with a book recommendation.

Responsible advertisement managers were getting uneasy; the proliferation of such hard sells made many users install "web cleansers," eventually –

11 Cf. *Spiegel Online*, Networld of 2.11.2001.

something proxy servers of large companies' intranets already did. Investigations have shown clearly that commercials getting through to the user in the end are met with either total rejection or total disregard.

Courts have meanwhile warned "push technology" companies that unsolicited marketing activities on the Internet fall under the consumer protection code and will be prosecuted like unsolicited marketing by phone. Companies are now mobilizing in order to circumvent an opt-in/opt-out solution by applying new feedback options. Future technology will not be accommodating commercial flashes or ad bubbles; UMTS, for instance, could be tariffed according to data volume. In that environment, unsolicited ads in the guise of e-mail, SMS or MMS, will be as unpopular among users as any advertisement banner clogging up an entire web page. On the one hand, commercials will not go away; on the other, pressure on volume tariffing will increase, as through flat rates, for instance. The companies with "the push" will find no cure against the fast growing number of filter systems. Public as well as suitable private information services could be set up via a so-called 'door message service' with the help of a trusted third party operator. An exhaustive discussion of this proposal at this time is not called for, because most potential stakeholders are not even aware of the future existence of the problem.

The organizational antidote to unsolicited e-mails, the so-called *Robinson Lists*, is still in a nascent state. The German Internet association, IDI, doubts that "such naming" could offer solutions against unwanted mails. "Notorious spammers would simply disregard the Robinson lists," said Torsten Schwarz, head of the Ecoworking group, Online-Marketing. "The list is nothing but a placebo."[12] The assertion that the Robinson Lists could be a lucrative target for crackers is probably also true. The addresses stored there are particularly interesting for spammers, because Robinson members are not usually found in spam distribution lists and are not regular recipients of e-mail ads. In this particular area, an entire army of software agents is sorely missed; without their help, the individual user might indeed be inundated by spam having no other option than repeatedly changing his e-mail address. Protection from those industrious automatic mail servers could be provided through a method involving several cumulating mail addresses or sender's passwords. However, no one has so far accepted responsibility for the development of such tools.

12 as opposed to *heise* online, 8.11.2001.

V. URL Snatchers

At first, there is amusement in the phenomenon of URL dealing. To prepare for a presentation in May 2000, I looked up some keywords in the context of "ethics" under the appropriate web addresses, the so-called URLs (Unique Request Location) and especially in the Top Level Domains (TLDs) on the web and jotted down the results. Under *wirtschaftsethik.de,* which translates as 'businessethics.de,' I found a leasing agency's advertisement page for holiday homes in Sardinia, *"abitare al mare"* (living by the sea); under *moral.de,* I encountered the first presentation of an online shopping company, *OK-Onlinekaufen.de,* while the address '*gutes-benehmen.de*' ('goodmanners. de') produced a total blank: "The requested URL could not be retrieved."

Those examples shed some light on the phenomenon and nature of domain snatching. Here, it is not only agencies at work, who are trying to secure a label for themselves and their potential clients, but a majority of 'regular folk,' who stake out their petty claim, enjoy their small protection right and hope for a trade-off that makes them rich and famous one day. Most of them will be disappointed, like most goldrush diggers.

It might be possible to become famous, if only as a later-day Herostrates[13] by destroying instead of creating. One of the best examples is that of an Internet trader, who claimed 'd21.de' as an URL just days after the official roll out of the government-backed D21 Information Society Initiative of German industry. The hundreds of companies supporting the D21 initiative had no option other than adopting an URL variation, "initiatived21.de." Hopes of getting rich by URL trading are ill founded not least because, if need be, the actual label owners can sue such 'info claims' into oblivion. In this context, it may be important to know that the number of lawyers admitted to the bar in Germany increased from 88,000 in 1998 to 104,000 in 2000 reaching 120,000 in 2003. Moreover, U.S. style litigation is becoming increasingly popular[14] in Europe.

---

13 So named after Herostrates who set fire to one of the Seven World Wonders, the Artemis Temple in Ephesos in the year 356 B.C in order to become famous.

14 Cf. JOHN HORVATH: *The Next Wave: Internet Insurance*, Telepolis of 04.03. 2000: "Following this came the lawyers. Whenever a large sum of money is involved, you can expect to find them. With their talents at twisting and manipulating reality beyond all reasons, many were sure that we have now reached the end. Yet, although there has been a marked increase in litigation involving copy-

At the end of the day, that type of information dealing is but a gamble. Not exactly a true expression of *'homo ludens'*, because long and tedious periods of waiting for 'the prey' are not that conducive to the anthropomorphic instinct to play. Despite all protests coming from ICANN and the Net scene, there are no solutions for the domain structure, unless there is agreement on fundamental Internet overhaul. Should it come to a new definition of the Internet, within the framework of redefining network structures – here, one should think of the efforts of the U.S. administration in creating a secure "gov.net" – an individual numbering plan for end users could emerge, such as for the telephone. The game with snatching, claiming and trading would then only work with aliases, nicknames or nom de plumes.

Today, one can already get a taste of things to come *@T-Online* or *@AOL.com* or by reviewing those fantasy 'combat' names adopted by hardcore chatters. Net-Zine *Heise-Online* said about TLDs: "There are seven international TLDs as well as 250 national TLDs that can somewhat mitigate domain name competition by allocating same names at different levels, for example. However, the urge to take complete possession of a name in all its variations seems to be overwhelming." Online mediators may not be that effective, after all, even if TLDs were expanded, significantly.

VI. Address Trafficking

In a country such as the United States that does not know any compulsory residential registration, the possession of valid addresses is a valuable asset. That gives rise to notorious website teasers – such as "do you want to mail this item to a friend?" – that seek to extricate those coveted addresses, usually for direct marketing purposes. Many eCommerce models depend on building a geographically classified dragnet comprising thousands of addresses. The e-mail address is not enough for that purpose, as is widely known.

The German Data Protection Agency in Berlin found:

> Every other advertising Euro spent by businesses in Germany goes to direct marketing. That includes advertising that directly targets the individual cus-

---

right and domain name disputes, online civil disobedience against the long arm of the law has been effective in keeping at least a portion of computer-mediated civic discourse alive."

> tomer by way of direct mail. That type of direct marketing is all the more successful, the more detailed the information is on consumer behavior. The going rate for address data on the address market is, therefore, linked to the accuracy of the customer profile that is sold along with the address.

Consequently, the Internet can serve as the ideal dragnet gathering such information, although the position is unequivocally clear on the legal side in Germany: "… Direct advertising by telephone, fax and e-mail is inadmissible as a matter of principle. According to ruling by the Federal Supreme Administrative Court, telephone advertising is only admissible under prior consent or under an established business relationship; the Court has in 1995 applied those principles to the conveyance of advertising by means of facsimile messages. As for e-mail advertising, the State Administrative Court in Berlin has in several rulings in 1998 clarified that unsolicited advertising by e-mail constitutes an inadmissible infringement of privacy."

List brokering is a term used to capture "the making available of data." According to the German data protection law, list brokering is not merely "making data available" but constitutes 'transmission' of personal data, instead, which is a criminal offense. When data is conveyed for a purpose other than the original purpose, i.e. when the conveyance serves as a conduit for a subsequent business transaction, it is a matter of data transmission. German courts are bound by that interpretation and, subsequently, their staunch legal attitude triggers a cross-border trade of some degree, "completely unbeknownst" to the traffickers, of course, in case they get caught in the act.

Solutions on the consumer side appear to be rather clumsy. The Berlin Data Protection Agency recommends some kind of boyscout game: "Should you want to find out the path your address is taking, alter the spelling of your name or address when placing an order or when taking part in a competition, for example by adding the first letter of an additional first name. Should the modified spelling appear on new mail from senders hitherto unknown to you, then you can find out who acquired your address from whom."

The Marketry Company of Bellevue, Washington DC, sells e-mail addresses of Internet users gleaned from newsgroups, and in its press reports claims:

> These are e-mail addresses of individuals who are actively using the Internet to obtain and transfer information. They have demonstrated a substantial interest in a specific area of information on the Internet. They are regularly accessing information in their interest areas from newsgroups, Internet chats and websites.

The list is growing by 250,000 mail addresses monthly, all of them revealing user preferences, such as "adult, computer, sports, science, education, news, investor, games, entertainment, religion, pets." Further, the Washington Post writes that Marketry's president refused to name the current proprietor of the list containing users both U.S. and non-U.S. on the grounds of confidentiality. The webpage citing this case recommends: "Either let yourself be inundated with junk mails or together with all friends and their friends send *very, very many protest mails* to 'listpeople@marketry.com'."

In other words, should an attack be launched against the culprit, which would contravene pertinent codes of ethics, it would then become clear that those "good" addresses come with a price tag. Picture this: A user's one-year data record is in this day and age commercially more interesting than his entire Genom. It's not the disposition that counts but the actual behavior. At this point it ought to have become clear that such address trafficking is brought to a halt only by a complete Internet overhaul after which addresses are temporarily stored with to-be-defined "trusted third parties" and for organizational purposes, only.

Public administrations face a particular dilemma: Their portals are linking up jointly with private enterprise in the so-called electronic government ventures, those partnerships between the public and private realms that are coveted for their popularity – and for lack of funds. If only one of the addresses – which are also found in the telephone directory, by the way – got into wrong hands, the citizen's somewhat delicate trust in 'his' virtual City Hall would wane rapidly.

VII. Hauling "Trash"

What to some is access to the world's knowledge is to others nothing but an abominable pile-up of 25 billion websites that will have grown by a further 100,000 before this presentation is over. Surrendering to that rising mountain can, at times, take ludicrous forms even in the realm of science. There, for example, a search engine is to gauge 'knowledge performance' from representative random results that re-labels everything that is not explicitly listed as "information trash." Conversely, applying the same gauge to an expert recommending one book out of a hundred, one would have to dump the 99 other books he also read but never recommended. In that case, information selection does not lead to an accumulation of knowledge, but to its reduction, instead.

That example should not be ignored when digging for information treasures under the heading “data mining.” In eCommerce, however, flimsy methodology does not make you keel over. Under the title “M-Marketing on the Move” – released on August 23rd 2003 – the chairman of the executive council of business consultants Mummert & Partner decries the technical and legal hurdles that thwart wide-spread use of mobile advertising messages:

> The starting position is not an ideal one: Companies’ data bases have not had sufficient customer information to allow a direct approach (…). Companies should, therefore, compile data employing all the media at their disposal. This would enhance the effective usage in terms of personalized customer approaches. Having such a data warehouse, we would get closer to the ideal of the “transparent customer”. The sad reality currently is that customers are inundated by mass mailings that are a far cry from a personalized approach; mostly it is trash that no one responds to. A correctly personalized approach could lift the return mail percentage by 70 points.

Although direct and personalized advertising on the Internet is prohibited in Germany, advertising messages on mobile phones remain in a legal grey area. EU law is more liberal at this point. For as long as it remains unclear whether or not ‘mobile’ marketing is allowed, companies have a back door open: In so-called permission marketing, clients consent to their service provider or to another company transmitting information to their mobile phones.

Here again, the simple “Click, Drag’N Paste” methodology described in the beginning is back again and up to no good: A user identifies a car by mouseclick, buys it and then is being bombarded for years on end with car commercial trash. Opting in, i.e. permitting service providers to send information – which, in fact, is a great achievement of the Internet – can and should be done for a limited period of time only (“feature timer”). Upon expiry, no formal termination notice would be required. Such a plausible and simple model has not yet been thought of in the worlds of databases and the Internet and, for this reason, has not materialized.

VIII. Tying with Megabytes

Office communications procedures all over the world require that a more or less sizeable document be forwarded along with a brief note or comment and, subsequently, often inform a third party with a need to know about it. In the traditional 'paper' office that is being done by using a code 'copy w/o attachment' or, as a variation, 'cover page only.' Often, that proved to be a helpful and even self-disciplining measure to stem the paper floods, especially when handling large documents. Before making an assistant, an office administrator or oneself work at the copy machine, it payed to think carefully who was indispensable to receive the comprehensive original.

The common mail systems of the wired office no longer provide for that forwarding option[15] of "copy only first page without enclosure" and even if it did, it would most likely not cause a moment's hesitation. A click on the "forward" or "reply with history" button and all the 'CCs' as well as the 'BCCs' will be convinced for a while that they received complete and flawless information. Of course, 1.5Mb is a speck of dust when hooked up to a pipe of 100Mbps, but even DSL and ISDN lines can cope. However, a simple analog link in a hotel room would not be that accommodating and mobile reception would just be overstrained. Even UMTS bandwidths – the beckoning new frontier for pushers – would fail to make those megabytes available by pressing buttons: Instead there will be 122kbps, rather.

Amendments to the 'Netiquettes' for senders or, conversely, appeals to filtering capacities of addressees will be about as effective as a teenager's will power to ignore the telephone ring – the average user can hardly suppress reflexes to click on incoming mail. And this would be perceived as nuisance by both sender and receiver: Flashing queries such as "would you really like to send 1.5 megabytes of attachment to all recipients?" or "would you really like to download 1.5 megabytes of attachments now?". As regards the latter, popular programs like Acrobat Reader often bring twice the aggravation especially concerning time wasted: If you leftclick, you can read the document, but you cannot store it after reading; if you rightclick for options, then click on 'link' to store the document, which works – but then the documents is stored unread. In the end and after wallowing in ritually abusive

15 One can, of course, prepare a separate mailshot without enclosures – but I have never seen it done in myriads of mails.

language hurled at that "slow coach network provider," you get engaged in double action in double time[16] – leftclick and load, read, review and relish; then return, rightclick, re-load and – store.

It may be safe to say that even the "gigabyte-richest" hard discs of our offices would have burst at their seams long ago if it weren't for the server's default '*temp*' files that catch downloaded documents in most offices and where they are often disposed of overnight – to the early morning chagrin of expensively qualified personnel. One way to avoid waste and duplication would be to re-introduce to the networked world the 'good old' mail classifications of the postal system. So, in analogy to the postal system, it is quite imaginable to complement the now universal e-mail by a to-be-negotiated, hierarchical classification such as "eNote, eLetter, ePackage, eBox, eCase" and even "eContainer." The individual "eClasses of mail" could be separated by urgency, importance and 'verifiability'– just like today's mail sorting does. As an example: A mobile phone user would receive an 'eNote' with a sender statement[17] informing the recipient of a 10 Mb 'ePackage' on hold for retrieval on the net, or even of a 100Mb 'eContainer' to be picked up from '*net restante*' under the URL indicated. Also thinkable: A new "Personal Mail Portal"[18] substituting the mailbox of the paper world and being adapted fully to the electronic age.

For sure, no one will be cautioned under any rules of ethics when their megabytes mindlessly litter the network landscape. But it would be worth a "Netiquette" rebuff because limitations will continue to exist even in the real broadband era – and also because you might never spot that 'famed mobile user' pulling a fiberoptic cable.

An "infrastructural" solution that adopts classes of information volumes is being impeded by the simple fact that no one is in charge any longer to define and implement such generally valid infrastructural norms[19]. Also technology associations fail to produce "recommendations". Deutsche Post can be expected to assess the impact of concepts like "ePackage" on their own brands

16 Such tedious waiting cannot be delegated away to a software agent as yet. All users are mindful of the 'hourglass' and mini breaks like this contribute overall to massive waste of time.

17 Not just a short message, this is frequently being abused as 'cheap SMS'.

18 Details will not be given here for reasons of patent law.

19 Cf. H. KUBICEK, D. KLUMPP, A. BÜLLESBACH, A. ROSSNAGEL: *Innovation@Infrastruktur*, Heidelberg 2002.

and mail business in general. Others would – if that has not already happened – secure the brand rights for such concecpts and, subsequently, let Deutsche Post, UPS and all other transport service providers know that the adoption of that scheme might not come cheap, after all.

A friend to whom I described in a telephone conversation that possible scheme ranging from "*eGram*" to "*net restante*" almost got beside himself with excitement and urged me to get those terms protected without delay and, most important, secure the corresponding domain names, as well. I replied that this was actually a bad moment – and the wrong thing to say – because I was currently working on a discourse in the context of ethics in eCommerce and that I was going to slam precisely that type of behavior pejoratively as information trafficking. My friend, who had meanwhile started his search engine, made all the right noise to confirm he had empathy for my stance and then he suggested that he would take care of everything for me until I would have shed my scruples after my speech in two weeks' time. There was no question, he said, that someone in the audience was going to walk off with that idea right there and then and, by the way, the domain "*net restante*" would exist already, but the others were up for grabs. Now, that phone conversation is an intro that takes us straight to a new quality of plagiarism linked to Click, Drag'N Paste, which can be termed the most severe of all modern, illicit information dealing.

IX. Dealing with Counterfeits

Our "*cognitopes*"[20] are not exactly being invaded by spectacular forms of plagiarism; instead, what we are witnessing is more like a ground swell of accepted petty habits using "Click, Drag'N Paste" to turn a plethora of information into grey goo. It would make much better sense, for instance, to plagiarize the text of this treatise because re-editing it would take longer than simply jotting it down after having read it. Plagiarism creeps into this world not so much by the use of WORD, but rather clandestinely through Power Point. Even in dissertations (doctoral thesis), one of the last havens of objec-

20 "Cognitope," in its capacity as an 'instant' creation and ostensibly claiming Latin-Greek parentage, has but one raison d'etre: to replace the dreaded expression 'world of knowledge.' Why did I create it? Everyone does it.

tive verification, Click, Drag'n Paste is used, if at all, to glean impressive reference lists and other sources. Straightforward text plagiarism would stand out like a sore thumb and would be spotted easily, especially when big, fat dissertations are read selectively with word processing search functions.

However, plagiarism can save an awful lot of time when you can tap resourceful 'chartware' for lavish or complex graphics and – everyone does it. A simple template caption change and the 'newly-made' will slip by search programs; even the best sleuth would need a photographic memory so as not to be dazzled by those illustrations. Thesis examiners should more practically – and in the spirit of the old Roman tenet "plagiatur et altera pars" – download the entire graphics glitz onto the hard disc. There is, however, no generally applicable remedy in sight. In order to separate the corn from the chaff in the process of academic qualification, one may have to rethink the value of the written work and give more emphasis oral exams.

In the eighties I characterized the "copy" command as an "assault on human creativity worse than the Xerox machine." The temptation of "multiple use" of an authentically created content is "plausibly even greater when access to the individual building blocks of the original work is made easier."[21] At that time, I could still see a solution in a blend of full text retrieval and "legal action;" today, I am not so sure. There is the irrefutable fact that I can find older texts on my hard disk much easier and much quicker than, in stark contrast, I am able to think of new, fresh formulations – which, evidently, is a strong hint of a creativity trap.

In the realm of eCommerce, we are therefore dealing with numerous design-oriented providers of "portals," "platform" and "websites"and their myriads of templates that are poised to rip off the next customer coming round the corner: "We no longer build in first-rate quality components, because they can and will be copied, and we also don't copy other's first-rate quality, because one would recognize those copies;" such was the information we acquired from design whiz startup who did not want to be named. We can therefore discern a trend towards making of software that takes from what has been known to be around, that counterfeits without stealing and that reproduces sustainable, genuine novelties – and makes a killing in so doing. It

21 DIETER KLUMPP: "Neue Medien – alte Probleme: Das Gestaltungspotential kann durch neue Fragestellungen vergrößert werden", in: ECKART GOTTWALD, REGINA HIBBELN, JÜRGEN LAUFFER (Eds.): *Alte Gesellschaft – Neue Medien*, Opladen 1989, pp. 93-98.

is somewhat reminiscent of Michelangelo students who, to begin with, do not need Michelangelo at all. Maybe it's not that new a phenomenon, after all. You can see such forms of legal plagiarism in many shop room windows with a variety that surprises – and creates.

X. "eEthics" – All But A Famous Last Word?

The Finish information society expert Illka Tuomi[22] referred to issues of ethics as "a focal point in future research work, and even more important than technological research." He also said, however, that there was hardly any other field with fewer tangible concepts; at the end of the day, no one knows how and where to implement 'eEthics' in this globalized world.

There is the reality of the everyday world in eCommerce, which forms an even *starker* contrast to the "commandments" already accepted elsewhere. There is one Commandment from the Decalogue – the Fourth – that has been honored far and wide even during the Industrial Revolution: "Remember the Sunday." And, in a matter of speaking, it was remembered over and beyond the call of duty. In the information society, no ethical code even comes close. From the concretely existing *ethics in institutions* today to a conceivable *ethics in infrastructure* in the future: When you're on the Net, "this incredible lightness of being" takes you across hang-ups and inhibitions that would have been nigh inconceivable to overcome just a short while ago. The phase of info pushing and trafficking will persist for some time to come, especially as the concept of knowledge is undergoing rapid and sustaining change.

One of the surprise elements in the "everyone-does-it society" is its *collectivizing* trend that is in juxtaposition to *individualistic* "fun society." "*Homo ludens*" is being evicted. Playing the game, in the true sense of this expression, is being played according to rules and by players honoring those rules – and that separates playing from cheating, it separates living from pretending.

Monetarism guru Milton Friedmann used to tell his Chicago Boys that one had to go about business "within the rules of the game," something they

22 Remarks by Tuomi, made at first workshop of the Stiftungs-Verbundkolleg Information Society of the Alcatel SEL Foundation in Berlin, November 8th, 2001. Tuoni is a renowned scientist with Nokia.

deliberately ignored. Nico Stehr was right in his analysis "that the modern economy, as it transforms itself into a knowledge-based economy, loses much of its immunity from societal influences it once enjoyed, at least in advanced societies".[23]

It may be that also in eCommerce, ethics can be found only when you read the small print. One is reminded of ecological issues and their commonplace use in today's world: Nigh everything has an eco tag, even appliances are sold along with mantras that, naturally, production and design are 'human-centric,' 'people-friendly' so, in analogy to ethics, each call for ethical compliance remains just like a whiff of lip service, a habitual last word that no one heeds. The allurements of Click, Drag'N Paste, "smokeless retrieval," or the 'off' button for harassing software agents, in short: the allurement of information dealing in these pioneering days of online communication is overwhelming the users, be they providers, users or regulators in the market. One might also argue, that by putting on the agenda the all-too familiar but nevertheless difficult concept of 'parallel' context it creates a new and even more complex communications concept, the 'hyper context.'

Models of society that are without adequate protective mechanisms of their own, without authentic values and accepted, calibrated standards have in history remained ephemeral. *Ceteris paribus* (i.e. all else being equal) this may become applicable to the information society concept. As human beings we cannot predict a future parallel context, but we can nevertheless presume.[24]

23 NICO STEHR: "Knowledge, Markets and Biotechnology", Sustainable Development Research Institute, University of British Columbia, Vancouver B.C. Canada, March 2000; in: JOHN DE LA MOTHE, JORGE NIOSI (Eds): *The Economic and Social Dynamics of Biotechnology*, Boston (Kluwer Academic Publishers) 2000.

24 A word of heartfelt gratitude goes to Mr. Harry U. Elhardt, a Brussels-based regulatory and policy expert in European electronic communications, whose advice, expertise and guidance were invaluable in producing this treatise in the English language.

Chapter 8

Power Redistribution and Ethical Challenges in E-Commerce

PAUL WHYSALL

I. Introduction

This paper reviews a range of ethical problems pertaining to e-commerce, which are interpreted largely in terms of a redistribution of power as a consequence of developments in electronic commerce. It then asks whether these are really new problems, and argues in fact they can readily be seen as new formulations of existing problems rather than genuinely new problems or issues. Finally a range of responses is examined with a view to generating an ethical response to these problems of e-commerce.

A luminary of British, and indeed European business ethics, Professor Jack Mahoney, suggested:

> one way of summing up the concern and content of modern business ethics is to see it as the study and evaluation of the power possessed by business

> throughout society, and of the ways in which businesses acquire, retain and exercise that power, whether for good or ill. (Mahoney 1994)

Power is recognised as an important component for understanding marketing channels (Gaski 1984), and thus aspects of power and conflict in supply chains are likely to constitute ethical as well as operational problems, following Mahoney's contribution. In virtual supply chains, new power relationships emerge, suggesting a new range of ethical problems also will be manifest. In this paper, examples of those new relationships will be explored, with a view to asking if a need exists to generate responses to potential abuses of power in e-commercial environments. However, it can also be contended that these new challenges have much in common with past ethical challenges, and thus we may beneficially look both forwards and backwards in contemplating appropriate responses to these new challenges.

II. Consumer Empowerment in a Digitally Divided Society

An optimistic scenario of e-commerce as a liberating force for consumers can be developed. In this scenario, consumers are freed from constraints on mobility and limited access to local provision (Prabhaker 2000), while notions of local monopolies or retail 'deserts' (Department of Health 1999), become irrelevant. The e-consumer is empowered with a global search capability of unprecedented power, which permits the best deal in terms of price, source, quality, service, or whatever to be accessed from a personal computer, or, increasingly, such a device as a WAP telephone. Traditional supply chain barriers can be overcome with ease, and intermediaries may become irrelevant.

Yet Internet access, and thus such consumer empowerment, is limited across society, with the 'Digital Divide' a concern in Europe and North America. Studies by the US National Telecommunications and Information Administration (1999) found high income urban households were 20 times more likely to have Internet access than low income rural households, and 9 times more likely to have access at home. Distinct ethnic contrasts existed in Internet access, with white households more likely to benefit from access from home than Black or Hispanic groups from any location. At lower income levels, Internet access is approximately twice as high in urban than rural communities. Gaps between ethnic groups, and gaps based on income and education continued to widen after 1997. Lerner (2000) adds that rural-urban contrasts may exist not just for underprivileged groups, but also generally in the quality of access (e.g. bandwidth).

The UK government has also identified the digital divide as an area of concern. In the summer of 2001, UK home Internet access was available to about 37% of homes (National Statistics, June 2001). Yet rates of 35% – 40% in London, South East and South West England, contrast with markedly lower levels for North Eastern England (25%), Scotland (24%) and Northern Ireland (20%). In early 2000, poorest to richest segments contrasted with rates of 3% and 48% respectively, and the most rapid growth was still occurring among richer households (Tran 2000). According to figures updated to September 2000, disparities were still increasing (Timmins 2000).

Of course, Internet shoppers are a specific subset of all Internet users. Information on Internet shoppers from the USA suggests they tend to be older and wealthier than non-shopping Internet users (Donthu and Garcia 1999). For some disadvantaged groups, though, e-commerce can represent a major benefit. Morganosky and Cude (2000) found some 15% of American on-line shoppers used the medium to counter difficulties associated with physical or care-giving considerations, while 6% of their sample mentioned "grocery shopper stressors" as motivation for on-line shopping.

Several themes emerge then. Some evidence exists to suggest that any digital divide for shopping purposes may be more strongly related to income than the generic digital divide, but there is also evidence that disadvantaged shoppers may buy into e-commerce to overcome difficulties. A concern emerges, then, that advantages of an expanding e-commerce, be they cheapness, better service, convenience, wider choice, or whatever, will largely accrue to consumers already enjoying advantaged status in conventional markets through higher purchasing power. These already financially empowered shoppers may find added power in a digital marketplace; disadvantaged shoppers, conversely, lacking on-line shopping access, could suffer greater disadvantage, or struggle to 'buy into' a potentially beneficial medium.

How might vendors respond to a future wherein the more affluent have the power to seek out better deals while the less affluent remain hostages to conventional retailing? One scenario might be of a highly polarised market. On one hand would be more affluent on-line shoppers, targeted by efficient suppliers who drive costs, margins, and thus prices down consistently. Contrastingly, other suppliers could face dwindling patronage focused increasingly on less affluent groups. To maintain profitability such suppliers might require increased margins from consumers with less potential to switch to electronic channels and increasingly trapped in conventional geographical markets. In short the rich could get richer and the poor could get poorer in an electronically generated manifestation of the model of circular and cumulative patterns of growth and decline depicted by Myrdal (1957).

III. Activists, Protestors and Internet Vigilantes

Consumers' empowerment is paralleled by an empowering of consumer activists. Many groups and individuals have found the Net to be a powerful medium to harangue, expose, and attack companies seen as displaying unacceptable standards of corporate behaviour and poor customer service. For example, Canadian Dana Peters created Web sites to channel his frustration at telecommunications companies' shortcomings. According to Peters, "The average citizen doesn't have the ability to project their opinion ... The Internet gives them a chance to project their opinion out to the world. Despite the large marketing budgets and slick web graphics a company might have, they simply cannot prevent an individual's protest site from popping up alongside their pages in a web search" (quoted from MacGregor and Riga 1997). There are echoes here of what Badaracco and Useem (1997) termed, in reviewing problems of Intel, 'Internet Vigilantes'. There are also wider resonances of the findings of Kozinets and Handelman (1998) who quoted 'Jacques' on his Internet boycotting behaviour: "Yes, I feel empowered, I feel that even tho it's only me I can in fact stand on my own two feet and stand up to corporate greed and not participate in the fleecing of america". Indeed, we can envisage a categorisation, almost a spectrum, of Internet activism targeted at what are perceived as unethical corporate practices, from individuals to major pressure groups and charities (Whysall 2000). While such examples may all be interpreted as principled attempts to exploit the Internet for reasons of ethical conviction, a quite different sort of agenda applies to those who seek to use the Internet as little more than vandals, with purely destructive objectives in many cases. Costs of viruses and such are high, not only in repair costs, time and data, but also, possibly more crucially, lost consumer confidence (Coleman 2000, Cerf and Patrick 2000). Yet we need to tread carefully here.

'Hacktivism' is ethically justifiable to some, but to others little more than vandalism (Denning 2000, Thomes 2001).

IV. Effects on Established Businesses

Any expansion of e-Commerce is likely to impact on to established business, including traders who do not enter e-commerce. German laws dating from the 1930s restricting discounting and special offers are expected to be abolished to gain compatibility with a European Union directive on e-commerce, and it has been suggested that a further effect might be a relaxation of Germany's relatively strict laws on store opening hours. These changes may pose significant threats to traditional stores; the Association of German Retailers questioned the need for such changes when retail prices in Germany were among Europe's lowest and when German consumers enjoyed strong protection from "confusing" discounts and offers (Atkins 2000).

The contraction of traditional chains raises concern, particularly in sectors where on-line trading offers significant economies and efficiency gains over conventional business. Banking in the UK has been radically restructured in the wake of new technologies. Many UK banks have downsized branch networks. In Spring 2000, Barclays warned that despite having already closed a tenth of its branches (171 branches) in a single week, further closures were possible. Midland had operated 2090 branches in 1988, but its successor HSBC's network numbered 1,622 in 2000. NatWest's branch network reduced from 3,086 in 1988 to around 1,700 in early 2000, although further closures were terminated after takeover by the Royal Bank of Scotland (Ibison 2000). That policy shift underpinned a widely televised advertisement, screened over the Christmas period of 2000, with an apparently stressed older lady finding several ex-bank premises converted to bars and restaurants before being reassured the NatWest branch would remain a conventional bank. The message was clearly that among those disadvantaged from bank branch closures were the elderly, whilst this new policy reflected a wider social responsibility. Alternatively, running e-commerce alongside a traditional retail network raises the prospect of supply chain duplication which may be environmentally wasteful (Reynolds 2000).

The innovative nature of e-commerce can lead to ambiguity and conflict between editorial and advertising roles. From a marketing viewpoint, Amazon.com may have "successfully positioned itself as a service provider rather than a book retailer" through its reviews, book suggestion service, and rankings information (Reynolds 2000). However, when Amazon were seen to be taking payments from publishers in return for recommending books, its claim to be following traditional practice on shared promotional expenditures contrasted with those seeing a conflict of interest between the retail role and editorial functions (Alsop 1999). There is a general concern that a clear distinction ought to exist, but at present is hard to discern in on-line publications, between editorial and advertising content (Berry 1997).

V. Identity Problems, Monopolies, and Traffic Diversion

Identity problems include domain name rights, 'cybersquatting', pirating of names, intentional mis-spelling of names, and parallel registration. The EasyGroup of companies provide an example where exclusivity of name is problematic. EasyGroup threatened legal action against companies they see as 'passing themselves off' as related to the group which includes EasyJet (the low cost airline), and its related businesses EasyRentacar and EasyEverything. Yet Easy car (a two year old pan-European car rental business), Easyspace (a web hosting company) and Easyshop (a UK on-line lingerie outlet) have no links to EasyGroup. The World Intellectual Property Organisation (WIPO), which rules on domain name disputes, has dismissed some EasyGroup complaints already, however (Grande 2000).

Related to the theme of exclusivity of domain names is 'cybersquatting', the opportunistic occupation of a site with commercial potential by a total outsider. When Chevron and Texaco merged in 2000, they found permutations of their combined names had already been taken up. Similarly, 'jpmorgan-chase.com' had previously been usurped before the merged banks sought registration. Cybersquatter rights had been upheld in the USA, forcing some companies to negotiate to 'regain their own names', but in 1999 a new law allowed companies to sue for damages over domain names. ICANN (International Corporation for Assigned Names and Numbers) instituted a dispute procedure in 2000, but only for trademarked names, which thus does not tackle problems of new, unregistered names resulting from mergers (Spiegel 2000). In Britain in 1997, the retailer Marks and Spencer and others brought a case against cyber-dealers trying to profit from domain names pertaining to well known brands. The High Court accepted the 'threat of passing off' when a stranger came to possess a famous brand or trademark and allowed injunctions to be used to stop the practice. A similar case involving Harrods had previously been heard in 1996, again with support for the established business (Abel 1998).

Abel (1998) identifies three related problems regarding domain names. Firstly there is pirating, where an outsider takes and registers a company's domain name. Abel lists many famous brands pirated in the 1990s. Mis-spelt names generate further concern. Examples have included MacDonald's and McDonaldz, and some less likely misspellings (e.g. MuckDonalds). An intention here may simply be to intercept misdirected web traffic, but in several cases there is a clear intent to undermine the reputation of the mis-spelt company. Then there is parallel registration of domain names in other nations, but ones that search engines may still find. Suffixes like Azerbaijan ('.az') have been exploited by those seeking a parasitic relationship to a name likely to attract high volumes of web traffic.

Abel (1998) traces, mainly from a US perspective, the history of litigation in these areas, and attempts by the USA's main registry of domains to respond to problems. When domain names remain disputed, as when more than one legitimate claim exists to a name, a Committee of the Internet Society has proposed the introduction of more 'top level domains' (TLDs) to reduce the appeal of the '.com' suffix. Yet problems of consistency across registration agencies globally (over 80 in late 1997) seem unlikely to disappear.

The main income source for web sites is advertising, and advertising revenues reflect a site's traffic volume, shown by numbers of 'hits', however brief. Industry data reveal that 71% of US 'dotcom advertising revenues' goes to the 10 most popular sites, with only 9% of revenue reaching companies below 50th in popularity. While often seen as a free and open market, the 'frictionless business' of e-commerce is also potentially a source for the emergence of "miniature monopolies" wherein players "aggressively pursue market power" (Kuttner 1998, Reynolds 2000). The shake out of 'dot coms' was seen by many as a source of market concentration. While barriers to entry to e-commerce may be low, that does not necessarily translate into ease of access to funding. Further, as popular sites gain greater advertising revenues, so they can be developed to generate additional growth. Consequences of such trends remain an area for speculation: the Internet may become but a further marketing channel for existing powerful 'real' corporations, or it could see the evolution of a small elite of Internet-based leviathans with power to deter new entrants (Tomkins 2000). The idea of cyberspace as a level playing field as open to entrepreneurial innovators as much as to large corporations is not necessarily the future, then, and clearly there are ethical and consumer welfare implications here.

Revenue issues also relate to the practices of 'linking' and 'framing'. Linking employs a hyperlink to another site, such that the user may assume information gained has been provided by the site operator from where the link originated (even though the URL will change). An apparently useful site could actually be little more than a shell accessing sites developed at cost to others, but that shell may generate substantial traffic and thus advertising revenue. Framing is somewhat more sophisticated, allowing a number of other sites to be seen as windows on a host site. Abel (1998) cites disputes of this nature between news providers, and a case involving Microsoft being accused of 'pirating' a Ticketmaster site. Such practices may allow a third party, perhaps a competitor or activist, to divert users' traffic to another location for a variety of motives, both commercial and otherwise. Diversion of web traffic also raises concerns around what is known technically as meta tagging. Words can, unknown to users, be inserted into a site's keywords field to make that site a destination for search engines seeking a frequently searched word. Cases involving Playboy magazine concerned so-called 'adult' sites; the words 'Playboy' and 'Playmate' were present on a web site as black print on a black background, invisible to users but read by search engines (Abel 1998). 'Spoofing' operates similarly, typically by attracting innocent searchers to pornographic sites (Desmond 1997). There are issues here both of links to sites that may be unwanted or unsuitable (say to children) in terms of content, but also advertising revenue implications.

VI. Rights, Freedoms and Regulation

A conflict exists in relation to market efficiency and individual rights. Miyazaki and Fernandez (2000) saw a double role for policy makers regarding e-commerce: on one hand to facilitate on-line shopping in order to generate potential market efficiencies, but on the other to protect and inform consumers by making the risks of e-commerce known to all. This is complicated by concerns for vulnerable consumers on the Web. Littman (2000) discusses issues pertaining to young teenagers on the Web, quoting studies suggesting that American parents' concerns rose between 1998 and 1999. Littman suggests parental ability to monitor child behaviour on the Net is less effective by comparison with traditional media, notwithstanding methods to screen content. In particular, parents are unable to know what data may be being collected on their off-springs' Internet activity.

Consumer privacy has emerged as a key issue in electronic commerce, notably in the USA. Site owners' ability to collect data on individuals is widely recognised: "as prospects visit Web Sites they leave a trail that includes e-mail addresses and clues about their lifestyles and interests" which "can be built into databases for future solicitation" (Bush et al. 2000). Contrasting interpretations of the use of this new found power exist. Many marketers claim there will be benefits to consumers: "There has never been a better opportunity to get closer to customers and focus on their needs" (Pitt et al. 1999). However, the language employed can suggest manipulation, even exploitation, of consumers, such as when it is suggested retailers can "focus their marketing efforts on managing their customers more effectively" (Doherty et al. 1999). Against such criticisms are claims that e-retailers act cautiously in compiling data on visitors (McCune 1999), and that data is collected on 'general trends' rather than specific visitors (Littman 2000). However Greening (1999) suggests "the value of knowing who is visiting your site, which people are generating the most revenue, and what advertisements are working most effectively can often generate profits and savings far exceeding the cost". Mullin (2000) claims abuse is not widespread, relating to a "few bad actors who steal and abuse consumer data", yet Prabhaker (2000) contends "It is unrealistic to expect profit driven businesses not to infringe on consumer privacy in an environment that makes it increasingly profitable and a technology that makes it easier than ever to collect and share personal information".

A response is to gain customer acceptance that data may be collected, but this is not necessarily a full solution. Waldmeir (2001a) suggests consumers might be mislead by the 'fine print'. She contends that "Merchants have all the powers and consumers have little". Given time pressured consumers seeking to get quickly to the electronic point-of-sale, a balance between consumer protection, legal precision, and commercial interest may be elusive.

From the earliest days of Internet commerce, there has been concern about a lack of regulation. McLeod (1995) saw the Internet as "an unstructured network with no one central control responsible for its use and future direction ... home to a plethora of special interest groups: extreme right- and left-wing political factions, hobbyists of every kind, even groups proffering pornographic materials". Even if we accept a need to regulate the Internet, this will be complex (Lessig and Resnick 1999). For some, though, its anarchistic tradition is a positive feature of the Net, and one that should be preserved. The Internet does not recognise political boundaries, and attempts to regulate may be thwarted by sites relocating to 'safe havens' (Studeman 1996). Yet, even legitimate businesses can face problems as a result of the Internet's transnational reach (McClenahen 2000). Cerf and Patrick (2000) suggest that governmental interventions, to be effective, require international and intergovernmental consensus and coordination, yet also must reflect the Web's flexibility and dynamism, an optimistic combination perhaps!

Moves to regulate e-commerce are underway, even if for some they pose a threat. Business-based critics attacked Britain's Regulation of Investigatory Powers Bill on grounds of costs and efficiency, while it has been criticised by civil liberties groups on grounds of basic human rights. The small e-pressure group STAND called the resulting Investigatory Powers Act (2000) "deeply flawed legislation" (http://www.stand.org.uk/). A wider issue is law enforcement agencies' access to decryption keys, and this is a pressing matter for governments in many countries. The annual costs of Britain's proposed solution have been estimated at around £0.25m for a large ISP, and around £10,000 for smaller operations. Industry sources suggest such costs could reduce the international competitiveness of UK businesses and also result in lower UK security standards (Eaglesham and Grande 2000).

Attempts to resolve legal problems arising out of cross-border e-commerce in the European Union have also proved challenging. Two main conflicts with ethical/power dimensions emerge. Firstly, clashes occur between consumer rights and market efficiency arguments: should consumers have a right to their own national legal protection against a 'foreign' e-trader, or should 'country of origin' rules apply? Secondly there are fears that international consumer protection will be costly and disadvantage smaller e-traders lacking an international presence. Internet regulation is likely to prove especially difficult given the Net's unique lowering of barriers of time and distance, its database potential, its flexibility in information handling and display, and its integration of previously separate media (Bush et al. 2000). The idea of an organisational code of ethics for Internet marketing received substantial support in the study by Bush et al. (2000), but the authors noted that a code alone is at best part of a process for establishing an ethical climate for Internet marketing, and difficult questions about implementation and enforcement are likely to remain. Nonetheless, in an industry where such as pornographers have been at the forefront of much technical innovation, the case for self-regulation remains problematic.

VII. Are These Really New Ethical Concerns?

The 'new world' of e-commerce can be portrayed as fundamentally different by comparison with traditional commercial (and societal) practices:

> Cyberculture is being nurtured by the young, the risk takers, and the uninitiated, rather than the established guardians of the markets. The risk-takers do not seem to carry the burdens of the past. The only burden they seem to be carrying is the burden of constructing the future. (Venkatesh 1998)

That might seem to imply that we face new ethical problems which require new ethical solutions, but not all agree:

> It's a mistake to think we need to reformulate our concepts of right and wrong to fit cyberspace. No, the real challenge is to find a way to apply our existing ethical principles within these new structures". (Plotnikoff 2000)

Richard de George (1999, p. 265) similarly interprets ethical problems in the Information Age: "We do not need a new ethics, but we have to apply and possibly revise our ethical concepts and norms to fit the new environment".

Most of the issues raised in these discussions do have parallels in conventional commerce. For example, ideas of a digitally divided e-commerce echo earlier debates over Out-of-Town Shopping in Britain. If a digital divide persists alongside an expanding e-commerce (presumably expanding since it is perceived to be adding consumer value), we can expect ethical concerns to emerge. Benefits will fall mainly to advantaged consumers: those in urban areas with higher disposable incomes. Conversely those in rural areas and/or with lower incomes, will be least advantaged, and arguably disadvantaged. This broadly parallels arguments around the social costs of out-of-town hypermarket-style shopping such as were heard during the 1970s and later (Hillman 1973, BDP Planning/Oxford Institute of Retail Management 1992).

Rural residents responded to limited public transport by rating car ownership a higher priority than did urban residents with similar disposable income. Perhaps in a future with attractive e-retailing opportunities, rural residents will have to respond similarly with higher computer ownership and capability? Lack of mobility was seen as the main source of disadvantage in the hypermarket debate, yet this is largely counteracted in cyberspace. Certain caveats need to be added here. Probably the greatest practical obstructions to widespread e-retailing as yet lie with logistical problems of delivery, and such obstacles are likely to be greater in rural areas, or, if reflected in costs, may add to rural disadvantage. Further, the solutions often voiced as ameliorations to a digital divide, such as Internet access through schools, libraries, and the like, are more realistic in urban environments.

A contrast with the hypermarket comparison is the lack of a regulatory body. The focus of the 1970s arguments was the British Town and Country Planning System, which many wanted to use to restrict out-of-town store developments whilst encouraging in-town retailing accessible particularly to disadvantaged inner urban residents. Regarding the digital divide and Internet access, no such regulatory framework exists or seems likely to appear. It is inconceivable to foresee government restricting Internet access in order to safeguard potentially disadvantaged consumers; such a policy would lack political, social and economic credibility. Even in the hypermarket context, social costs carried comparatively little weight, while factors such as environmental impact, which were more prominent then, could arguably be seen to favour virtual shopping. So the digital divide scenario has parallels with earlier social welfare arguments in relation to retailing, but also differences. However, the core *ethical problem* appears comparable – change generating disadvantage for some groups, while simultaneously empowering already advantaged groups.

Parallel ethical discourses in conventional business also exist for other issues. Consumer privacy concerns are raised in direct marketing (Evans 1999, Patterson et al. 1996). Trademark dilution issues have much in common with look-a-like branding (Davies 1998, Burt and Davis 1999). Advertising claims have long generated ethical discourse. And is consumer activism on the Net really unrelated to wider counter-corporate protest and lobbying? Some may suggest that the Internet raises distinctive problems in terms of regulation, while others take somewhat different views (Rowland 1998). While many may accept the view of Zugelder et al. (2000) that: "It is evident that the evolution of international Internet marketing is years ahead of the law's ability to handle it", those who have struggled with grey markets, parallel imports and globally traded fake goods (Alberts 1992, Clarke and Owens 2000) may feel international regulatory difficulties are not unique to e-commerce, notwithstanding the search for international legal solutions to the challenges of e-commerce (Waldmeir 2001b).

VIII. Towards an Ethical Response

It is often easier to identify ethical problems than to provide solutions. Moreover, there may be a temptation to ignore some of these challenges on the grounds that they have yet fully to crystallise in a period of rapid change. De George (1999) cautions against such an attitude:

> Business ethicists and society in general could wait for ethical problems and injustices of the information age to arise, and do our analysis after the fact. Far preferable, however, is to anticipate injustice and prevent it from appearing, forming structures that are ethically justifiable, rather than having to undo and attempt to reform structures that are unfair, socially disruptive and harmful to some of the parties.

Cataloguing ethical concerns is a step to anticipating injustices, but the real challenge is to prevent potential injustices becoming manifest. Broadly, three types of response are seen. We could seek to eradicate unethical practices through a regulation of cyberspace by governments. As an alternative, self-regulation of e-commerce could be advocated. Thirdly, there is the view that an ethical community could be generated by example and reward.

The idea of effective regulation of cyberspace has already been touched on. Until September 11, 2001 it looked extremely unlikely that effective regulation might develop. Governments seemed slow, cumbersome and disinclined to react to the fluid nature of cyberspace. Then there were serious international differences of opinion on core issues such as privacy (Despeignes 2001). However, since the traumatic events of September 11, 2001, it might be that a new international dynamic has emerged in relation to the so-called 'war against terrorism'. Given the importance of the Net in such a 'war', it is more likely than previously that western nations will seek to intervene in cyberspace, with clear consequences for e-commerce. If hacking and protest activities are seen as problems, these could be targeted by governments acting in a new spirit of international concert. However, a danger here would be if justified, legitimate opposition to corporate agendas became demonised alongside the worst terrorist excesses. Further, the likelihood remains that global support will not be total and thus while there could be effects in some societies, the prospect of 'safe havens' for cyberspace's pariahs would remain.

Self-regulation by a responsible industry also seems a flawed approach. While responsible businesses may represent the majority of e-commerce, the minority of unethical actors in e-commerce are unlikely to accept self-regulation, and indeed may even take it as a shield for less scrupulous activities. As has already been argued, such as pornographers have been at the forefront of innovation in cyberspace, and are likely to continue in such a vein in the future, regardless of calls to act more responsibly.

So our best hope for an ethical future for e-commerce may lay in the evolution of a virtuous community in cyberspace, although this may seem a very optimistic scenario perhaps. The idea that an ethical community might evolve in cyberspace has parallels in classical ethics. This approach could accept that e-commerce is but the latest manifestation of an old practice – commercial exchange – which may be as old as civilisation itself. Many ethicists have addressed the theme of fair exchange, as with Cicero's musing on the moral and social responsibilities of the first grain merchant to arrive in Rhodes after a famine, or more recently R.M. Hare's hypothetical example of the baker who short-weighs his bread. However, it is Aristotle who perhaps best addresses the concept of virtuous exchange, and who has been most frequently revisited by modern authors seeking to explore the ethics of exchange (e.g. Cordero 1988, Koehn 1992). Cordero suggests that, following Aristotelian thinking, three sorts of unfair exchanges are possible:

- in which at least one party does not agree to the exchange;
- in which at least one party agrees unwittingly;
- in which at least one party agrees only under pressure of circumstances.

Many concerns raised here seem to fall into the second category, where site owners either portray themselves as someone else, or devise ways deviously to divert web traffic. Issues of privacy can also be associated with this category if interpreted as instances where users are unaware that part of the transaction involves personal data collection. Perhaps empowerment/disempowerment issues are less readily interpreted in the framework. Something like 'where one party is unable to participate in a potentially advantageous exchange' might appropriately be added. Nonetheless, the Aristotelian model of free, fully informed and open exchange as the basis for a virtuous community seems an appropriate one when contemplating ethical e-commerce.

Thus a tentative model of ethical e-commerce (and *many* more issues require addressing before a general model emerges) stresses concerns such as:

- ethical e-commerce would be transparently fair and open, with no hidden costs (e.g. hidden data collection; opaque legal conditions);
- all parties to an electronic exchange should be able to be fully aware of all pertinent facts about other parties' identities and motives, and in particular vendors' status should be clear and 'visible' to consumers;
- e-commerce should be as widely accessible as possible (which can generate further scale benefits), or equivalent benefits should be available via alternative media, especially for the less advantaged (cf. Rawls on justice);
- the empowerment of individuals created by the Internet brings with it significant responsibilities, and while legitimate protest is justified, purely destructive activity is not acceptable.

These may well be idealistic objectives, and will surely benefit from debate and reworking, but it is in the interests of the majority of legitimate, well-intentioned members of our societies that the opportunities generated by e-commerce are as widely accessible as possible, exist in an environment of trust and openness, and are used to generate progressive communities. Only then will the full empowering potential of e-commerce be released.

On a more pragmatic basis, such an ethical community may evolve more on grounds of self-interest than ethical enlightenment. Even pornographers need to generate consumer trust in e-commerce. However, there may also be a self-destructive force at work here. Two contrasting hypothetical scenarios can be seen. On one hand we can mirror the thinking of Dubinsky and Gwin (1981) who hypothesised "that some type of 'Gresham's Law (upper case) of Ethics' operates in a business environment. That is, 'the ethic of corporate advantage invariably silences and drives out the ethic of individual restraint'." If bad practice does drive out good, then probably e-commerce is doomed as the sustainable community of trust it requires will not evolve. Or, we can hypothesise a virtuous circle of exchange whereby ethical behaviour is rewarded. One reason Mahoney (1994) gave in response to the question 'What makes a company ethical?' was that it pays, especially in the long run. While that may not be a satisfactory *ethical* argument for ethical behaviour, as Mahoney himself implied, it does offer a basis for a more optimistic future for e-commerce perhaps.

References

ABEL, S. M.: *Trademark issues in Cyberspace: the brave new frontier*, Palo Alto Cal. (Fenwick & West LLB) 1998. *(http://www.fenwick.com/pub/trademark_issues_-in_cyberspace.htm)*

ALBERTS, S.: "Trademarks and gray market goods: why United States trademark holders should be held strictly liable for defective gray market imports", *George Washington Journal of International Law and Economics*, 25 (1992), pp. 841-873.

ALSOP, S.: "You can trust me on this – really", *Fortune*, 139 (1999), pp. 175-176.

ATKINS, R.: "Net threat to German shop law", *FT.com*, 7 April 2000

BADARACCO, J. L., JR.; USEEM, J. V.: "The Internet, Intel and the Vigilante Stakeholder", *Business Ethics. A European Review*, 6 (1997), pp. 18-29.

BDP PLANNING / OXFORD INSTITUTE OF RETAIL MANAGEMENT: *The Effects of Major Out-of-Town retail development. A literature review for the Department of the Environment*, London (HMSO) 1992.

BERRY, J.: "The ethics of online publishing", *Webreview* (*http://webreview.com/wr/-pub/97/10/03/feature/ethics.html*) 1997.

BURT, S.; DAVIS, S.: "Follow my leader? Lookalike retailer brands in non-manufacturer-dominated product markets in the UK retailing sector", *International Review of Retail, Distribution and Consumer Research*, 9 (1999), pp. 163-185.

BUSH, V. D.; VENABLE, B. T.; BUSH, A. J.: "Ethics and Marketing on the Internet: practitioners' perception of societal, industry and company concerns", *Journal of Business Ethics*, 23 (2000), pp. 237-248.

CERF, V.; PATRICK, J.: "New ways to police the internet", *FT.com*, 27 June 2000.

CLARKE I. III; OWENS, M.: "Trademark rights in gray markets", *International Marketing Review*, 17 (2000), pp. 272-286.

COLEMAN, K.: "Sensible security: how e-tailers and on-line shoppers can protect themselves (Parts 1 & 2)", *KPMG Insider, from http://www.ideabeat.com/Exchange/-KPMG/KPMG_Article.html (2000)*

CORDERO, R. A.: "Aristotle and fair deals", *Journal of Business Ethics*, 7 (1988), pp. 681-690.

DAVIES, G.: "Retail brands and the theft of identity", *International Journal of Retail & Distribution Management*, 26 (1998), pp. 140-146.

DE GEORGE, R. T.: "Business ethics and the information age", *Business and Society Review*, 104 (1999), pp. 261-278.

DENNING, D. E.: "Activism, Hacktivism, and Cyberterrorism: The Internet as a Tool for Influencing Foreign Policy", *http://www.nautilus.org/info-policy/workshop/-papers/denning.html* (2000)

DEPARTMENT OF HEALTH: *Improving shopping access for people living in deprived neighbourhoods*, Paper for Discussion, Policy Action Team 13, London (Department of Health) 1999.

DESMOND, E. W.: "The erotic allure of home schooling: web porn sites", *Fortune*, 136 (1997), p. 151.

DESPEIGNES, P.: "US and EU clash on privacy", *FT.com*, 28 March 2001.

DOHERTY, N. F.; ELLIS-CHADWICK F.; HART, C. A.: "Cyber retailing in the UK: the potential of the Internet as a retail channel", *International Journal of Retail & Distribution Management*, 27 (1999), pp. 22-36.

DONTHU, N.; GARCIA, N.: "The Internet shopper", *Journal of Advertising Research*, 39 (1999), pp. 52-58.

DUBINSKY, A. J.; GWIN, J. M.: "Business Ethics: Buyers and Sellers", *Journal of Purchasing and Materials Management,* 17 (1981), pp. 9-16.

EAGLESHAM, J.; GRANDE, C.: "The price of policing e-business", *FT.com*, 31 May 2001.

EVANS, M.: "Food retailing loyalty schemes - and the Orwellian Millennium", *British Food Journal*, 101 (1999), pp. 132-147.

GASKI, J. F.: "The theory of power and conflict in channels of distribution", *Journal of Marketing*, 48 (1984), pp. 9-29.

GRANDE, C.: "'Easy' traders step up fight over website names", *FT.com*, 8 November 2000.

GREENING, D. R.: "Tracking users. What marketers really want to know", *Webtechniques*, July *http://www.webtechniques.com/archives/1999/07/greening/*, 1999.

HARGREAVES, D.: "E-commerce: Europe caught in legal tangle", *FT.com*, 1 November 1999.

HARGREAVES, D.: "Boost for e-commerce", *FT.com*, 9 May 2000.

HILLMAN, M.: "The social costs of hypermarket development", *Built Environment*, 2 (1973), pp. 89-91.

IBISON, D.: "Internet growth may lead to more Barclay closures", *FT.com*, 11 April 2000.

KOEHN, D.: "Toward an ethic of exchange", *Business Ethics Quarterly*, 2 (1992), pp. 341-355.

KOZINETS, R. V.; HANDELMAN, J. M.: "Ensouling consumption: a netographic exploration of the meaning of boycotting behavior", *Advances in Consumer Research*, 25 (1998), pp. 475-480.

KUTTNER, R.: "The Net: a market too perfect for profits", *Business Week*, 11 May 1998, p. 20.

LERNER, D.: "Rural US may trail web revolution", *FT.com*, 28 March 2000.

LESSIG, L.; RESNICK, P.: "Zoning speech on the Internet: a legal and technical model", *Michigan Law Review*, 98 (1999), pp. 395-431.

LITTMAN, M.: "How marketers track underage consumers", *Marketing News*, 34(10) (2000), pp. 4-5.

MACGREGOR, K.; RIGA, A.: "Rogue web sites target firms", *Ottawa Citizen*, 6 September 1997.

MAHONEY, J.: "What makes a company ethical?", *Business Strategy Review*, 5 (1994), pp. 1-15.

MCCLENAHEN, J. S.: "Doing it e-right. What's acceptable business behavior on the 'Net?'", *Industry Week*, 21 August 2000, pp. 13-14.

MCCUNE, J. C.: "Big brother is watching you", *Management Review*, 88 (1999), pp. 10-12.

MCLEOD, J.: "Let the buyer beware of Internet commerce", *Industry Week*, 244(9) (1995), p. 58.

MIYAZAKI, A. D.; FERNANDEZ, A.: "Internet privacy and security: an examination of online retailer disclosures", *Journal of Public Policy and Marketing*, 19 (2000), pp. 54-61.

MORGANOSKY, M. A.; CUDE, B. J.: "Consumer response to online grocery shopping", *International Journal of Retail & Distribution Management*, 28 (2000), pp. 17-26.

MULLIN, T.: "Internet Issues Abound", *Chain Store Age*, 76(7) (2000), p. 30.

MYRDAL, G.: *Economic Theory and Underdeveloped Regions*, London (Duckworth) 1957.

NATIONAL TELECOMMUNICATIONS AND INFORMATION ADMINISTRATION: *Closing the Digital Divide*, *http://www.digitaldivide.gov/*, 1999.

PATTERSON, M.; EVANS, M. J.; O'MALLEY, L.: "The growth of direct marketing and consumer attitudinal response to the privacy issue", *Journal of Targetting, Measurement and Analysis in Marketing*, 4 (1996), pp. 14-33.

PITT, L.; BERTHON, P.; WATSON, R. T.: "Cyberservice: taming service marketing problems with the world wide web", *Business Horizons*, 42 (1999), pp. 11-18.

PLOTNIKOFF, D.: "Talking about ethics in a society that is dominated by the Internet", *Silicon Valley News*, 15 April 2000.

PRABHAKER, P. R.: "Who owns the online consumer?", *Journal of Consumer Marketing*, 17 (2000), pp. 158-171.

REYNOLDS, J.: "eCommerce: a critical review", *International Journal of Retail & Distribution Management*, 28 (2000), pp. 417-444.

ROWLAND, D.: "Cyberspace: a world apart?", paper presented at *British and Irish Legal Education Technology Association Conference*, Dublin 1998.

SPIEGEL, P.: "Planning a mega-merger? Don't forget to register the internet domain name", *FT.com*, 23 October 2000.

STUDEMAN, F.: "Internet controls may open route to sex havens", *The European*, 22 February 1996, p. 22.

THOMES, J.L.C.: "Ethics of Hacktivism", *Information Security Reading Room*, Sans Institute, *http://www.sans.org/infosecFAQ/hackers/hacktivism2.htm*, 2001.

TIMMINS, N.: "Digital divide grows in UK", *FT.com*, 19 December 2000.

TOMKINS, R.: "Dotcoms devoured", *FT.com*, 22 October 2000.

TRAN, M.: "The digital divide", *GuardianUnlimited*, 11 July 2000.

VENKATESH, A.: "Cybermarketscapes and consumer freedoms and identities", *European Journal of Marketing*, 32 (1998), pp. 664-676.

WALDMEIR, P. (2001a) "Ethics are a few clicks behind", *FT.com*, 18 April 2001.

WALDMEIR, P. (2001b) "Treaty threatens e-commerce", *FT.com*, 31 May 2001.

WHYSALL, P. T.: "Retailing and the Internet: a review of ethical issues", *International Journal of Retail & Distribution Management*, 28 (2000), pp. 481-489.

ZUGELDER, M. T.; FLAHERTY, T. B.; JOHNSON, J. P.: "Legal issues associated with international Internet marketing", *International Marketing Review*, 17 (2000), pp. 253-271.

Chapter 9

Transcultural Ethics: Beyond the Electronic Economy of MTV

ROBERT VAN ES

The electronic economy crosses the borders of countries and cultures. A moral theory that fits the electronic economy is therefore faced with cross-cultural issues. In international business ethics the established theory of cultural dimensions is helpful for a first orientation in cultural and moral differences. However, it assumes a concept of culture that is not adequate for the study of present day cross-cultural morality. Where do we find cross-cultural morality? Neither in books nor behind desks. We'll have to go and study places that are less obvious for philosophers but are familiar to marketers. Institutions like Music Television offer us trend-setting moments of cross-cultural morality. It is in the commercial concentrations of youth culture that the electronic economy may find its inspiration to develop a fitting moral theory that crosses borders.

I. Cultural Dimensions and Criticism

Geert Hofstede's famous empirical research into cultural differences was based on IBM as a clear constant. In each country the multinational had a business office or a plant, Hofstede looked for variety in cultures. His study first appeared in 1980 and was elaborated in 1991. The most important improvement was adding a fifth dimension to the four he already found. Although Hofstede frequently speaks of one aspect of a dimension "versus" another, his five dimensions to track cultural differences are in fact ranges. These five dimensions or ranges are:

1. Individualism to Collectivism. The extent to which individuals are integrated into groups. In short: individualism.
2. Masculine behaviour to Feminine behaviour. From assertiveness and competitiveness to modesty and caring. In short: masculinity.
3. Weak Avoidance of Uncertainty to strong Avoidance of Uncertainty. The extent to which uncertainty and ambiguity are tolerated. In short: uncertainty avoidance.
4. Small Power distance to large Power distance. The extent to which the less powerful accept and expect that power is distributed unequally. In short: power distribution.
5. Short-term orientation to Long-term orientation. From social obligation and saving face, to thrift and perseverance. In short: long term thinking.

When we use the Hofstede dimensions to look at two strong business cultures, Germany and Hong-Kong, the following pattern emerges. In Table 1 the five dimensions are scored on a scale from 1 to 100.

Table 1. The Hofstede Dimensions of Germany and Hong-Kong

Dimension/Range	Germany	Hong-Kong
Individualism	67	25
Masculinity	66	57
Uncertainty avoidance	65	29
Power distance	35	68
Long term thinking	31	96

Comparing the scores from these indexes is instructive. Hong-Kong Chinese can infer from Figure 1 that in communication Germans are more individualistic (67), don't like uncertainty (65) and are more orientated to short-term thinking (31). Germans in turn must know in their communication Hong-Kong Chinese are orientated to collectives (25) and long term thinking (96), can handle uncertainty (29), and are used to large power distances (68). On the dimension of masculinity both cultures differ only slightly.

No one will deny the usefulness of such comparisons. The five dimensions of Hofstede's research are insightful and instrumental for a quick orientation on a foreign culture. Preparing business transactions certainly benefits from this information. However, some of us have experienced it does not always work that way: the predictive force of the theory is not without limits. Like any theory Hofstede's cultural dimensions must be understood in the context of its time. In the early 1970-ies national cultures were more compact and tight. Nowadays cultural reality is more complex due to the accelerating process of internationalisation.

The basic criticism of the Hofstede research is of two sorts. The first basic criticism concentrates on the external validity of the findings. The sample, IBM co-workers in the early 1970-ies, is not representative for a culture or a country. One cannot simply generalize these findings for an entire national culture. Although this criticism as such is right, research corrections didn't make much difference. Follow-up research with other samples in main lines confirmed the early findings of the IBM sample.

The second basic criticism can be summarized in three points. All three concern the concept of culture used in the Hofstede research:

- Culture is not just coherence or hierarchy. Culture is not typified simply by pointing out the dominant view. In one and the same nation there are larger and smaller subcultures and between these subcultures there are power differences. Sometimes the struggle for power makes it clear there is not one culture dominant in a nation state (Bourdieu 1979). The same goes for organizations: in a single organization a differentiation or even a fragmentation of subcultures may occur (Martin 1992).
- Culture is not simply "software of the mind". As a concept culture does not only represent the mental but also the physical aspects. Culture is about artefacts too, about body movements and about behaviour, especially important in non-verbal communication (Hall 1966).

- A single photograph cannot catch culture. To capture the dynamics of culture we need moving pictures. Cultures develop in interaction and exchange with other cultures. Cultures are not really authentic, but always in a process of change, although the speed of change might differ. This dynamics was already noticed by Robbert Redfield (1962).

For a more differentiated view in the study of culture and values in the 21-th century we need an approach in which this criticism is taken into account. This means

1. We take culture to be a dynamic concept the study of which requires moving pictures of both psychological and physical aspects.
2. Culture only rarely is a harmonized unity; in most cases culture is a set of subcultures involved in some kind of power struggle.

Struggling subcultures cannot only be found within countries or within organisations. Power differences are also present on a global scale in the laborious construction of world culture. In the last decade this process often is called globalisation: a form of internationalisation with a controversial twist.

II. Power Differences in Globalisation

The general process of globalisation is of course as old as mankind. From the early beginning people migrated, bringing with them their cultures and convictions, and coming across other people with different cultures and convictions. It led to curiosity and trade, or to abhorrence and conflict. In the last decade a more controversial process of globalisation forced itself to the front. This process is all about profit and power. It is also about perspectives and positions: that's where we start first.

Seen from the perspective of a West-European the magic term 'globalisation' refers to four trends. First, politics is in a process of internationalisation. A point in case is the forming of the European Union and the introduction of the Euro. In worldwide politics globalisation can be found in the national civil rights giving way to international Human Rights. Second, the world economy stimulates uniform patterns of consumption: drink Coca Cola, eat with McDonalds, be entertained by Disney, listen to the Top-40, look at MTV, watch the next Hollywood-block buster, play Nintendo Mortal Kombat and spend your vacations at standard exotic places like Burma or Ibiza.

Third, an increasing number of people use airplanes to reduce distances and travelling time. Four hours of flying to spend one week on Cyprus; or six hours flying for a long weekend in New York. The sky no longer is the limit. Fourth, cultural products like literature, photographs, paintings, films and music are produced, reproduced and distributed on a worldwide scale. Quality products in the form of books, video's and discs are available for relatively low prices for an increasing number of people worldwide. There you have globalisation. Most Americans find it a matter of course, because it is for the greater part their culture that is exported. Most Europeans like it, because they prefer to identify with that rich and powerful nation state, so strong in mass culture and consumerism.

Now most African and Asian people will have a different point of view because they have different experiences. First, what they hear in times of war is foreign politicians talking about human rights while their own politicians are talking about their tradition and family values. In times of war they sometimes see blue helmed soldiers drive by, and once and again packets of strange food are dropped out of trucks or out of planes. Second, what they see in times of peace is the opening of new shops. Cola, hamburgers and sunglasses are sold, but they cannot afford the prices for these consumer goods. Third, in Africa and Asia travelling by airplane is only for the happy few. Vacations, if any, are always nearby. In most cases, on walking distance. Of course, the Japanese are an exception, but tourists from Burma, Uganda or Pakistan hardly exist. Fourth, in Asia the new compact disc from Jennifer Lopez also is hot, but the only way to get it is by buying an illegal copy made on a personal computer on the local black market. Western entrepreneurs and lawyers in expensive suits get angry when you do that. They say it is an invasion of their property rights; illegal copiers are stealing their money. That is difficult to understand when you hear that these people are paid more in two weeks then you will earn in a year. If you are lucky you can get a job with a multinational that produce jeans or sport shoes. You get paid a little bit more than with local companies, but management positions are not open for you. First of all, you are considered cheap labour. That was the whole idea of coming to Taiwan, Korea or Indonesia in the first place. There you have the other side of globalisation. Most Africans and Asians find it confusing. Western values are imported by capital force. Their own local values are not considered equal: they are primarily seen as targets for marketers.

These differences in view and interests invited Leslie Sklair (1998) to distinguish between the class of transnational capitalists and the class of anti-globalists. The transnational capitalists are in favour of globalisation: managers, media tycoons, consultants and diplomats. Managers because of promising fusions and investments. Media tycoons because of the increase of power and impact on consumerism worldwide. And diplomats, politicians and consultants because they like to intensify their professional fields. At the opposite side we find the anti-globalists, a diversity of local, national and international groups (or individuals) who are against further globalisation because it is in fact, they say, capitalist imperialism disguised as a free market on its way to democracy.

Now Sklair's distinction may be too simple, but his rigorism makes one thing clear. The evaluation of this specific process of globalisation directly depends on your position and your perspective. First, the classical distinction between the rich north and the poor south is confirmed: between the West and Africa and South-Asia there are large power differences. It is not at all clear how globalisation will be in the interest of poor countries. It is more likely that it will not be in their interest at all. To show the public what is going on, these countries need worldwide watchdogs that use multimedia to monitor the behaviour of foreign companies. To increase their independency these countries are in need of reinforcement of their negotiating power. Both needs are well served by information technology. Second, within the culture of the rich north there is again a distinction between the culture of the established and the youth cultures. Most "transnational capitalists" can be found among the established; most "anti-globalists" can be found in youth cultures. These stereotyped groups have major differences, but both of them make intensive use of Internet as a mean of communication and organization.

Looking for the highest common factor, could Internet be an instrument to bridge the classes of the rich and the poor countries, or the culture of the established and youth culture? What does cyberspace have to offer?

III. Cyberspace for the Electronic Economy

Cyberspace is the worldwide non-physical space in which transactions are mediated between people and computers, independent of time, distance and location. Elements of cyberspace are digital computers, digital electronics (transport systems, control systems, and robots) and communication networks. Cyberspace got an enormous push in 1993 when the World Wide

Web, an integration of telecommunications and computers, became active. The early surfers were radical spirits aimed at experiments and innovations. But after a decade www has become more and more the mirror of everyday transactional society. Day to day interactions can now be arranged by using Internet. All sorts of virtual communities have come into being.

From a commercial point of view this is highly attractive. For sales people www has become the giant catalogue of a department store: books, compact discs, clothes, tickets, food, flowers, cars and houses are offered in full colour. For marketing people virtual communities are attractive target groups. Well-collected e-mail addresses are worth a fortune for marketers. For *b2b* Internet offers quick information exchanges useful for shareholders, for the stock market, for banking, for research labs, but also for newspapers and television. Internet appears to increase the freedom of choice for the customer. At the same time Internet offers ample opportunity to create monopolies and has serious limitations as a mean of communication. Two examples:

Example 1. The search-and-find systems on Internet do not always search the entire net. Most of them do their work in neatly selected data bases of sellers who had to pay to join that particular database.

Example 2. Communication by e-mail tends to fall back on stereotyping and projection towards the relatively unknown other, be it an informer, a seller, or a chatter. Non-verbal communication is missing. For the time being web cams only offer small compensation. The missing non-verbal communication is a serious flaw, as we already noticed in the criticism of the Hofstede research.

Manual Castell (1997) foresees the integration of all information in shared frames of knowledge. Switching between positions and views within the same frame reduces the distance between cultural products. Multimedia, Castell says, will integrate all cultural forms: prints, audiovisuals, the distinction between popular and elite, between entertainment and information, education and propaganda. Virtual images will capture reality. This might be so, but it will be a long-term process, and in the next twenty or thirty years it will not be accessible for anyone, anytime or anyplace. A recent Human Development Report (2000) offers an interesting schedule. Table 2 gives us only a short selection of all data on the differences in access to means of communication for every 1000 inhabitants of a country.

Table 2. Access to Means of Communication for every 1000 Inhabitants

Nation-state	Televisions	Personal Computers	Internet Providers
USA	847	459	113
Netherlands	543	318	40
South Korea	346	157	4
Turkey	286	23	0.7
Uganda	26	1	0.01

The greater part of the South and most countries in the East have little to no experience with personal computers, not to mention internet providers. The rapid implementation of the electronic economy will be a cultural invasion in Africa and Asia in the next two decades. This calls for extra attention for the moral, cultural and political dimensions of globalisation as the cross-cultural struggle for profit and power.

The Dutch IT company Explainer dc that has set up business in Ghana shows that it can be done carefully. It started with a small initiative and immediately fine-tuned with the cultural context of the country. The basic way to do this was operating in close connection with local government and local technology specialists. At present eight out of the nine IT specialists of this company are from Ghana. This shows us the way to go in small-scale projects. For large scale sociological developments we have to study everyday moral practices at the junction of transcultural fields more closely.

IV. Transcultural Fields in Junction

One step away from Hofstede's research Pierre Bourdieu (1979) offers us another way of looking at the reproduction and transformation of cultures. In industrialised countries, he says, cultural reproduction takes place in more or less autonomous societal fields: sports, politics, literature, fashion, law, music, medicine, and business. These fields have their own rules, vocabulary and capital. Capital not only in the sense of money, but also in the sense of knowledge, know-how and competences. Next to these fields there is a more general field, or rather a sphere, where common sense rules and everyday normativity goes without saying. In principal all fields are equal, but some fields are more equal. In the West the economical field is dominant because of its financial power, not because of its cultural or moral quality.

On the basis of his experience with intercultural training programmes Nico Vink (2001) elaborates on Bourdieu's distinctions. He points out there is a significant difference between the field or sphere of common sense and the other fields. The sphere of common sense is the everyday morality you are used to and you expect that morality to be operative tomorrow: the usual mix of manners and morals of this particular locality. Culture shock for almost 90% concerns differences between the common sense spheres of different cultures. The other fields are rapidly becoming transcultural, that is why he calls them 'transcultural fields'. These fields result from the interaction between the local and the global. In that process the nation state is surpassed. Location is more important than nation. At the opposite side of the common sense sphere we see globalisation in its most impersonal form. Worldwide there is a growth of "non-places". These places look the same wherever you are. Airports, gas stations, coffee corners, fast food outlets, and high ways hotels: they have no real identity. In between the non-places with their lack of identity and the common sense fields bursting with identity there are transcultural fields. They are linking globalism and localism, and therefore changing both.

Now I think Vink is on to something, and I am going to elaborate his concept by going one step further. Not only are these field becoming transcultural, they use each other to reinforce the process. On significant moments transcultural fields are intertwining. By using prominent figures or symbols the sum total of these moments creates a surplus value for all fields involved. This creates a winning situation for all those present, and a loose situation for all those absent. I call these meaningful moments junctions of cultural fields. They are the breeding places of cross-cultural morality. The commercial youth culture in the rich north is an excellent example of the places I have in mind.

The basic market of present day rich youth culture is made up of seven components: music, movies, books, clothing, sports, television, and Internet. 90% of this market in the USA and over 50% of the worldwide market is in the hands of only five companies. Two of them are well-known, older companies: Disney and AOL/Time Warner. The other three are much younger: Newscorp, Universal Vivendi and Viacom International. The latter has an eye catching and influential show-piece: Music Television or MTV. In 2000 it yielded Viacom a billion dollar profit. MTV is big business. Let's look into this everyday moral practice more closely.

V. The Case of Music Television

The concept of MTV is simple and effective. Right from the start in 1982 it used music videos as a creative program, but in the process it sold everything that could be sold. What MTV puts on screen never is serious journalism or criticism. The screen is filled with straight commercials or with a range of infomercials. Marketer Todd Cunningham speaks of ethnographic research as he frequently visits average MTV fans to get to know them. However, the aim is not to produce services and products that make fans happier. You have to know what fans want and how they think, "so that you can give them what you want them to have" as researcher Crispen-Muller puts it (Goodman 2001). What you want them to have is what you can sell by Viacom. There can be no misunderstanding, according to Brent Hansen, Chief Executive of MTV Europe: "MTV is a global brand. Alongside the Cokes and Nikes of this world" and it "creates a constant changing environment for every aspect of youth culture" (Duerden a.o. 1997).

MTV started presenting music awards for best groups, albums and clips of the year. That turned out to be a success. Soon American and European awards were distinguished. In this way each continent could have its own rewards, globalism was softened with a touch of localism, and producers could get a more focused grip on the European market. The MTV Europe Music Awards 2001 was held in Frankfurt. 140 million people saw the programme. Most of them in Europe and America, but a couple of million viewers were Asians and Africans. 90% of the viewers are between 10 and 30 years old. It is the MTV-generation.

Table 3 focuses on the Music Awards as they were presented in Europe in 2001.

Table 3. MTV Europe Music Awards 2001

The biggest sponsors of this event were Intel (hardware for personal computers) and Sony Ericsson (audio, games and mobile phones). People of all sorts of cultures were present. The event was structured like the Oscar presentations in Hollywood: a small number of nominees for each prize, the famous envelope and of course the cliché "... and the winner is ...". Prices were awarded in several categories, not only for popular music video's but also for the best website on music. The prices were introduced and handed out by stars from different fields: sports (Boris Becker), fashion (Claudia Schiffer), and the film world (Ben Stiller, Pedro Almodovar). Several gimmicks of comics and cartoons assisted the presenters and introduced the clips. The way of presenting the entire program and of introducing the film and television-stars was critical and ironical. Sometimes even insulting. As a presenter the British comic Ali G. was responsible for this. MTV officially announced it regretted to have asked this presenter to do the job. This was communicated on MTV's own website, alongside lots of information on the event and opportunities to buy books, discs, clothes films and software.

At this junction of transcultural fields we are confronted with a statement of what it is to be young and cool "right here, right now!" What we experience at this junction is a prescription of how to do things with words, emotions, body language, clothes and trinkets that go way across national cultures. What we have here is global morality in the making. The prescriptive character is closely linked to the commercials and the electronic economy of international business. Millions of fans agree. Normativity, power and profits join hands to the advantage of everyone present at this multimedia event.

At the junctions of transcultural fields such as these the morality of the electronic economy is already developing. What we need now is the moral theory that can keep pace with this moral practice.

VI. Towards Transcultural Ethics

The moral theory we are looking for should not have the intention to pass sentence on these practices, but instead to handle these practices conceptually and practically. Not one theory fits the junction of transcultural fields entirely, but some theories offer elements for setting up transcultural ethics. What kind of discourse is transcultural ethics? How do we create cooperation? How can we understand each other's identity? Does applied ethics has something to offer? I will try to give a first answer to these questions, seen from the perspective of western ethics.

First, there is Ulrich Beck (2000) who claims that world society will not be based on nation states but on a cosmopolitan order of human rights. Cees Hamelink (1999) agrees, in stating that human rights are the moral seal for a decent society. However, Asian countries in particular deny that human rights are really universal. They would in fact reflect a western political, liberal and Christian point of view on moral values and norms. Some western philosophers in turn denied that bias, and among themselves started to discuss the Asian objections. That is not a viable way to go. The ethics we are looking for can only be authoritative if it is constructed in a dialogue between all concerned, not a debate about the argumentation of others in their absence. On the basis of her long term research Stella Ting-Toomey (1999) pointed out the basic values in intercultural communication. The promising way to start a dialogue is to hold onto the values respect, trust and inclusion.

Second, there are Jurgen Habermas and Sheila Benhabib operating in the realm of communicative action. Habermas' distinction between system and lifeworld corresponds to Bourdieu and Vink distinction between the transcultural fields and the sphere of common sense. With all due respect for his integration of sociological insights, Habermas' idea of economy is not the strongest part of his action theory. Benhabib rightly stressed the fact that political-economical interaction is in need of another approach: more down to earth. Habermas therefore tried to develop the application discourse as a tool in between justification and everyday practice. In fact what Habermas is referring to are notions of constructive negotiation, as I pointed out elsewhere (1996 and 2001). The basic value in constructive negotiation is reciprocity. Recent research shows a basic attitude and behaviour of constructive negotiation is more successful in creating cooperation than building forth on the idea of shared values (French, Hasslein and Van Es 2002).

Third, Aldous MacIntyre (1981) and Martha Nussbaum (1986) stressed the importance of the cultivation of human values in becoming a full-grown person. Education only formally is a collective enterprise belonging to a nation. In fact the sphere of common sense is bounded to location, while the other fields are becoming transcultural. Each individual has to cope with a multitude of moral appeals and temptations, and has to write its own biography along the way, changing it from station to station. This narrative concept of identity seems to be the most fitting to the present condition of human development, whether you are born in Uganda, Hong-Kong or Germany. Of course the definition of individuality in Germany refers to one person, while in China individuality refers to the core family. But the moral appeals, the temptations and the rewriting of the autobiography are the same.

Fourth, the rise of applied ethics in the past two decades is for the greater part characterized by a tale-telling imperfection. Moral questions are carefully broken down in relevant elements and arguments. Then surprisingly a conclusion jumps up on the basis of simple thumb rules like "principles go before consequences". The justification of those simple rules in that particular situation usually is missing. Especially when pro and contra arguments are more or less in balance most theories of applied ethics go boy scouting ("Apply thumb rules!") or go post modern ("Anything goes!"). The missing piece of course is serious attention for personal morality. In professional ethics this remains the finishing touch. Joseph Badaracco experienced this at Harvard and came up with the right questions to ask when a moral actor is thrown back upon herself (1997).

Five, personal ethics is concerned with the sphere of common sense. Common sense moral notions are bound to the life world of the individual. The individual is seen as a narrative unity shaping and reshaping its biography. Changing by learning is possible. Even the now culturally closed societies will open up because of the moral appeal of the multitude of stories, images and music that flows around the globe in the multimedia. Being the backbone of the multimedia Internet is an important instrument to create that cultural dynamics. The transcultural fields will especially be the concern of professional and public ethics. In these domains we must try to start or continue dialogues on moral issues. The most challenging task will be to get a grip on the dominance of the economical field with its everlasting craving for efficiency, power and profit at the expense of the ignorant and of the poor countries.

From a Western point of view nine indicators for the development of transcultural ethics can be distinguished. Transcultural ethics:

- is characterized by dialogue
- is guided by the values respect, trust and inclusion
- uses constructive negotiation about what is right and true
- uses reciprocity as guide during that negotiating process
- takes identity to be a narrative concept open to change
- let moral decisions be inspired both by the common sense sphere and by the transcultural fields
- sees the common sense sphere as not static: change is not only possible but likely due to the multimedia
- sees the transcultural fields as change agents because they link the global and the local
- takes the world-wide differences in power and profits to be an important topic for dialogue

These indicators are formulated from a Western point of view. Not all of them will be valid in Eastern and Southern cultures. Hopefully insiders will consider these closing lines as an invitation to point out the similarities and the differences between our perspectives on transcultural ethics.

References

BADARACCO, J.: *Defining moments. When managers must choose between right and wrong,* Boston (Harvard Business School Press) 1997.

BECK, U.: "The sociological perspective; sociology of the second age of modernity", *British Journal of Sociology*, 50/1 (2000), pp. 79-105.

BENHABIB, S.: "Communicative Ethics and Contemporary Controversies in Practical Philosophy" , in: S. BENHABIB, F. DALLMAYR: *The Communicative Ethics Controversy*, Cambridge (MIT-press) 1990.

BOURDIEU, P.: *La Distinction*, Paris (Ed. De Minuit) 1979.

CASTELL, M.: *The Power of Identity*, Oxford (Blackwell) 1997.

DUERDEN, N.; GITTIN, I.; PHILIPS, S.: *MTV-cyclopedia*, London (Carlton) 1997.

FRENCH, W.; HASSLEIN; VAN ES, R.: "Constructive Negotiating Ethics", *Journal of Business Ethics*, 22/9 (2002).

GOODMAN, B.: *Cool!*, London (Channel Four-documentary) 2001.

HABERMAS, J.: *Theorie des kommunikativen Handelns*, Frankfurt (Suhrkamp) 1981.

HALL, E.: *The Hidden Dimension*, New York (Doubleday) 1966.

HAMELINK, C.: *Digitaal fatsoen: mensenrechten in cyberspace*, Amsterdam (Boom) 1999.

HOFSTEDE, G.: *Culture's Consequences: International Differences in Work Related Values,* Beverly Hills (Sage) 1980. (Reviewed edition 2001).

HOFSTEDE, G.: *Cultures and Organizations, Software of the Mind,* London (McGraw-Hill) 1991.

MACINTYRE, A.: *After Virtue*, London (Duckworth) 1981.

MARTIN, J.: *Cultures in Organizations. Three Perspectives*, Oxford (University Press) 1992.

MTV Website *www.mtv.com/mtvinternational*

NUSSBAUM, M.: *The Fragility of Goodness*, Cambridge (University Press) 1986.

REDFIELD, R.: *Human Nature and the Study of Society*, Chicago (University Press) 1962.

SKLAIR, J.: "The transnational capitalist class", in: J. G. CARRIER, D. MILLER: *Virtualism, a new political economy*, Oxford (University Press) 1998.

TING-TOOMEY, S.: *Communicating Across Cultures*, New York (Guilford Press) 1999.

UNITED NATIONS: *Human Development Report 2000,* New York (UN Press) 2000.

VAN ES, R.: *Negotiating Ethics. On Ethics in Negotiation and Negotiating in Ethics*, Delft (Eburon Press) 1996.

VAN ES, R.: "Global Moral Debates. The turn from discourse ethics to negotiation ethics", *www.edu/~isbee/papers/Vanes.doc* (2001).

VAN OUDENHOVEN, J.-P.: "Do organizations reflect national culture? A 10-nations study", *International Journal of Intercultural Relations*ˆ, 25/1 (2001), pp. 89-107.

VINK, N.: *Grenzeloos communiceren. Een nieuwe benadering van interculturele communicatie*, Amsterdam (KIT Publishers) 2001.

Chapter 10

Consumers v. E-Business: Who Should Pay? An Ethical Discourse on the Right to Privacy

ANASTASIA H. CORTES

I. What Is Privacy?

The notion of individual privacy is a core belief of the American consciousness.[1] People demand that their privacy be respected, although, it will be argued, they do so without a very good understanding of what they are asking for.

The word privacy does not appear in the United States Constitution or Bill of Rights. Our commonly held notions of privacy rights are in fact not as legally protected as many people assume them to be. In the United States, privacy laws have been enacted piecemeal, patching together various Constitutional concepts in narrowly constricted ways in order to protect highly specific privacy situations. According to Alderman and Kennedy, the reason these individual pieces of legislation fail to provide adequate protection is

1 ALDERMAN and KENNEDY (1995), p. xiv.

that they have been created without an overall conception of privacy. "Congress has been sporadically creating individual pieces of legislation that not only do not mesh neatly but also leave gaping holes."[2] For example, it is against the law for video rental stores to publicize the rental choices of any individual patrons.[3] The sweeping privacy protection so many Americans believe that they have does not legally exist.

Privacy needs often actually contradict Constitutionally guaranteed rights such as the First Amendment right to free speech. Since the courts are reluctant to abridge Constitutional rights, the *expectation* of privacy is often sacrificed to the *right* of free speech when a case makes it to court. Privacy rights do gain definition through court cases, however, beginning with Supreme Court Justice Brandeis' 1890 opinion that privacy is the "right to be let alone." The "phrase seems to sum up what most Americans have in mind when they think of privacy … [however,] legally it offers no guidance at all."[4] Brandeis' statement is not a guarantee of an individual's right to isolate him- or herself; it simply says that citizens have a right to protection from *government* intrusion into their private lives. The Constitution and Bill of Rights are statements of citizens' rights with respect to the *government*,[5] and can be applied to interactions between people and businesses only through legal (court) interpretation. The promisingly named "Privacy Act" "bars *federal agencies* (italics added) from disclosing information for purposes other than the reason it was collected."[6] Protection against privacy violations by businesses or individuals is not explicitly dealt with except through legal precedent, and the legal system can be slow, tortuous, and specific.

An individual's expectation of privacy in daily life in the United States must have evolved through other means than the Constitution. In some European countries, privacy is a constitutionally defined right, sometimes because those countries have specific experience of life without privacy and the potentially disastrous consequences that can arise.[7] Instances of imprisonment, torture, or execution because of political or religious beliefs abound, and other countries are careful to draft constitutions that try to prevent these acts.

---

2 ALDERMAN and KENNEDY (1995), pp. 330-331.
3 ALDERMAN and KENNEDY (1995), pp. 330-33; ROTENBERG (2000).
4 ALDERMAN and KENNEDY (1995), p. xiv.
5 HARTMAN (2000), p.14.
6 ALDERMAN and KENNEDY (1995), p. 330.
7 ALDERMAN and KENNEDY (1995), p. xv.

Since the U.S. Constitution has never given the government power to persecute citizens on the basis of those types of beliefs, it is not necessary to legislate hiding those beliefs from the government.

However, people seem to find it necessary to hide those beliefs from each other. The view that no others have a right to know details of my own life – from my religious or political beliefs to my medical status or sexual orientation – is so widely held that it is often assumed that such information is protected. Although some of this information is protected from a government standpoint, outside of that arena, most of it is not. A notable exception, HIV-status, is protected in most instances, but even that is available to medical personnel if they feel it is necessary. Hospital admission consent forms specifically grant medical personnel the right to know an individual's HIV-status when relevant.

"Freedom of information" is a foundation of the government of the United States. Thomas Jefferson said "that educated and enlightened citizens could govern themselves. 'Whenever the people are well informed, they can be trusted with their own government.'"[8] Initially, legislation prevented the government from harboring secrets from its citizens, but the notion has been expanded to apply to any number of situations in the public and private arenas. For example, the market is supposed to reflect the vast amount of information available when valuing stock. "A free and prosperous society also requires the free flow of information."[9]

In the end, though, the widespread belief is that privacy is sacrosanct in the United States.[10] This has been elevated to the status of moral belief – it is *wrong* to violate the privacy of another, because this amounts to some type of lying (betrayal of trust), another *wrong* thing:

> Three separate claims are advanced in support of keeping secrets confidential. First, that we have a right to protect ourselves and those close to us from the harm that might flow from disclosure; second, that fairness requires respect for privacy; and third, that added respect is due for that which one has *promised* to keep secret.[11]

"The core fear underlying the privacy debate is a concern for our loss of autonomy … [w]e recoil at intrusions into that space from government, busi-

8 WENTWORTH (2000), p. 24.

9 JORSTAD (2001), p. 11a.

10 JORSTAD (2001), p. 11a; ALDERMAN and KENNEDY (1995), p. xiv.

11 BOK (1978), p. 149.

ness or our neighbors."[12] "It comes down to one's ability to be autonomous in controlling one's personal information."[13] We each want our privacy to be *respected*, and believe that we are morally due this type of respect from others. Both the inherent respect due persons as rational beings and the idea of a universal maxim support this desire.

In fact, "Privacy is a fundamental human right recognized in all major international treaties and agreements on human rights … Most recently drafted constitutions include specific rights to access and control one's personal information."[14] Privacy meets the test of Integrative Social Contract Theory's standard of a hypernorm.[15]

I extend these ideas by discussing (for the sake of the later part of this paper) the products of business. Goods and services are provided for people by businesses, and these goods and services are available through the work of producers and because of the pay given workers in exchange for their work. That is, one works to make or provide goods and services, and the pay one receives enables one to purchase desired goods and services. This is more important to the big picture than might be assumed, and is a point made along the way by Solomon, who describes it as a benefit to society at large for tolerating the whole system of private enterprise.[16]

II. Privacy Online

E-business has a special place in the argument regarding privacy between consumers and business. Because e-businesses are able to collect and process large amounts of information automatically, the issue of consumer privacy is amplified.

Televisions and radios seem archaic when compared to computers and wireless phones – one can have information literally at hand, and can get information about almost anything almost instantly. Consumers do not complain about this availability of information; in fact, they buy the latest tech-

12 JORSTAD (2001), p. 11a.
13 HARTMAN (2000), p. 11.
14 HARTMAN (2000), p. 17.
15 HARTMAN (2000), p. 11.
16 SOLOMON (1993).

nology as soon as possible, and complain to their service providers if information is not constantly or instantly available. The Internet updates news almost instantaneously; a constant stream of information flowing through computers, pagers, and wireless phones worldwide updates everyone on the status of an election, the wedding of a celebrity, sports scores, or weather around the globe.

The paradox, though, is that these same consumers expect that none of this vast flow of information should ever be about *them*. Information has become a valuable commodity in today's world, and everyone is prepared to pay to have the latest, most, and best information. Consumers pay for cable television and Internet access and wireless telephones, yet they do not consider the possibility that they generate information themselves, by their very activity within this digital world. This information is easily collected, recorded, and can even be transformed into a financial asset by the companies that have to process the transactions. Although people don't protest at a store's scanning of all purchases in order to facilitate inventory control and track purchasing trends (this concerns only the *products*, not the *buyers*), these people often do not consider the fact that swiping their credit card through the cash register in order to pay for these products can record their personal preferences. Visa and Mastercard have been collecting and selling consumer preference information for decades, and Visa and Mastercard, by definition, have vast amounts of financial data about us – these different types of data can be used in targeted marketing.

Companies anticipate the next consumer need by analyzing what consumers do and want *now*. Internet businesses, whether they be merchants, search-engine portals, or Internet service providers, all have a vested interest in keeping abreast of consumer wants. The technological environment is changing so quickly that information about trends must be constantly generated, analyzed, updated, and available to those who need it in order to be ready to meet tomorrow's demands. Computers that process transactions can easily record them – from clicks on web links to actual purchases. Transaction and clickstream data can be analyzed for trends and the resulting information is a valuable commodity, both for the company that creates the information and others.

Websites target advertising based on a surfer's activity. For example, if you search for information on a tourist destination, Yahoo will offer links for that information, as well as a banner ad at the top of the page for a major airline. This ability to target advertisements to potentially more interested consumers, in addition to high traffic volume, is what allows Yahoo and other sites to charge more to advertise on their sites. So the analysis of their customer activity by Yahoo (volume and interests) creates added value for Yahoo's advertising customers, and advertising revenue currently makes up about 90% of Yahoo's revenue. Consumers access Yahoo for free, and use its search services without charge. The link can be more subtle, too: "One of TimeWarner's users could click on an ad for the movie Pearl Harbor … buy tickets through the [Entertainment Channel's] MovieFone service [and] months later … could be targeted with a promotion to purchase the video."[17]

Since a large portion of Internet services are available to consumers free of charge and goods are available at a reduced rate over traditional retailers, consumers have grown to expect that the Internet *should* be cheap or free. The contradiction inherent in consumer expectations is evident in consumer disappointment when their Internet stocks lose value or when they are asked to register and provide information in order to use the free sites. The vast infrastructure of servers, customer service agents, technicians, order fillers, and distribution agents must be supported with money. If consumers are not paying money, then the websites must generate revenue in other ways. Web operators earn money in the information society by selling information that they gather from consumers. This is the payment that consumers make – they contribute to the database rather than directly to the coffers. In addition, Internet companies are valued by the stock market in growing part based on revenue – when a stock loses value, it is often because the company is not generating enough revenue to satisfy analysts that it will continue to be viable. The free ride that the market gave Internet stocks based on reputation and hype has ended (as shown by the NASDAQ's recent performance), and analysts are looking for evidence that Internet companies are financially viable businesses.

III. Ethics and the Limitation of the Law

Ethical analysis of this situation cannot satisfy those who cry for absolute privacy. Ethics cannot solve the contradiction between consumer privacy expectations and consumer demand for a constant stream of free information.

17 Fox (2001), p. 24.

What ethics can answer is the question of what consumers *should* be expecting. Although they may not like the answer, the public at large should be aware of the inherent contradictions in their demands. An ethical discourse is necessary to come to an agreement as to what people are and are not willing to tolerate in order to benefit from the potential of the Internet.

Ethical discourse is necessary because the law cannot help yet. In the United States, we often look to the law to guide our ethical decisions, and even confuse law and ethics in some cases. In this area, however, there is little law to guide us, and, in fact, ethical discourse is needed in order to shape good laws.

> ... an animating principle of cyberspace is the free flow of information. It is the ultimate democracy, where principles of open records and unfettered speech prevail. As a practical matter, the digital world is extremely difficult to police. In addition, courts are only beginning to consider how First Amendment freedoms will apply.[18]

Reconciling free speech, information access, and privacy is the challenge. Instead of simply declaring privacy to be the most important consideration, thought must be given to the value of free speech and information access. Are they worth sacrificing in order to protect privacy? Some privacy advocates think so. More often, however, people seem to want it all; unlimited access to the information they want should be free, and come without the penalty of having to provide any information about oneself. Businesses must provide the latest in goods and services without disclosing any data about what it is doing. The cost of such privacy will be enormous – data protection does not come easily, or free.

The trouble with this approach is that it puts the burden on business to shoulder the costs and penalties inherent in cyber-existence. Consumers are let off, with a full set of rights and privileges to boot. An impartial ethical discourse would reveal the imbalance of this position. Consider, for example, another version of the categorical imperative: "Act only according to that maxim whereby you can at the same time will that it should become a universal law."[19] Imagine if absolute privacy were a universal law. What we would gain in our own privacy, we would lose in information access. Our own lives would be shielded from public view, and much of what we consider to be

18 ALDERMAN and KENNEDY (1995), p. 331.
19 KANT (1785, 1981), p. 31.

"news" would be protected information. In fact, the First Amendment would have to go, which reveals the inherent untenability of this position. Since "a press that is free to investigate and criticize government is essential to the preservation of democracy,"[20] Americans should not be willing to give up First Amendment protections regarding free speech, and so must concede that they face a certain amount of exposure where others' rights to free speech are involved. Since September 11, the clamor for government control of terrorist activities in the United States has been tempered and countered by those who say that if Americans are willing to give up Constitutional rights in the hopes of reducing terrorism, then the terrorists have won. This is not to say that absolute freedom of information is the solution. As a society, we have already decided that some things are worth affording privacy protection (those video-rental histories, for example), so we have conceded that information does not need to be absolutely free and available. Kant's universal maxim can point to the flaws in the privacy argument, but it cannot offer an acceptable solution.

Americans must reach a compromise with regards to the Internet. Business simply cannot afford to take all of the responsibility; and it is not reasonable to expect that they should, regardless of financial viability. Rawls' theory of distributive justice and his "veil of ignorance" may primarily address the equitable distribution of goods and services, but it can be extended to apply to costs as well. The veil would encourage a sharing of costs, since neither business nor consumers would want to pay the price alone. With respect to supporting the Internet financially, there are three options for consumers: provide information as part of doing business in cyberspace, don't participate, or pay for services and share the dollar cost of data privacy and information availability.

Accepting the Internet as a valuable provider of goods and services (that is, deciding to participate) requires some sort of responsibility on the part of consumers. Business has been taking the initiative so far by providing privacy notices that have largely promised that consumer information will not be misused. In fact, however, "privacy advocates [say] that online companies amass large and potentially valuable customer databases and have little incentive to adhere to privacy policies once they go out of business."[21] Mounting financial pressures have forced e-businesses to reevaluate their offers of

20 WENTWORTH (2000), p. 24.

21 ABA (2000), p. 4.

data protection. Two examples illustrate the different ways this phenomenon may be manifested.

IV. Toysmart.com

A former Internet toy merchant, Toysmart.com, failed in May 2000. The company decided to sell its customer information in the course of its bankruptcy. From the shareholders' point of view, this information was an asset, and could be sold to reduce the overall financial loss of the bankruptcy. The catch to this case is that Toysmart's privacy policy promised its customers that data would not be sold or shared with third parties. In addition, Toysmart had signed up with TRUSTe, an organization providing an Internet privacy "seal of approval" program.[22] Toysmart maintained that their privacy promise was no longer valid due to the bankruptcy situation.[23] Consumer outrage prompted 39 state attorneys-general to file suit to prevent the sale of the customer information.[24] In July, the company settled with the FTC, agreeing not to sell their "customer information except to a 'qualified buyer' who will agree to continue Toysmart's privacy policy unless consumers 'opt-in' to any changes."[25] Toysmart's majority (60%) shareholder, the Walt Disney Company, tried to buy the customer list for $50,000 in order to "retire" it altogether.[26] This did not settle the matter, however, because a new suit was filed claiming that the settlement did not sufficiently protect customer data, and the settlement was thrown out.[27] TRUSTe also filed a brief with the bankruptcy court, saying that "Toysmart had signed a contract with TRUSTe, in which TRUSTe certified the company's privacy statement and put its seal on its site,"[28] and essentially charged that Toysmart had breached its contract with TRUSTe.

22 DISABATINO (2000), p. 10.
23 ABA (2000), p. 4.
24 VERDISCO (2000) p. 15.
25 ABA (2000), p. 4.
26 DISABATINO (2000), p. 10; MARK (2000), p. 31.
27 REILLY (2000), p. 36.
28 MARK (2000), p. 31.

On the face of it, Toysmart is about a company lying to its customers by disregarding a promise made to them, and in that context, Toysmart is clearly in the wrong. No code of ethics allows lying for convenience's sake, and Toysmart wants to violate its promise to its customers solely to ease the financial burden faced by its investors because of its bankruptcy. Clearly that is not reason enough to change a key provision of its privacy policy unilaterally.

Although the primary issue is clear, Toysmart's case raises another, broader issue. The particular instance of the Toysmart data sale can be decided on the basis of its original promise.[29] Lying to customers cannot last as a universal maxim; lying is one of the first examples Kant provides to prove that wrong things may not successfully be universalized.[30] But what happens with the companies who have learned the lesson Toysmart has to teach, and to their customers?

V. Amazon.com

In September 2000, in the wake of the Toysmart flap, Amazon.com, one of the Internet's brightest stars, altered its privacy policy:

> We receive and store any information you enter on our Web site or give us in any other way. You can choose not to provide certain information, but then you might not be able to take advantage of many of our features. We use the information you provide for such purposes as responding to your requests, customizing future shopping for you, improving our stores, and communicating with you …
>
> As we continue to develop our business, we might sell or buy stores or assets. In such transactions, customer information is generally one of the transferred assets. Also, in the unlikely event that Amazon.com, Inc., or substantially all of its assets are acquired, customer information will of course be one of the transferred assets.[31]

So, Amazon has learned a lesson from Toysmart: don't make promises that you may not want to keep later. This may not be the direction that privacy advocates want the Internet to go in; activists want more security and

---

29 BOK (1978), p. 149.

30 KANT (1785, 1981), p. 31.

31 AMAZON.COM (2000).

privacy. But one thing they unanimously call for, informed consent, is available at Amazon.com's website. Customers are told that their information is a company asset, and from a business and contractual standpoint, this should be sufficient. Consumers may choose to take advantage of Amazon's services, or may avoid the website altogether if they prefer not to share data with Amazon.

VI. The Trouble with the Status Quo

In an ideal free-market society, consumers should make choices, rather than demanding government restriction on businesses. Privacy advocates, realizing the difficulty of enacting meaningful and timely legislation where the Internet is concerned, have universally called for "opt-out" provisions, which enable consumers to exit a site before any personal information is collected.[32] This option not to participate strongly echoes Hirschman's description of "exit." According to Hirschman, it is an American tradition to decline participation rather than force change, starting with the original exit from England in the 17th century.[33] This may not be the best answer to the Internet privacy situation, however, since an American exit in this case would require that most Americans refuse to use the Internet.

Facing the probability that the Internet may not be truly "exit"-able, Congress is attempting to force change, inspired in no small part by the European Union's strict Internet privacy regulations. U.S. Internet-based businesses are, for the most part, currently operating with standards that fail to meet EU requirements. The implications are enormous for e-commerce: EU standards prohibit businesses from operating in any EU nation unless they can show that they can comply with the EU standard. The 1998 Data Protection Directive "says that data cannot be transferred from Europe to a site in a country outside the Union unless that country's laws provide comparable privacy protections and a regulatory agency to enforce them."[34] In 1998, an FTC

32 TRUSTE (2000); ROTENBERG (2000); EPIC.ORG (2000).

33 HIRSCHMAN (1970).

34 BRAKEMAN (1998) p. 50.

survey revealed that only 2% of websites had a full privacy statement posted.[35]

The situation is better now in terms of percentages, but perhaps not significantly different as to results. In testimony presented to the Senate Commerce Committee on October 2, 2000, Mark Rotenberg of the Electronic Privacy Information Center stated:

> In fact, privacy notices without other substantive rights operate more like warning labels or disclaimers than actual privacy safeguards. Although it would be tempting to pass legislation based simply on the notice requirement, we believe such a bill over the long term would reduce the expectation of privacy and the level of online protection. A substantive privacy measure must provide more than notice.[36]

Challenging Rotenberg's position, we should ask: what is wrong with reducing the expectation of privacy? In Kantian terms, could this be a universal law (ignoring for the moment the EU's move away from this standard)? Why isn't a warning label sufficient? Possibly because mere warnings would lead back to the exit choice; consumers would have to accept the conditions or refuse to use the Internet, and Rotenberg's position is that the conditions offered by mere warning are tantamount to declaring that privacy will *not* be respected. There does not appear to be an option of compromise in this scenario. Rotenberg does not seem to believe that e-businesses can be *expected* to operate with any reasonable measure of respect for their customers' rights or privacy, and so should be required to do so by law. Although Rotenberg's view seems harsh, Richard Kovacevich, CE of Wells-Fargo, was quoted in January 2001: "If we can't use the information about people to offer them goods and services, then why be in the business?"[37] Although customer information for Wells-Fargo is an internal asset, used to expand company offerings to existing customers, the view is not unique.

35 BRAKEMAN (1998) p. 50.

36 ROTENBERG (2000), p. 2.

37 ROMBEL (2001), p. 28.

VII. Movement Towards a Solution

In the spirit of fairness, shouldn't consumers share the financial burden of running the Internet? One of the key objections to the EU directive is that many U.S. e-businesses cannot afford to comply. Compliance would require upgraded hardware, software, record-keeping, or failing that in the U.S., any company which wishes to conduct business in the EU must maintain a separate, local operation, so as to avoid transfer of data outside the EU. This is not a reasonable standard for smaller operators, and it is clear, upon reading Amazon's privacy policy, that larger operators (who might have deeper pockets) may not be willing to comply, either. The financial issue is an important one; even some apparently large and successful Internet companies have been operating in the red for as long as they have existed. To make matters worse, individual users polled about the possibility of having their own home-computer security hardware were not willing to pay for it (82%) or even install free hardware if it would be inconvenient to do so (30%).[38]

The expense of making the Internet's vast resources available should not fall solely on the shoulders of businesses. The expectations of the privacy lobby are that business should attempt to achieve this sort of standard, and that the Internet will go down the drain unless privacy is absolutely guaranteed:

> ... it is possible that the amount of information that this bill requires to be disclosed [in a privacy policy] will likely overwhelm the average Internet user. The speed and convenience of shopping online will quickly hit speed bumps if all consumers are expected to read such notices before transacting business. Consumers should be assured that baseline principles to safeguard their privacy apply to every site they visit. They should not be burdened with having to examine and comprehend each line of a privacy policy before they decide whether or not to transact business with that specific company.[39]

The dire prediction that consumers will flee the Internet unless their privacy is absolutely protected is both unfair and naïve. Why should consumers enjoy more protection at Amazon.com than at Wal-Mart? Using a credit card at any retailer, whether real or virtual, creates a stream of customer preference data. "The auto industry has known our names, addresses, and our an-

---

38 COMMUNITY BANKER (2001), p. 47.

39 ROTENBERG (2000), p. 4.

nual income for almost 100 years."[40] Using a discount card at a bookstore or grocery store enables those merchandisers to amass customer preference data. Although so-called "club cards" have come under some of the same sort of fire that the Internet is facing,[41] the decades of information that has been collected by credit card companies and traditional retailers has been largely ignored in this fight.

The alternative to exit or information gathering is for consumers to share the costs. It is not reasonable to expect the Internet to be an unlimited free resource if the companies providing the services (information, discounted goods) cannot generate the revenue needed to maintain their existences. Public libraries are supported as a "free" service through tax revenues, but the Internet is supposed to survive without receiving tax support or direct customer (consumer) revenue. Network television and radio currently support their operations through advertising revenues, but both have larger audiences and can charge more for their advertising space or time than Internet companies currently can. With the devaluation of NASDAQ, many Internet businesses have folded because they could no longer trade on paper value; even that has deteriorated. Consumers can start supporting the Internet with money, especially if they are not interested in providing information that the companies can use as an asset.

A new program started by Amazon, the Honor System, allows websites to register with Amazon and collect from their own website visitors (presently on a mostly voluntary basis) small fees. Amazon provides the hardware and software structure to process the credit card payments, and charges a commission-like fee (a combination flat amount and percentage from each dollar collected). So far the program is small, but Amazon has a resource of 29 million registered users whom they can steer to these sites (Amazon maintains a page of links to registered websites), and a financial interest in encouraging its users to visit and make payments. At this point, the system operates like a charity, with web surfers contributing what they want to, if they want to. Few sites have collected any significant amounts yet, and donations are not large (sites have default suggested payment amounts of $5-$10, but the minimum is only $1).[42]

---

40 SCHWARTZ (2000), p. 54.

41 JANOFF (2000), p. 79.

42 AMAZON.COM (2000); COHEN (2001), p. 81.

There are other websites which charge a fixed amount for a fixed service. For example, Sony charges $1.99 to let a user download a song, and *The New York Times* charges $2.50 to see a newspaper story from their archive.[43] These "micropayment" systems on both individual sites and at Amazon allow websites to collect money without obligating users to spend large amounts of money for information they may not be interested in. Since most users already pay for Internet access and some level of online services, through access subscription fees and companies like America Online, it does not seem unreasonable to extend the money flow downward to web operators. "Free" content, although some of it may not be strictly expensive to post, is never free to generate or maintain online. Consumers may have to become willing to pay for what they use or even view online, as they already have become willing to pay for cable and satellite television.

Although consumer privacy advocates have complained about industry practice, and Amazon's policy change received press attention, Amazon's stock price barely registered a change on the days surrounding the change in its privacy policy. Wall Street has refocused Internet stock attention on profits (or lack thereof), and Amazon's stock price has taken a heavy toll. But the new privacy policy does not appear to have significantly harmed company value – in fact, in the long term, it may send a signal to Wall Street that Amazon is making the most of its company assets and making a real effort to be a sustainable, profitable business. And Amazon's continued expansion of its business offerings, especially with the Honor System program, may also indicate an interest in being among those who finally manage to squeeze actual cash out of web users. In the short term, it is not clear if consumers will accept the request for payment, but in the long term, Internet survival may depend on it.

VIII. Consumer Choices

Surveys have revealed that consumers are quite reluctant to reveal personal information on the Internet, most likely because they seem to fully realize that their information is not private. Lobbyists have been trying to get Congress to pass legislation to protect consumers. There is an inherent lack of

43 COHEN (2001), p. 81.

respect, however, in an appeal that states, as quoted from Rotenberg earlier, that consumers would be unable to wade through a thorough privacy policy, and therefore should be forcibly protected. There are more moderate voices:

> In your privacy policy, list the companies and brands that share customer information. If you state the policy and your customers agree to it, there's no privacy violation. If they don't agree they can take their business elsewhere. It's a matter of mutual consent, as it should be.[44]

Although Congress is likely to legislate this minimum, "opt-out" standard as a requirement for all Internet businesses,[45] Rotenberg's criticisms[46] and Lewis' statement above both show that this minimal standard does not offer a consumer much protection.

Businesses will have to take a reasonable care approach to customer privacy in order to turn consumers into paying customers. This idea is beginning to grow among some businesses. In general, businesses "care about what their primary stakeholders consider to be ethical, because they are perceived to have the greatest impact on the business."[47] More directly, though, a strong privacy stance can be an asset in and of itself: at FleetBoston "We want to communicate to our customers that we have a proactive privacy policy ... It's a competitive stance."[48] It may soon evolve from being competitive to being necessary: a July 2001 survey found that 75% of internet users shop online, but "nearly one-third (32%) say that these worries [about privacy] limit the amount they will spend in a single online purchase."[49]

In the end though, it is possible that consumers will have to become the Internet's primary stakeholders in order to have their privacy respected. Businesses need a financial incentive to put consumers on top – either customer purchase revenue, or, if the business does not sell tangible products, direct payments of either money or information assets. Although buying products is relatively straightforward (either Amazon sells books or they don't), it remains to be seen whether people will be willing to pay money to access the Internet's information or if they would rather provide their own personal information as a substitute asset.

---

44 LEWIS (2000), p. 84.
45 EPIC.ORG (2000).
46 ROTENBERG (2000).
47 HARTMAN (2000), p. 6.
48 COLKIN (2001), p. 54.
49 COMMUNITY BANKER (2001), p. 46.

References

ANONYMOUS: "Online Privacy Concerns Continue to Linger", *Community Banker* (September 2001), pp. 44-47.

ANONYMOUS: "FTC Settles Privacy Violations With Bankrupt Toysmart.com", *ABA Bank Compliance*, 21, no. 8 (August 2000), p. 4. [cited as ABA]

ALDERMAN, E.; KENNEDY, C.: *The Right to Privacy,* New York (Alfred A. Knopf) 1995.

AMAZON.COM: *http://www.amazon.com.*

BOK, S.: *Lying: Moral Choice in Public and Private Life,* New York (Pantheon Books) 1978.

BOWIE, N.: "A Kantian Theory of Capitalism", *Business Ethics Quarterly, The Ruffin Series: Special Issue* No. 1 (1998), pp. 37-60.

BRAKEMAN, L.: "Europe's Strict Protections Motivate Security Concerns", *Managed Healthcare*, 8 (November 1998), p. 50.

CAMP, L. J.: "Web Security and Privacy: An American Perspective", *Information Society*, 15 (October-December 1999), pp. 249-256.

COHEN, A.: "For Pennies a Day", *Time* (February 19, 2001), p. 81.

COLKIN, E.: "Privacy Law Requires Hard Work", *Informationweek* (August 20, 2001), pp. 52-54.

DISABATINO, J.: "Disney: We'll Retire Toysmart Customer List", *Computerworld*, 34 (July 17, 2000), p. 10.

FITZGERALD, K.: "Poll: Consumers Sharply Divided on Privacy Issue", *Advertising Age*, 71, no. 47 (November 13, 2000), p. 80.

FOX, P.: "Online Privacy Should Be a Right, Not an Option", *Computerworld*, 35, no. 23 (June 4, 2001), p. 24.

HARTMAN, L.: "Technology and Ethics: Privacy in the Workplace", Bentley College Center for Business Ethics, February 28, 2000.

HIRSCHMAN, A.: *Exit, Voice, and Loyalty,* Cambridge, MA (Harvard University Press) 1970.

JANOFF, B.: "Private Practice", *Progressive Grocer*, 79, no. 1 (Jan 2000), pp. 79-82.

JORSTAD, E.: "Tread Carefully on the Issue of Privacy", *Star Tribune* (Minneapolis, MN) (January 29, 2001), p. 11A.

KANT, I.: *Grounding for the Metaphysics of Morals*, transl. by James W. Ellington, Indianapolis (Hackett Publishing Company) 1981.

LEWIS, B.: "Where Everyone Knows Your Name: There's No Use Confusing Privacy Issues With Courtesy", *Infoworld*, 22 (September 18, 2000), p. 84.

MARK, A.: "Toysmart.com: The Saga Continues", *Catalog Age*, 17 (October 2000), p. 31.

NASH, K.: "Amazon Alters Privacy Policy", *Computerworld*, 34, no. 37 (September 11, 2000), p. 46.

REILLY, T.: "Toysmart Case Can Set Bar for Online Privacy", *Computerworld*, 34, no. 36 (September 4, 2000), p. 36.

ROMBEL, A.: "Navigating the Privacy Law Divide", *Global Finance* (January 2001), p. 28.

ROTENBERG, M.: "Prepared Testimony and Statement for the Record Before the Senate Commerce Committee, October 2, 2000" (Available online at *www.epic.org/privacy/internet/testimony_1000.html*).

SCHWARTZ, E.: "Popularity of Online Data Gathering Leads to Potential for Abuse of Your Information", *Infoworld*, 22, no. 38 (September 18, 2000), p. 54.

SCHWARTZ, N.: "Inside the Market's Myth Machine", *Fortune*, 142, no. 7 (October 2, 2000), pp. 114-120.

SOLOMON, R.: *Ethics and Excellence: Cooperation and Integrity in Business*, New York (Oxford University Press) 1993.

TRUSTe, *http://www.truste.org*.

VERDISCO, R.: "Consumer Privacy is Coming to a Boil", *DSN Retailing Today*, 39, no. 19 (October 2, 2000), p. 15.

WELLBERY, B. and C. WOLFE: "Privacy in the Information Age", *Business America*, 119, no. 1 (January 1998), pp. 12-13.

WENTWORTH, J.: "Public's Right to Know is Foundation of Democracy", *The Quill*, 88, no. 5 (June 2000), pp. 24-25.

WICKS, A.: "How Kantian a Theory of Kantian Capitalism?", *Business Ethics Quarterly, The Ruffin Series: Special Issue* No. 1 (1998), pp. 61-73.

Chapter 11

Ethical Crisis on the Internet: the Case of Licra vs. Yahoo!

MARK HUNTER, MARC LE MENESTREL,
AND HENRI-CLAUDE DE BETTIGNIES

I. Introduction

In the early spring of 2000, a Paris-based anti-hate activist and member of the International League Against Racism and Anti-Semitism (LICRA) launched a media and judicial attack on the business practices of Yahoo! Inc. and its subsidiary, Yahoo! France. The specific issue in question was the right of Yahoo! Inc., a U.S. corporation, to allow visitors to its American auction sites, including the French, to buy and sell Nazi items. In France, unlike the U.S., commerce in such items is illegal; the activist contended that allowing

allowing the French access to it, via the Internet, should likewise be considered a violation of French law.

The case and its aftermath, including a series of rulings and judgments against Yahoo!, established numerous precedents across a number of interrelated domains. From the legal perspective, although not the first case of its kind[1], the affair has become an international landmark; jurists[2] regard it as the best example of the risks that companies must face when marketing their products on the Internet, in light of the lack of consensus among states about international jurisdiction and applicable law in cyberspace. The notion of the Internet as a medium without frontiers, transcending national territories and regulations, took a severe beating in this case, not least because Yahoo! is among the companies that helped to define the Internet. A related issue, the technical specificity of the Internet, was likewise shown as perceived radically differently within the Internet business community and by activists and the court. The case should also be read as a landmark in a continuing trend – namely, rising pressure on business to assume responsibility for the social consequences of commercial activities. When it erupted, demands for regulation (and self-regulation by access providers) of hate content carried by Internet sites was already evident worldwide, in spheres ranging from online and print media to political elites. Yet Yahoo!, so far as our research[3] shows,

---

1 *Inter alia*, see ASHLEY CRADDOCK: "Nottingham v. Net: Game, Set, Match to Net", *Wired News*, August 4, 1997; JON WIENER: "Copyright as Censorship", *The Nation*, May 22, 2000.

2 *Inter alia*, see LIONEL THOUMYRE: "Consultation internationale sur les implications de l'affaire Yahoo! Inc.", *Juriscom.net* 2001 (available at *http://www.-juriscom.net/uni/doc/20010131.htm*); BRENDON FOWLER ET AL.: "Can you Yahoo!? The Internet's Digital Fences", *Duke Law and Technological Review*, 0012 (2001) (available at *www.law.duke.edu/dltr/articles/2001dltr0012.html*); MICHAEL GEIST: "Is there a there there? Toward greater certainty for internet jurisdiction", *Berkeley Technical Law Journal*, 16 (2001), pp. 1345-1406; JEFFREY BARLOW: "Jurisdiction and you: Yahoo!", *The Internet Law Review* (available at *http://www.internetlawjournal.com/content/litigationarticle03080102.htm*).

3 Research for this paper included interviews, in person and by telephone, with top managers of Yahoo!, including associate general counsel for international affairs Gregg Wrenn, corporate communications director Scott Morris, and the general director of Yahoo! France, Philippe Guillanton and his staff. On the plaintiffs' side, Marc Knobel, who initiated the action against Yahoo! and his lawyer were interviewed. The presiding magistrate in the case, Jean-Jacques Gomez, was also

failed to fully appreciate the impact of what appears, in retrospect, as a rising international tide, and the empowerment it conferred on determined opponents and national regulators. Finally, specific business issues raised by the affair – and which impacted both on its ethical and judicial content – include the nature of e-business, coordination between headquarters and a foreign subsidiary, leadership, and relations with domestic and international media.

A central finding of this article is that Yahoo!'s actions in the case cannot be explained solely by a more or less cynical search for profits. Our research suggests, on the contrary, that Yahoo! adopted mainly principled attitudes, basing its strategy from the outset on a sincere belief that it was participating in the making of a new (and better) society. Yet the principal results of this stance were sustained damage to the firm's brand, and a humiliating defeat in the French courts. The issue thereby raised is equally unsettling for those who decry or justify the absence of ethical behavior in business, and those who contend that companies should place ethical concerns at the center of their activity. If a company that tries to do good according to its ethics runs into trouble like this, it may be because problems of business ethics are irreducible to a purely ethical standpoint, as they may be to a purely business perspective.

This article begins with a detailed review[4] of the context and history of the affair, taking as its starting point a rising international wave of protests against hate literature and sites on the Internet in the summer of 1999. It is crucial to note that Yahoo! became an actor in this initial phase of the story only months after it began, and was able to resolve its initial conflicts in this domain, in the United States, without serious difficulty. We continue through the onset of the conflict in France and its judicial developments, underlining points at which Yahoo!'s proposed solutions, based on its own ethical princi-

---

interviewed, as was the president of the U.K.'s Internet Watch Foundation, Roger Darlington. Documentary research included all public court documents and an extensive review of coverage of the case and its antecedents over a period of one year in print and online media. The authors wish also to thank Joaquim Barbera of IESE for his contribution in documenting judicial commentary and analysis of the case.

4 A much shorter version of this chronology has been published in M. LE MENESTREL, M. HUNTER and H.C. DE BETTIGNIES: "Internet e-ethics in Confrontation with an Activists' Agenda: Yahoo! on Trial", *Journal of Business Ethics*, 39 (2002), pp. 135-144.

ples, were explicitly rejected by its adversaries and the court. The story concludes at the point where a U.S. court of appeals granted Yahoo!'s demand to declare the French judgment unenforceable on U.S. soil.

The chief advantage of this structure (aside from its inherent narrative force, like any courtroom drama) is that by following the chronology, we are able to identify Yahoo!'s ethical positions as they emerge in confrontation with specific situations. A thematic structure would miss some of Yahoo!'s ethics, simply because they were often tacit – that is, previously the company had neither explicitly defined nor expressed them, very likely because it was never obliged to. (A good example is Yahoo!'s position on freedom of expression, which corresponds largely to a consensus position in U.S. society, and thus barely requires explication or reflection in the firm's home base.) A further advantage is that shifts in Yahoo!'s ethical positions become visible through its responses to the successive issues raised by the case. We will argue that at least one of those shifts, in which Yahoo! altered its relationship to user-generated content, was radical indeed.

Throughout, we are concerned on the one hand with the practical implications of Yahoo!'s positions: Did they work from a legal standpoint, from a business standpoint, and in terms of public opinion? In other words, was the company's ethical stance manageable? Inevitably, the question arises as to whether Yahoo! could have handled this affair more successfully – in terms of avoiding both conflict with social institutions (activists, public opinion, the courts and media), and damage to its business interests. But the more interesting question is why, if this were indeed the case, and assuming that the firm had the opportunity to pursue other courses of action, Yahoo! did not do so. In this sense, we are suggesting that ethical principles may become an obstacle to resolving ethical crises, when followed without attention to the context in which they are exercised.

II. Protests Against Hate for Sale on the Web, Aug. 1999-Feb. 2000

At the end of the last decade, the appearance of objects with a Nazi provenance in e-commerce sites became an object of outraged protest, in the U.S. and internationally. Thus online booksellers Barnesandnoble.com and

Amazon.com stopped selling Adolf Hitler's *Mein Kampf* to German customers in August 1999, after the Simon Wiesenthal Center of Los Angeles notified the German Ministry of Justice that the companies might be violating the Federal Republic's laws against hate literature. A skilled Internet user could nonetheless find alternate sources for these materials, as the online magazine *Salon* reported: "While German extremists can't buy their books from the Internet's biggest vendors, they can find them if they dig a little deeper."[5] Indeed, the impossibility of enforcing absolute censorship on the Internet was and remains a given among experts interviewed for this article, including all the protagonists in the Yahoo! affair. Absolute censorship was apparently not the goal, however: The Wiesenthal Center sought instead to compel opinion and business leaders in the Internet community to abandon commerce in Nazi memorabilia.

That became explicitly clear three months later, when the Center attacked what it called the U.S.-based online auctioneer eBay's "current policy of marketing Nazi memorabilia", adding that it intended to ask German leaders to "review existing anti-Nazi laws and possible legal actions." Executives at eBay argued that its German subsidiary "adheres to German law and does not allow the posting of Nazi items" – which is legal in the U.S. – and that they were "hesitant to perform the role of censor." (Very similar arguments would later be employed by Yahoo! Inc.) One eBay manager publicly compared the Center, known for pursuit of war criminals, to "a Nazi Gestapo force [that wants to] police everything that goes on the market."[6] In an attenuated form, the charge that protest activists had become more dangerous enemies of freedom than their targets would also figure in the Yahoo! case.

The Wiesenthal Center was among the victors of this first round of conflict, as it swiftly widened to include other actors. In February 2000, a New York-based anti-hate group, BiasHELP, asked eBay to remove all listings of items related to the Ku Klux Klan, arguing that "the incredible size and reach of [eBay's] audience creates special responsibilities."[7] While denying that the protests had any effect on its decisions, eBay nonetheless announced a

---

5 See CRAIG OFFMAN: "Hate Books Still for Sale on the Web", *Salon.com*, August 17, 1999.

6 See ED RITCHIE: "No Tolerance for Nazi Items", *Auctionwatch.com*, Dec. 1, 1999.

7 ED RITCHIE: "BiasHELP Wants Klan Items Banned From eBay", *Auctionwatch.com*, Feb. 3, 2000.

change in its practices, declaring that its site "will not become a platform for those who promote hatred toward their fellow man." The company's new stance attempted to balance the interests of legitimate collectors (such as historians) against the concerns of protestors:

> Relics of groups such as the KKK or Nazi Germany may be listed on eBay, provided that they are at least 50 years old, and the listing is not used as a platform to glorify or promote the organization or its values... eBay will judiciously disallow listings or items that promote hatred, violence or racial intolerance, including items that promote organizations with such views. eBay will review listings that are brought to its attention by the community, and will look at the entire listing to determine whether it falls within this rule.

Yahoo! Inc. now also felt the rising heat. On Feb. 23, 2000, the Anti-Defamation League (ADL), an American non-profit group founded in 1913, accused Yahoo! Inc. of hosting an entire category of "White Pride and Racialism" clubs. Noting that Yahoo!'s "Terms of Service" agreement prohibited users from posting content of a "racially, ethnically or otherwise objectionable" nature, the ADL demanded that Yahoo! cease to "ignore its own policy and us." Two days later, the ADL triumphantly reported that Yahoo! had "apologized for not addressing the violations sooner," and had encouraged the ADL's Internet Monitoring Unit to report such abuses.

The responses of Yahoo! and eBay reflected an emerging consensus among leaders of the New Economy, to deal with offensive materials largely through a policy of "notice and take down." While refusing to establish broad pre-emptive standards for user-generated content, Yahoo! and eBay removed materials that aroused significant protests from users or spokespeople for legitimate causes. Thus Internet companies could hope to avoid both heavy-handed government regulation that might harm their industry, and accusations of censoring their users.

The stakes were high, and not only in the virtual world of e-business hype. At the moment these cases erupted, the C2C (consumer to consumer) sector of the Internet, including online auctions – an outgrowth of the online forums that first created a mass public for the Internet in general and Yahoo! in particular – was rising fast, led by eBay, QXL and iBazar. Within a single year, eBay's revenues, mainly derived from a fee on transactions, practically doubled, from $150 million through the first nine months of 1999 to $297 million for the same period in 2000. In the latter period, eBay's gross profit was $225 million and net income reached $39 million.[8] In January 2001, *Forrester Research* reported that online auctions in Europe had passed the billion-euro landmark, and would attain 8.8 billion euros by 2005, with 62 percent of transactions taking place in C2C sites.[9] These spectacular successes, at a moment when few e-businesses were generating profits, clearly contributed to attracting the attention of activists.[10] In retrospect, one may ask why neither eBay nor Yahoo! were prepared for that attention.

III. The Public and Governments Intervene Against Hate on the Web, Jan.-Feb. 2000

Meanwhile, the issue of Internet hate steadily widened into judicial and political spheres around the world. In January 2000, the United Kingdom's Internet Watch Foundation (IWF: *www.iwf.org.uk*), an industry self-regulatory group established in 1996, announced that it was extending its authority from child pornography to hate materials on the Internet. Under an agreement with the British government, the IWF investigated complaints received on its hotline, to determine if pages on a given site contained illegal pornographic or hate content. If so, the IWF would ask the service provider to take down the site. Providers that complied were guaranteed immunity from criminal prosecution, though not from civil actions.

For British civil liberties activists like Chris Ellison, founder of Internet Freedom, the IWF's goal was to "extend their ability to censor," at a moment when the Blair government sought to improve its "politically correct" image.[11] But for IWF chairman Roger Darlington, self-regulation, and not cen-

8 Figures are taken from eBay's quarterly reports (form 10Q) to the Securities and Exchange Commission.

9 HELLEN K. OMWANDO ET AL.: "Europe's Online Auction Prize: SME's", *Forrester Research*, Jan. 2001, pp. 1, 2, 6. The report quotes a competitor of eBay who estimates that 10 percent of the site's inventory, and 80 percent of its gross auction value, is accounted for by businesses posing as consumers (p. 4). The mascarade is presumably designed to profit from the fad for C2C auctions.

10 See note 4.

11 LAKSHMI CHAUDRY: "British ISPs Crack Down on Hate", *Libertarian Alliance*, Jan. 25, 2000 (via *www.codoh.com*).

sorship, was the issue: "We have no formal legal powers – Parliament hasn't legislated this. The strength [of the IWF] is that the industry is more sensitive to a body it set up, and it works faster than a public body. The weakness is that [its actions] could still be challenged in the courts."[12]

Government leaders in other countries were likewise calling for stricter regulation of Internet hate. On Jan. 27, 2000, German Chancellor Gerhard Schröder, inaugurating the first International Forum on the Holocaust in Stockholm, asked for international cooperation to keep neo-Nazis off the Internet.[13]

The debate over misuse of the Internet was particularly intense in France, where a new "Law on the Liberty of Communication" was under debate in the National Assembly. The law held Internet service providers responsible for illegal content that transited by their servers, exactly as printers could be held responsible under French law if the authors and publishers of a defamatory printed work could not be located.[14] Noting that access providers were increasingly accused of promoting "defamation, pedophilia, violations of authors' rights, and incitation to racial hatred," the daily newspaper *Libération* remarked that they "are trapped, at once guarantors of the freedom of expression and subject to the pressure of plaintiffs."[15] This was the precise quandary into which Yahoo! was now plunged.

---

12 Interview with the authors, March 30, 2001. The whole interview is reproduced in LE MENESTREL ET AL. (2001a, exhibit 1). Useful information can be found on Roger Darlington's personal site: ***http://members.tripod.co.uk/rogerdarlington/-index.html***.

13 KIM GAMEL: "Forum: Keep Neo-Nazis From Web", *Associated Press*, Jan. 27, 2000.

14 This is the substance of Article 43 of the Loi du 1er août 2000 "relative à la liberté de communication". Even before the law was passed, a leading French access provider, altern.org, had paid ruinous damages when French model Estelle Hallyday discovered her photographs on an unauthorized site that used altern.org's server and sued. In effect, the new law confirmed and extended that jurisprudence.

15 FLORENT LATRIVE: "Les hébergeurs priés de sévir", *Libération*, April 7, 2000 (via *www.liberation.com*).

IV. An Activist Sounds the Alert: February 2000

Marc Knobel is a Paris-based researcher who tracks neo-Nazi groups for the Wiesenthal Center, and whose Jewish ancestors, he recalled in a bitter euphemism, had "tasted fascism in every flavor."[16] Since 1997, when he began conducting his research online, he had become convinced that the Internet was changing the landscape of hate for the worse. Said Knobel:

> The Internet didn't invent anything. These groups existed, they distributed their propaganda, forged bonds among themselves, met with each other. That hasn't changed. But before Internet, they were largely confined to specific geographical zones. What's new is the very great ease which allows me today to connect to the web pages and sites created by these groups, and to see what they distribute, who they are, what they're doing, and to have access to their very essence.

He acknowledged that this shift had greatly facilitated his own research. And yet, said Knobel, "I would prefer, frankly, to never see a site that was created by the extreme right. Every time we leave open ground to the extreme right, it moves in."[17]

One day in February 2000, an American acquaintance called Knobel to ask if he were aware that yahoo.com's auction site was selling Nazi goods. Knobel said that until then, he regarded Yahoo! as "the great community of Internauts where you find everything right away, and even better, for free. A wonderful new world." On yahoo.com, after typing the word "nazi" into the auction site's search window, he discovered 800 items for sale. He was particularly shocked by a box of Zyklon-B, the poison gas used at Auschwitz,

---

16 Marc Knobel's quotes are drawn from an interview with the authors, February 6, 2001, and from follow-up telephone calls, unless otherwise indicated.

17 Recent research on extreme right movements in Europe supports Knobel's opinion; France's National Front and its more radical satellites, for example, were the first political forces in France to establish a presence on the Internet. The promotional power of their websites can be disputed, but their utility as a communications tool within the movements seems clear. See MARK HUNTER: "Beat the Press: How the extreme right runs rings around the media", *Columbia Journalism Review* (March-April 1997) (via *http://www.cjr.org/year/97/2/france.-asp*). For the rise, fall and rise of the extreme right in Europe, see LE MENESTREL ET AL. (2001a, exhibit 2).

identified as a "museum-quality replica."[18] Though Knobel was aware that visitors to yahoo.com, and not the firm, were responsible for the objects on auction, he claims to have felt betrayed by Yahoo!. In conjunction with his lawyer, Stéphane Lilti, he decided to pressure Yahoo! to stop these auctions, starting with a pressure campaign in the media:

> I thought I could make Yahoo! understand that it's no big problem if they take these things off the site. They'd get the idea, they'd contact me. I said to myself, "They're Americans, they'll understand that the French see this differently, that it isn't good to sell this stuff. It's their responsibility and it's in their power to do something." And I said to myself – not to them – "Maybe they will. I'll give them two months."

Knobel convinced the UEJF (Union of Jewish French Students), and the LICRA (International League Against Racism and Anti-Semitism), where he sat on the executive board, to join his cause. Their press campaign began on Feb. 17, 2000 in the weekly *Paris-Match*, which announced its "discovery" of Nazi goods on the Internet – "nearly 500 on Yahoo!, and over 3,500 on eBay," noted the reporters. An illustration of a Waffen SS, a member of the Nazi party's armed forces, was captioned: "On Yahoo! Auctions: A mouse pad glorifying the SS troops." The article ended with a threat from Knobel: "It's up to Internet companies to regulate themselves. If not, we'll launch a boycott [of Yahoo!]."[19] The LICRA did so two days later, but the boycott had no immediate measurable effect on visits to yahoo.fr, according to company officials.

Knobel's next coup targeted a particular vulnerability of online auction sites in general, and Yahoo! in particular: reliance on advertising revenues, which in 1999 accounted for 90 percent of Yahoo!'s income[20]. Among 25 auction sites surveyed by Forrester Research, advertising generated an aver-

---

18 Comments Greg Wrenn, Yahoo associate general counsel for international affairs: "The vendors didn't say, 'Throw this at your Jewish neighbor and scare him.' Nothing to indicate they were offered by Nazi supporters – or not offered to legitimate collectors who don't want to forget the atrocities committed in World War Two", Interviewed by telephone, March 29, 2001.

19 FRANÇOIS LABROUILLÈRE and LAURENT LÉGER: "Quand Yahoo et eBay deviennent les supermarchés des souvenirs Nazis", *Paris-Match*, No. 2647, February 17, 2000.

20 According to its quarterly SEC filings, Yahoo! Inc. earned $799 million through the first nine months of 2000, of which $722.8 million came from advertising.

age 22 percent of revenues, second only to commissions.[21] Knobel perfectly understood this aspect of Yahoo!'s business, and during an interview with the French newsweekly *L'Express*, he suggested asking Yahoo advertisers what they thought about the Nazi goods. The reporter followed his advice:

> Questioned and informed by *L'Express*, Ford and Visa declared themselves stupefied to discover that their banners are displayed on the same page as the SS. "We aren't indifferent," said Ford, "but what can we do? The laws governing the Web are so complex." The London-based managers of Visa, however, claimed they demanded that Yahoo! stop this 'abusive use' [of Visa's ads].[22]

That article was read with foreboding at Yahoo! France, the American firm's subsidiary, whose General Director, Philippe Guillanton, recalled thinking, "This feels like a complicated affair." He added, "We could have called the LICRA to say, 'Listen, there's a problem, but *it's not something we control* [emphasis added], can we talk about it?'" He meant that Yahoo! neither created nor necessarily condoned user-generated content. As he explained to us:

> We don't work the same way as a traditional medium. We're not a minority of specialists who create content for a passive majority. In most cases, we put tools at the disposition of people so they can communicate; they're the stars. So groups form around little centers of interest, like sports cars, and in certain cases, around opinions like these [i.e., hate groups].

It was also a fact that Yahoo! France did not determine corporate policy on user complaints. Guillanton recalled that when he contacted Yahoo! Inc. to discuss the matter, corporate headquarters replied that the company received "five letters like that every day," implying there was no major cause for concern. (One of the consequences of the case, Guillanton noted, was that requests from Paris for guidance now receive closer attention.) No contact was made with LICRA.

On April 5, 2000, Yahoo! France received a registered letter from the LICRA, warning that if the auctions of Nazi objects did not cease within eight days, charges would be filed in Paris. The letter was forwarded to Ya-

---

21 *Op. cit.*, Omwando, pp. 3, 4.

22 CÉDRIC GOUVERNEUR: "Internet: Comment éliminer les sites nazis?", *L'Express*, No. 2541, March 16, 2000, p. 40+.

hoo! Inc. for reply. Three days later, before Yahoo! Inc. could prepare its answer, Yahoo! France learned from the press that it and its parent were being sued.

V. Yahoo! Stands Accused: April-May 2000

Under a special procedure called the *référé*, which allows a judge to ordain immediate preventive measures against a defendant without a full trial, the plaintiffs (LICRA, later joined by the UEJF) demanded that Yahoo! be fined 100,000 euros for every day the sales of Nazi objects continued. Further demands included removing all links to "negationist" (Holocaust denial) websites from Yahoo! France, and eliminating two sites, including one in French, that offered the text of *Mein Kampf* on Yahoo! Inc.'s geocities.com subsidiary.

Yahoo! Inc.'s associate general counsel for international affairs, Greg Wrenn, already knew LICRA: Prior to Knobel's press campaign, in response to a complaint from the group, Wrenn had contacted Inktomi, which provides Yahoo! France with web page search results, to ensure that the sub-contractor would remove sites considered illegal in France from its index. "It's an automatic system – they'd find French-language sites and index them," explained Wrenn. "They don't do human reviews." Now Wrenn faxed LICRA president Patrick Gaubert, taking a stance similar to that adopted by eBay in the U.S., and which would later form the basis of its defense:

> Yahoo! applauds the mission of your organization and in no way does Yahoo! endorse anti-Semitism or racism of any sort. In fact, as you may recall, Yahoo! France has cooperated extensively this year with LICRA regarding your concerns about Nazi-related sites.... Within the bounds of the law of the 23 different countries in which our international properties are located, we promote freedom of expression and choice and Yahoo! believes it should not act as a political censor... in the U.S., the removal of such items would be considered censorship and treated by many as more offensive than the isolated postings themselves.

Following the first dispatches on the case, French online media, notably transfert.net, began what turned into extensive coverage of the affair, including the posting of judicial documents. But outside France, coverage was nonexistent, with the significant exception of a major Israeli newspaper, the

Jerusalem Post.[23] It is interesting to note that in an April 17 story on "Weaving the Web in Paris," *Business Week* found it more interesting that in France, unlike Silicon Valley, "the locals smoke cigarettes in Internet cafés." Likewise, when CNN's Internet-savvy "New Show" discussed the international strategies of Yahoo! and eBay on April 25, the Paris affair never came up. Only scattered online media, like ZDNet News, picked up coverage by Reuters, while other leading online news sources, like *Hotwired*, remained silent. Market analysts in London and New York apparently saw no significance in the case, which appeared in not a single analyst's report through the spring. Yahoo! Inc. indirectly contributed to the silence, by following its established policy of refusing to comment about ongoing judicial proceedings. In sum, neither Yahoo! nor its various stakeholders treated the lawsuit in its initial stages as a crisis situation.

VI. The First Hearings: May 15-22, 2000

At the first hearing in the *Tribunal de Grande Instance de Paris* on May 15, Yahoo!'s position on the legal issues was based on three key lines of argument. The first pervades the firm's pleadings: Yahoo! and the Internet are *media freely created by their users*. Visitors to its auctions placed objects on sale themselves, and Yahoo! "received no remuneration" for these transactions.[24] Activity on the auction site could thus be considered user-generated (and not commercial) content, for which Yahoo! bore no direct responsibility. Indeed, declared defending counsel Christophe Pecnard, inasmuch as negationist or neo-Nazi literature is protected by the First Amendment to the U.S. Constitution, "it could not be evident" to Yahoo! that it might be of an "illicit" character.[25]

To a large extent this argument was aimed beyond the courtroom, to public opinion. Its apparent goal was to convince observers that the company was acting in an ethical and responsible manner, and that its position was not

---

23 This statement is based on a review of the Lexis-Nexis database.

24 "Conclusions pour la Société Yahoo ! Inc., A Monsieur le Président du Tribunal de Grande Instance de Paris", Audience de référé du 15 mai 2000 (via *www.juriscom.net*), p. 8.

25 *Ibid.*, p. 8.

based on a crude profit motive. That was partly true, but the stance was nonetheless extremely risky. It was not credible to Yahoo!'s adversaries, who by targeting the firm's advertisers had already demonstrated awareness of the firm's profit motives. (Lilti told us flatly: "We're not talking about free speech, we're talking about commerce.") More broadly, even companies that benefit from a positive public image are very unlikely to be considered credible when they justify their position in a conflictual situation by a philosophical or ethical stance. The role of business is to make profits, and attempts by a company to portray its position as socially responsible may well be regarded as mere promotional campaigns, if not hypocrisy.[26] And at least some public suspicion about such attempts appears justified. As shown by Litman (1999), far from sacrificing business interests in the defense of freedom of expression, New Economy companies act in concert with the government to pass laws that restrict free speech and protect their interests.

The second line of Yahoo!'s defense was that content on its U.S. site was outside French jurisidiction, because, as Pecnard explained: "Internet users who go to yahoo.com undertake a virtual voyage to the U.S." Much was at stake for Yahoo! in this part of the debate. Yahoo! had developed nearly two dozen local sites around the world, aimed at specific national or regional audiences. Its expansion was predicated on the fact that content on these sites was calibrated to local legislation and political reality. "We can work around local groups and mores," Wrenn told us. "What we can't do is make different countries happy with content on every site."

For the plaintiffs, Lilti counter-attacked that "American jurisdictions systematically retain the application of the law of the country of reception [of Internet-related content] – when the U.S. is concerned."[27] His argument intimated that if U.S. courts can impose their jurisdiction on Internet content originating abroad, it is because the U.S. is the major Internet market. As a

---

26 On the ambiguity of communicating about ethics when making profitable activities, see LE MENESTREL (2001).

27 "Conclusions en réplique de L'Union des étudiants juif de France, A Monsieur le Président du Tribunal de Grande Instance de Paris", Audience de référé du 15 mai 2000. On the issue of multi-jurisdictional compliance, see FARHOOMAND (2000). On more general issues about law on the Internet, see Diamond and Bates (1995), ARKDENIZ ET AL. (2000). A good synthesis has been published in *The Economist*, January 13th, 2001: The Internet and the Law. A seminal book is O'REILLY ET AL. (1997).

practical matter, Yahoo!'s principles are indeed dependent on the context in which they are expressed and exercised. The firm would certainly not have faced a crisis should the Taliban have asked an Afghan court to force the company to remove all images of unveiled women from its various sites. But was the company under-estimating the power of the French courts and public opinion?

The plaintiffs certainly thought so. Lilti argued that "Yahoo! Inc. has not seen fit, since the delivery of the lawsuit, to remedy the problems that were denounced, which it maintains in full awareness."[28] He noted in our interview that Yahoo! Inc. had removed certain Nazi-related content from its sites at the demand of the ADL. If Yahoo! would do as much for an American non-profit group, why would it not do so for the French, who could also be considered part of the company's international public? More important, the plaintiffs were arguing that the spread of extreme right movements on the Internet is inescapably a *universal* problem, which supersedes questions of what is or is not locally permissible.

Yahoo!'s ultimate defense was that it would be technically impossible to satisfy the plaintiffs' demand that it block all access to the disputed sites from France. The Internet simply did not work that way; its infrastructure is conceived to be open, and is thus uncontrollable. Consequently, Pecnard declared, "The plaintiff has picked the wrong enemy, and finds himself, unjustly and in spite of himself, putting Internet on trial instead of neo-Nazi propaganda."[29]

Jean-Jacques Gomez, who presided over the case, was concerned by two major points: Did French law apply here? And if so, did his court possess the means to enforce it?[30] In a ruling on May 22, Judge Gomez answered yes to the first question: "In permitting the visualization in France of [Nazi] objects and the eventual participation of a French Internaut in such a sale, Yahoo! Inc. commits a fault on French territory." True, said the judge, "the unintentional character [of Yahoo!'s 'fault'] is evident." But the sales were nonetheless "an offense to the collective memory of a nation profoundly wounded by

---

28 "Conclusions en réplique de L'Union des étudiants juif de France, A Monsieur le Président du Tribunal de Grande Instance de Paris", Audience de référé du 15 mai 2000 (via *www.juriscom.net*).

29 *Op. cit.*, "Conclusions pour la Société Yahoo! Inc.", pp. 4-10.

30 Interview with the authors, March 2, 2001.

the atrocities committed in the name of the Nazi criminal enterprise ... and especially to its Jewish citizens."[31]

Not once, now or later, did Gomez deny that Yahoo! could host any content it wished in the U.S. Instead, he focused on the issue of *access*, interdicting Yahoo! from distributing materials to the French that are forbidden under French law. That stance effectively bypassed the question of whether Yahoo! is or is not a content provider. It also turned the fact that a French court holds no jurisdiction over the U.S. into an advantage for the plaintiffs: By the same token, the U.S. cannot force France to allow the distribution of materials the latter considers illegal. It was therefore Yahoo!'s responsibility to restrict access to these materials. Yahoo!'s principled refusal to consider the spread of hate content on the Internet as a universal issue for which it bore responsibility was thus doubly flawed, in a practical sense: It locked the company into a losing battle over jurisdiction, at the same time that it fuelled further opposition from its activist adversaries and the court.

Likewise, Yahoo! lost the first battle over the technical issue of whether it was possible to restrict access by French Internauts to a U.S. site. Indeed it was, declared Judge Gomez: "[T]he genuine difficulties encountered by Yahoo! do not constitute insurmountable obstacles." However, he did not say how this might be done. Instead, he left it to Yahoo! Inc. to devise and "undertake all measures of a nature to dissuade and to render impossible all consultation on yahoo.com of the online sale of Nazi objects and *of any other site or service that constitutes an apology of Nazism or a contestation of Nazi crimes* [emphasis added]" – a formula far beyond the interdiction of a few negationist sites that the plaintiffs had demanded. A date of July 24 was set for Yahoo!'s presentation of those "measures".[32] In the meanwhile, Gomez ordered Yahoo! to pay the costs of the hearing, including the legal fees of the plaintiffs' lawyers, plus $1,390 in provisional damages to the LICRA and the UEJF.

The ruling turned the case into an international affair and a crisis for Yahoo!. For the first time, leading English-language media like the *New York Times*[33] and *Los Angeles Times*[34] covered the story. There was a short-lived

31 Tribunal de Grande Instance de Paris, UEJF et LICRA c. Yahoo! Inc. Et Yahoo! France, Ordonnance de référé, 22 mai 2000 (via *www.juriscom.net*).

32 *Ibid.*

33 ASSOCIATED PRESS: "French Court Says Yahoo Broke Racial Law", *New York Times*, May 23, 2000, Section C, p. 27.

impact on Yahoo!'s share price, which dipped from 126 to 118 on May 23 and rebounded to 122 the following day, before rising to 144 on June 7. However, damage to the brand was very apparent, particularly in Europe. As Wrenn said, "We're a global brand, not just a U.S. brand. And a lot of people just kept seeing 'Yahoo!-Nazi'." Within the industry, he noted, rivals profited from Yahoo!'s troubles to promote their own auctions, while content providers "were not publicly behind us, because of the Nazi issue – they were saying, "it's a good fight, Yahoo! Go to it! We're quietly behind you.'" In short, the more publicity the case received, the more Yahoo! was isolated.

Its response was to attempt to bring forward what it considered the underlying ethical issues of the affair. Said Wrenn,

> We needed people to understand that we didn't do this thoughtlessly. We realized we were getting beat up. LICRA and the others were very good – they didn't want a settlement, they wanted press and publicity for the issue. So we had to get more aggressive about doing interviews and getting the word out.

VII. The Chief Yahoo! Speaks

In early June 2000, Yahoo! co-founder and titular "Chief Yahoo!" Jerry Yang arrived in Paris for the inauguration of Yahoo! France's new offices, and was greeted by a call from *Libération* requesting an interview. The subsidiary's employees, at least one of whom had been pressured by her family to leave the company over the issue, urged Yang to meet the reporter. By now, tension was growing between the subsidiary and corporate headquarters. Yahoo!'s Paris staff wondered if Americans could appreciate the horrors of Nazism to the same extent as the French. Said Yahoo! Inc.'s international communications director, Scott Morris, whose mother is French: "From the cultural perspective, we [in California] didn't all understand how sensitive things would get when the word 'Nazi' was mentioned. In France, World

34 BLOOMBERG NEWS: "Yahoo Launches Stock Purchase Plan", *Los Angeles Times*, May 23, 2000, Part C, p. 3. Coverage of the French case constituted the second half of an article consecrated mainly to Yahoo stock market strategy, a clear indication of the priorities of American readers.

War Two is yesterday."[35] Moreover, Philippe Guillanton and his Yahoo! France team were at once in the front lines and without authority: Legal and communications strategies were decided in California. This represented a victory for the plaintiffs, who sought to portray the central issue as an American company advancing irrelevant or false ideals in the face of barbarism. Guillanton was clearly aware of that factor:

> One of our greatest successes in France was to have managed to insert ourselves perfectly into the local tissue. The site is very 'Frenchy.' Up until this affair, when we asked focus groups questions about our identity, one in four people thought we were a subsidiary of France Telecom, one in four thought we were American, and the other half didn't know .... It was terrible to be attacked [as American] when we were really pioneers of localization.

In the end, Yang agreed to an interview with reporter Eduard Launet, which appeared on June 16, 2000, under a bold-faced quote that Yahoo! executives say was taken out of context: "**The French court is very naïve**." The introduction presented Yang in an aggressive, defiant light: "Okay, he'll respect the laws that apply to his foreign subsidiaries, but it's not okay to intervene on the site of yahoo.com [in] the United States. Not unless an American court so orders." In fact, this was not far from Yang's remarks as transcribed in the body of the interview. Asked if Yahoo! Inc. would obey the French court's orders, Yang had replied: "This court wants to impose a judgment in a jurisdiction over which it has no control .... Asking us to filter access to our content according to the nationality of an internaut is very naïve." He went on to deny, apparently in response to persistent questioning from the reporter, that Yahoo! was practicing cultural imperialism:

> We don't think that American values should apply everywhere .... It happens that American style and business have been dominant until now [on the Internet]. But not American values. I am not the advocate of 'Americanism.' We have good and bad points. Every culture should be able to defend itself. But you can't impose your values on the rest of the world. If we're talking about American imperialism, then why can't we talk about French imperialism in the LICRA case? ... Can you imagine an American arriving in France and ordering, 'French sites can't say this or that'?

When asked what Yahoo! planned to do next, Yang answered that the company had no plans to filter French access to its sites. He made a final,

35 Interview with the authors, March 2001.

emotional plea on behalf of Yahoo!'s role as a neutral provider of an open, free cyberspace: "I would like people to understand: We can't favor one group of users over another."[36]

Yang's insistence that his company cannot discriminate among users (and their opinions) resides on classic U.S. free speech doctrine, which holds that offensive speech is the price a society must pay for freedom of expression.[37] Thus the First Amendment to the U.S. constitution provides that "Congress shall make no law [...] abridging the freedom of speech, or of the press." In recent years the U.S. Supreme Court extended that protection to the Internet in particularly strong terms.[38] Yahoo! Inc.'s reliance on these principles extended to French executives like Guillanton, who told us that the best defense against dangerous ideas is to subject them to open public debate – and in particular, that allowing hate groups on the Internet exposes, rather than promotes them. He said: "The Internet forces everyone to have a more skeptical approach, to be wary. There's a lot of crap, and the Internet forces you to put it aside. The tool imposes this revolution."

The crucial question is not whether the position taken by Yahoo!'s leaders in defense of free expression for their users is morally or intellectually right or not. More important, for Yahoo!'s adversaries and French public opinion its stance was not credible. During his interview with *Libération*, Jerry Yang candidly admitted that in operating Yahoo! China, "on Chinese soil, we re-

---

36 A complete translation of the interview is available in LE MENESTREL ET AL. (2001b, exhibit 2).

37 For example, the American Civil Liberties Union argues: "The best way to counter obnoxious speech is with more speech." See *www.aclu.org/-FreeSpeech/FreeSpeechMain.cfm.*

38 Among the first and most successful websites and forums, as the Internet expanded in the mid-1990s, were those offering pornography. Responding to public concern over the issue, President Bill Clinton signed the Communications Decency Act of 1996, which outlawed "indecent" communications online. But the Supreme Court unanimously struck down the law, agreeing with a lower court that the Internet constitutes "the most participatory form of mass speech yet developed," and was thus entitled to "the highest protection from government intrusion." In April 2001 the Supreme Court upheld the right of an anti-abortion website to publish a "hit list" of doctors who perform abortions, and to mark their photographs with a red cross when they died – or were murdered, which had in fact occurred. For more on free speech in the U.S. and in France, see LE MENESTREL ET AL. (2001a), exhibit 3; TAYLOR (2000).

spect censorship, including political matters." Knobel later cited that passage to us from memory, as proof of Yahoo!'s corporate hypocrisy. Moreover, the activists argued that defending free speech and avoiding responsibility for condoning neo-Nazi publicity are not synonymous. Noted Lilti, "The first thing I did [in preparing the case] was to read Yahoo!'s contractual conditions, which allow them to clean up their site."

Yahoo! also apparently over-estimated the universality of its own ideals, and in particular its belief that on the Internet, the good drives out the bad. In particular, Judge Gomez had studied the Internet assiduously since Web cases started arriving in his courtroom in 1996, and had concluded that it was promoting false ideas – which demanded attention from authorities:

> From 1996 to 1999, people said that if you regulate the Internet, you'll kill it. My answer resides in a very simple example: If you want to upload an application on the Web that enables someone to get my credit card number, I don't agree .... Some people try to make Internauts believe that the Web is totally free, without any obligation – and we all know it's not true. In real life, my freedom stops where the freedom of others begins. On the Internet, it's the same thing.

Judge Gomez's position reflects a European consensus that the free and open debate of ideas must be tempered by the possibility *and experience* that certain ideas (such as, precisely, Nazism) can destroy public order, and with it any semblance of debate. Thus the Declaration of the Rights of the Man and Citizen – a crucial summation of the principles behind the Revolution of 1789 – guarantees the right of free speech, "except in cases foreseen by the law," which are in practice fairly numerous. For example, it is illegal to discuss the private lives of public figures, or to insult the President and foreign heads of states. It is also illegal under article 645 of the Penal Code, the statute under which Yahoo! was prosecuted, to publish materials or to make public declarations that constitute an "apology" for Nazi crimes. Victims of Nazi crimes are permitted to initiate prosecutions by the State of violations of article 645, an exceptional privilege in French jurisprudence.

Moreover, Yang's intervention revealed an understandable but profound ignorance of the rules of public discourse in France. While to an American his words might have seemed refreshingly frank, and thus laudable, for the French they could appear merely "brutal". In succeeding days, his interview was widely quoted in the French press, and "definitely made the PR worse," according to Greg Wrenn. Among its readers was Judge Gomez, one of whose subsequent rulings ironically and pointedly referred to Yahoo! as "naïve." Moreover, the firm was accused by its adversaries of seeking to create an immoral confusion between neo-Nazis and anti-Nazi activists (just as eBay had done in attacking the Wiesenthal Center). The plaintiffs were particularly enraged by accusations, in the media and through private e-mails sent to Knobel and the LICRA, that they were promoting censorship. Knobel's reply appeared in an editorial published by *Libération* soon after Yang's interview:

> Are we dangerous, we who dream of a Net cleansed of [the] merchants of hatred? ... Are we dangerous, or are the others? Those who normalize Nazism on the Net? Those who sell the weapons of barbarism as if they were selling socks? ... Those who fall silent when these pages promote hatred, discriminate, call for murder?[39]

Significantly, from this point onward Yahoo! found itself constrained to move away from its ethical positions, which were submerged into and behind a debate over whether and to what extent the firm could obey the judge's orders on technical grounds. Here, too, it would lose.

VIII. Inside Internet Technology: Summer, 2000

Judge Gomez's demand that Yahoo! "render impossible" any and all consultation from France of Nazi-related content was met with resigned disbelief by Yahoo! Inc. Said Wrenn, "We knew it was impossible to do it, and we knew we'd have to come back and say that." Christophe Pecnard did just that on July 24, when he informed the court that "Yahoo! Inc. cannot obey the ordonnance of May 22."[40] Gomez's order ignored "the very nature of the Internet," he added.[41] Was not the Internet conceived and structured as "a space of freedom without central control"?[42] Thus blocking techniques based on the IP (internet protocol) addresses of netsurfers – a method Gomez had

39 MARC KNOBEL: "Non à l'Internet de la haine", *Libération*, 21 juillet 2000, p. 5.

40 "Conclusions pour la Société Yahoo! Inc., A Monsieur le Président du Tribunal de Grande Instance de Paris", Audience de référé du 24 juillet 2000, p. 5.

41 *Ibid.*

42 *Ibid.*, p. 6.

suggested on May 22[43] – would not satisfy the court's order as written.[44] Likewise, Pecnard argued that blocking methods based on keyword searches would mostly penalize sites "favorable to the cause of the struggle against racism and anti-semitism," because they were indexed by the same keywords used by neo-Nazis.[45]

Instead, Pecnard offered a compromise. Yahoo! would advise French internauts that content on the U.S. site might violate their laws. It would encourage users to monitor sites, in order to "make actors and users more responsible".[46] It would contact the publisher of a web page that offered the notorious anti-Semitic forgery, "The Protocols of the Elders of Zion", to see if he warned users that the content was fake. But Yahoo! Inc. steadfastly refused to "act in one way or another as a censor."[47]

Following the hearing, Wrenn invited Knobel and Lilti for a beer, and attempted to reach a settlement. But his offer was not what the plaintiffs wanted:

> I said, "If what you're trying to do is get racism off the Net, even if you win and shut down Yahoo!, that won't solve the problem. ... the nature of the Internet is that the sites will pop up elsewhere. What you need to do is win the battle for people's minds, and get out your message, and let them know the tools they can use to stop their children from seeing this. Why don't we talk about ways to get your ideas out – promote your sites, get better tools to users – instead of trying to shut these other things down?" Lilti said, "That's an American way of settling a dispute." And Marc [Knobel] said, "No, you'll find a way to do this blocking, and that's what we want."

The offer that Wrenn made to Knobel and Lilti was strikingly similar to the deal Yahoo! had struck in the U.S. with the ADL in February 2000. But in the present context, its failure was predictable (though no less disappointing to Yahoo!). And it presaged a larger failure.

There is reason to believe that Judge Gomez understood that his initial demand that Yahoo! "render impossible all consultation" of the contested services from France was unfeasible, not least because he gave Yahoo! two

---

43 Tribunal de Grande Instance de Paris, Ordonnance de référé, UEJF et Licra c/ Yahoo! Inc. Et Yahoo! France, 22 mai 2000 (via *www.juriscom.net*).

44 *Op. cit.*, "Conclusions pour la Société Yahoo! Inc .... 24 juillet 2000", p. 8.

45 *Ibid.*, pp. 12-13.

46 *Ibid.*, p. 26.

47 *Ibid.*, p. 27

months to propose solutions. But during those two months, Yahoo! concentrated on developing arguments to show that obeying the judge's order *to the letter* was technically impossible. The arguments are true, so far as they go. But though they respond directly to the text of Gomez's order, they do not address its *spirit*, which is to hamper access to Nazi content from France. The possibility that *partial* access-blocking solutions might be feasible was not addressed by Yahoo!. Instead, it argued that since no technical solution could be guaranteed as completely effective, Yahoo! could not reasonably be expected to implement *any* solution.

Yahoo!'s position that any solution would be valid if, and *only* if, it complied perfectly with Gomez's first order may appear as a mere (or cynical) tactical error; but on an ethical level, it is absolutely idealistic. That does not make it less of an error; for example, the fact that no ideal solution exists to the problem of people murdering each other does not mean we should tolerate homicide. However, a similar line of argument is pervasive in business ethics – for example, in the notion that "business cannot be ethical because it cannot be perfectly ethical." The essence of such arguments is the reduction of ethics to perfect compliance with a rule or norm. This refers to a recurring ethical issue: Is a norm valid only if it is applicable in all practical situations? Conversely, should a norm be invalidated merely because it is not universally applicable?

From the start of the case, Judge Gomez had answered in the negative, by holding that "the genuine difficulties encountered by Yahoo! do not constitute insurmountable obstacles." Yahoo!'s implicit affirmation of the contrary not only guaranteed more frontal conflict with the activists and the judge; less apparently, it reinforced their position, as a matter of law and of public opinion, because it invited them to widen the debate still further in search of support. On August 11, Judge Gomez named a panel of international experts – including Vinton Cerf, an American considered among the founders of the Internet, François Wallon, a French Internet authority, and English Web expert Ben Laurie – to study the technical issues. Their role was defined in a way that foretold Yahoo!'s defeat, because they were asked to determine not merely *if* a technical solution were possible, but *to what extent* it would be effective. The judge thereby indicated that a less than perfect solution was conceivably acceptable. At that point, the plaintiffs could not lose on technical grounds, assuming that a partial solution was indeed feasible. By the same token, the mere demonstration that a partial solution could be implemented would make it possible to accuse Yahoo! – as Gomez later did, explicitly, in his final ordonnance – of failing to demonstrate "even a little good faith."

Was Yahoo!'s interpretation of the technical issues merely a dodge, as the court and the plaintiffs eventually charged? Several elements contradict that conclusion. First, it is extremely difficult for any company to use its capabilities for technological innovation to imagine solutions that would restrict its own activities. In Yahoo!'s case, widening access to the Internet, and not restricting it, claims the overwhelming share of the firm's innovative energy. In a larger sense, private technological innovation is generally employed to generate private benefits. There may indeed be social benefits of the innovation, but they emerge indirectly, and do not inevitably serve as its primary motivation. It is hard to see how Yahoo! could spontaneously discover the positive impact for its stakeholders in implementing a technology that *constrains* certain aspects of the Internet. Finally, Yahoo!'s leaders clearly believe that it is *in principle* ethically wrong to try to restrain the Internet's development, precisely because they view the Web as a vehicle of freedom and enlightenment. Solutions that might partially satisfy the judge's demands are therefore not worth considering, because by circumscribing the freedom of individuals to use the Internet, they will have a negative impact on society.

The experts rendered their report in a public hearing on Nov. 6, which superficially seemed to turn to Yahoo!'s advantage. They agreed that no technical measures could ensure that Yahoo! would succeed in keeping all French Internauts away from Nazi writings or objects.[48] They nonetheless maintained that up to 80 percent of French visitors could indeed be identified, and hence potentially deterred, through various techniques. Confusion mounted as under questioning, Vinton Cerf implied that certain solutions envisioned by the court, such as asking users to voluntarily identify their locations, were futile and dangerous:

> [Users] can choose to lie about their locations. [And] it might be considered a violation of the right of privacy of European users, including French users, to request this information. Of course, if this information is required solely be-

48 Looking back on the event, Ben Laurie wrote that the use of current techniques offered nothing more than a "solution [that] is half-assed and trivially avoidable" by an experienced Internaut. The text is online at *http://www.apache-ssl.org/-apology.html.*

> cause of the French Court Order, one might wonder on what grounds all users all over the world are required to comply.[49]

Prosecutor Pierre Dillange, representing the State, asked the court to retreat: "French justice should rule within the limits of what is possible and doable."[50] His position may have reflected the desire of the French government that France appear as an attractive home for Internet enterprises. The plaintiffs maintained their demands.

Before Gomez's final ruling, Yahoo!'s international leadership – CEO Tim Koogle, Greg Wrenn, Jerry Yang, European general director Fabiola Arrendondo, Philippe Guillanton, and others – held a conference call on how to limit further damage from the case. Assuming that Gomez ruled against Yahoo! again, should the company appeal his decision in France? According to Wrenn:

> The main issue was timing. You don't get the order stayed while you appeal, you're required to comply immediately. It's not that we had no chance to get a stay, but we did not view the chances as favorable. And we're a public company. We felt more confident about our ability to resolve the questions sooner in the U.S. courts.

Instead, Yahoo! Inc. would file a complaint for declaratory relief before the U.S. courts, which hold the sole power to enforce foreign judgements against an American corporation's U.S. assets. Yahoo! Inc. has no assets in France that could be seized by the plaintiffs. And Wrenn thought it would be difficult for the French to win in the U.S.: "Our First Amendment case is as strong as it gets.... If U.S. companies can be threatened by judgments in other countries, that has a chilling effect on free speech." Thus Yahoo! could shift the debate away from the alleged promotion of Nazism, and toward the rights of Americans.

A second decision on the same occasion confirmed that the business dimension of the case, which Yahoo! had sought to avoid or downplay, had nonetheless remained pervasive, continuous and unfavorable to the firm. Yahoo!'s auctions would no longer be a free service, run by and for users. Auction users would pay for them in some form, and Yahoo! would decide what was proper for sale. Commented Wrenn:

---

49 JULIE KRASSOVSKY: "Procès Yahoo!, les experts, stars d'un jour", *www.transfert.net*, Nov. 6, 2000.

50 *Ibid.*

> We were already thinking of changing. We didn't want to be seen as making money off these things directly. But we wanted to make it a quality shopping experience, less of a flea market ... to get fees, and make it more attractive to sellers. We knew people would think it was because of the lawsuit. Then you just invite more lawsuits. But you can't let that be the reason to avoid what's right for your business.

Whether right for the business or not, the decision implied a shift in the ethical principle on behalf of which Yahoo! had fought this conflict – namely, that users must be allowed to freely define the content of the Internet. In a double sense, auctions on Yahoo! would no longer be "free", as the word is used in English: They carried a price for the user, and the firm would if necessary censor the user's content. The change, though limited to auctions (policy for user forums remained the same), was no less profound. For the first time, Yahoo! retreated from the position that its own future, and the future of the Internet, depend on free access and expression for all users everywhere.

IX. The Judge's Last Word: Nov. 20, 2000

On Nov. 20, Judge Gomez asked, in his final ordonnance, how it was that Yahoo! Inc. could "already refuse human organs, drugs, or works and objects related to pedophilia on its auction site," but could not do the same with Nazi objects. The firm, he said, was avoiding "a moral and ethical exigency that all democratic societies share."[51] He allowed that Yahoo!'s French subsidiary "had largely satisfied the letter and spirit" of his previous ruling.[52] But Yahoo! Inc. was again ordered to pay $1390 to each of the plaintiffs, plus the expenses of the court and the plaintiffs, and to satisfy the terms of Gomez's previous ordonnance within three months, or pay a fine of $13,900 per day thereafter.[53]

---

51 Tribunal de Grande Instance de Paris, Ordonnance de référé rendue le 20 Novembre 2000 par Jean-Jacques Gomez, p. 18.

52 *Ibid.*, p. 21.

53 *Ibid.*, pp. 20-21.

The ruling was international front-page news, often accompanied by headlines linking the words "Yahoo!" and "Nazi." However, Yahoo!'s belief that the affair was central to the future of the Internet was widely amplified by editorial commentators in major newspapers. The *International Herald Tribune* called the ruling "certain to reverberate through the uncharted world of the Internet".[54] The *Financial Times* quoted Nigel Hickson, head of the e-business unit at the Confederation of British Industry: "Despite the obnoxious nature of the [Nazi] material, this ruling sets a very bad precedent for the future development of services on the Internet."[55] An accompanying editorial warned that "similar cases in other countries .... Would be a sure way to hinder the growth of Internet business."[56] The *Wall Street Journal* saw "disastrous implications for free expression around the world," and an open door "for other countries to hold independent web site publishers or large corporations outside their borders responsible under strict rules about illegal content."[57]

The day following the ruling, Yahoo!'s share price on the Nasdaq exchange dropped from $48.87 to $41.68, and again to $38.18 on Nov. 22. It rebounded to over $40 on Nov. 27, and then slid below $37 the following day, simultaneous with the announcement that a Munich prosecutor was investigating charges that Yahoo! Deutschland had sold copies of *Mein Kampf*, banned in Germany.[58] Yahoo! executives dismiss the notion that the stock slides were related to its judicial woes. Indeed, the curve of its share price corresponds closely to that of the Nasdaq exchange in general, and of rivals like eBay. However, across the duration of the affair, a pattern of share price movements related to judicial events, in which Yahoo! shares declined slightly just before Gomez's rulings, then rebounded following them, can be

54 Victoria Shannon: "French Court Tells Yahoo to Block Nazi Items on Site", *International Herald Tribune*, Nov. 21, 2000, p. 1.

55 Jean Eaglesham, Robert Graham: "French Court Ruling hits Yahoo!". *Financial Times*, Nov. 21, 2000, p. 1.

56 Anon: "Offensive Ruling", *Financial Times*, Nov. 21, 2000, p. 20.

57 Mylène Mangalindan, Kevin J. Delaney: "Yahoo! Is Ordered to Bar Nazi Material," *Wall Street Journal*, Nov. 21, 2000, p. 1.

58 Steve Kettmann: "Germany's Kampf Furor Renews," *www.wired.com*, Dec. 1, 2000.

discerned.[59] In other words, at least some players appear to have speculated on the commercial impact of the affair.

X. Yahoo! Changes Jurisdiction: Dec. 2000-Jan. 2001

On Dec. 21, 2000, Yahoo! Inc. filed suit in U.S. District Court, asking for a ruling that Gomez's orders "are not recognizable or enforceable" in the U.S., plus recovery of Yahoo court costs and an injunction to prevent the French plaintiffs "from enforcing or attempting to enforce the Paris Court's [rulings in the U.S.]."[60] Predictably, Knobel was enraged: "They're still accusing French justice. [Supposedly] we're in a banana republic, a totalitarian country. It's disgusting," he told us. However, Yahoo!'s action may also be read as simple recognition of the futility of attempting to reconcile American and European approaches to the ethics of free expression on an issue such as Nazism.

On Jan. 6, 2001, Yahoo! Inc. announced the removal of all objects related to Nazism from its auction sites, except some 140 collectible coins, stamps, and anti-Nazi books and films. However, on Jan. 22, another French group, the Association of Friends of the Deported of Auschwitz and the Camps of High Silesia, in communication with Knobel, filed criminal charges against Tim Koogle, CEO of Yahoo! Inc., for "justifying war crimes, crimes against humanity, or crimes of collaborating with the enemy [and] for having deliberately maintained auctions of Nazi objects."[61] Attached to the charges was proof that the auctions had continued until Jan. 5, 2001. In March and April 2001, Tim Koogle resigned as CEO and Chairman of Yahoo!, citing personal reasons. He remains a member of the board of directors.

---

59 See LE MENESTREL ET AL. (2001b), exhibit 1.

60 "Complaint for Declaratory Relief, Yahoo! Inc., a Delaware corporation, v. La Ligue contre le Racisme et l'Antisemitisme, a French Association, and l'Union des Etudiants Juifs de France, a French Association," U.S. District Court for the Northern Dictrict of California, San Jose Division, Dec. 21, 2000, pp. 12-13.

61 Citation directe devant le Tribunal Correctionnel de Paris (17ème Chambre), à la requête de l'Association amicale des déportés d'Auschwitz et des camps de Haute Silésie, p. 8.

As Vinton Cerf commented in an interview with *Libération*, "We're at the beginning of ten years of conflicts."[62]

XI. Discussion

The chronology of this case suggests a tool that may be available to managers operating in ethically sensitive environments – namely, analysis of media content to discern patterns of rising opposition or activism. Certain parameters of such analysis are implicit in the events that immediately preceded the assignation of Yahoo!: A growing density of similar protests within a given time frame; a growing number of protagonists, including business firms, social or political leaders, and distinct protest organizations; and the scenarisation of protest along predictable lines of argument and action. It is worth noting that scholars of social movements, and most notably Luther P. Gerlach, have demonstrated the possibility of predicting events in the life of such movements through observation of their activities (Gerlach 1987). It is also worth noting that in our conversations with Yahoo! executives, they drew no spontaneous connections between protests against eBay and against their own firm in the U.S., and the LICRA case. That may reflect the fact that protests on either side of the Atlantic were first confronted by different executives. It is nonetheless remarkable that Yahoo! was caught by surprise on an issue that was first and best documented by Internet news sources.

Certainly, if Yahoo! had removed offensive items from its U.S. auction site in February 2000, instead of in January 2001, there would have been no LICRA case and no damage to the company and its brand. In theory, a company can neither respond to, nor give in to all pressures arising from society. But in practice, failure to appreciate the character of specific protests can have serious consequences. Surely Yahoo! committed this error at the outset of this case. Yet by July 2000, the company understood that it had a great deal at stake in the French courts, and continued to fight, despite growing signs of its inevitable defeat.

If one searches for a reason that Yahoo! did not arrive at its ultimate solution to the conflict earlier, it may well lie in the difficulty of altering its fun-

62 LAURE NOUALHAT: "Nous sommes à l'aube de dix ans d'affrontements," *Libération*, Nov. 10, 2000 (via *www.liberation.fr*).

damental conviction in the necessary freedom of the Internet. Certainly, that refusal was not motivated only by ethical concerns. Yahoo!'s analysis of the future evolution of the Internet, and hence of its own success, was that free access and expression are necessary prerequisites to the medium's social, and hence commercial, development. But its short-term business interests would clearly have been better served by saving itself nearly a full year of draining and humiliating conflict.

One managerial implication of this case is that responsibility for dealing with social protests cannot be the monopoly of the highest executive levels of an international corporation. Activists are not only or merely ideologues, they are "doers". They may be more effectively dealt with by operational managers who can propose workable solutions to their concerns, rather than by executives far away. The latter may be too preoccupied, and not sensitive enough to local issues, to appreciate the intensity of local concerns before an affair explodes. We note that Knobel said he was astonished that Yahoo! made no attempt to contact him during the press campaign that preceded his legal assault.

It is also significant that operational direction of the affair at Yahoo! Inc. resided from the start with the legal affairs department. A legal approach to the relation between business and society tends to interpret any initiative that follows the direction set by activists as a dangerous precedent. But that approach may preclude the opportunity to use activists as objective allies, who provide early warning signs of social concerns.

If the term "business ethics" has meaning, part of it is surely an effort to understand the social responsibility of firms *beyond the simple respect of legal constraints*. In the case at hand the laws governing the protagonists, like their ethical positions, were in conflict. It is thus of little use to contend that a firm in such a situation may simply go about making profits within the law. It may be more useful to ask whether the firm concentrates on respecting its principles or on gaining a practical benefit, and whether it is confronting or aligning itself with social pressure. As we see it, Yahoo! Inc. placed its principles first (at least insofar as its public statements are concerned), thereby accepting, consciously or not, the risk of growing confrontation. Yet simultaneously the firm's legalistic response implicitly reduced business ethics to a compliance issue, and prevented it from responding adequately to local social concerns and values.

This contradictory pattern is hardly limited to the New Economy. For example, many companies require employees to ask their headquarters before talking with journalists or activists, and approval for remedial action is often difficult to obtain before damage is done. Activists learn to play on such structural weakness. It is highly significant that several Yahoo! executives commented to us on the superb publicity skills of Knobel, without realizing that at the outset he lacked any experience of such confrontations. In effect, Yahoo! was training him.

In this particular sense, Yahoo! Inc. over-estimated its adversary. But more frequently, the firm under-estimated the gravity of the issues and the potential influence of its opposition. Its relationship to the court, whose ability to determine events was publicly dismissed by Jerry Yang, may be taken as one illustration of this tendency. It should be remembered that at the time of this case, it was fashionable to classify the Internet among the forces rendering national frontiers, and with them nation-states, impotent and obsolete. If this case is any indication, the contrary is also true: The Internet has opened a wide new field of action for national courts, enabling them to assert their powers in new domains.

Three interrelated beliefs seem to have contributed to Yahoo!'s errors of appreciation. The first was Yahoo!'s confidence in its own ethical values, as a champion for the rights of its users and a new medium for free expression. The second was its faith in the Internet as a vehicle for good, whose ultimate success is inevitable. The third was a belief that other parties, if properly informed, would naturally arrive at the same conclusions. These positions add up to a coherent ideological stance, that can be summarized as *the good comes by itself, and this process cannot and should not be constrained.* The strength derived from such an ideology should not be dismissed: Yahoo! never gave up in this case. Yet its efforts to persuade the judge and public opinion of the rightness of its cause nonetheless failed. Yahoo!'s opponents, too, were united by an ideology: *Evil occupies any vacuum, and this process must be constrained.* They too were determined, and fully confident of their ethical position. But their victory was predicated, in large part, on their growing capacity to convince others that their values were less dangerous and more credible than those of Yahoo!.

If this case is any indication, it is not enough for a firm to formulate ethical positions, or even to believe wholeheartedly in them. Its stance must also be able to withstand assault in the public arena, in the event of crisis. The firm must therefore be prepared to ask if its principles – even principles on which it has based its vision of the future – make as much sense to those outside the company as within it. If not, however valid its ethics may be in an ideal sense, they may compromise not only the firm's commercial assets in the short term, but its long-term attempts to align itself with society. Wise leadership, rather than seeking to suppress the inevitable tension between ethical positions and pragmatic concerns, may justifiably navigate between the two.

Additional References

ARKDENIZ, Y.; WALKER C.; WALL, D. (2000): "The Internet, the Law and Society" (CyberLaw Research Unit, University of Leeds, Longman Pearson).

DIAMOND, E.; BATES, S. (1995): "Law and order comes to cyberspace," *Technology Review*. Available at *http://209.58.177.220/articles/oct95/Diamond.html*.

FARHOOMAND, A. (2000): "Multi-jurisdictional Compliance in Cyberspace" (Center for Asian Business Cases, School of Business, The University of Hong Kong).

FEKETE, L. (2001): "Rights, rules and regulation in the cyberspace," paper presented during the 14th Annual EBEN conference, Valencia, Spain.

GERLACH, LUTHER P. (1987): "Protest Movements and the Construction of Risk," in: B. B. JOHNSON, V. T. COVELLO (Eds.): *The Social and Cultural Construction of Risk*, Boston (D. Reidel), pp. 103-145.

HUNTER, MARK (1998): *Un Américain au Front: Enquête au sein du Front National*, Paris (Editions Stock).

LE MENESTREL, M. (2002): "Economic Rationality and Ethical Behavior. Ethical Business between Venality and Sacrifice," *Business Ethics: A European Review*, 11, pp. 157-166.

LE MENESTREL, M.; DE BETTIGNIES, H.-C.; HUNTER, MARK (2001a): "Business e-ethics: Yahoo! on Trial," INSEAD Case Study N° 4956 (A). Available at ECCH.

LE MENESTREL, M.; DE BETTIGNIES, H.-C.; HUNTER, MARK (2001b): "Business e-ethics: Yahoo! on Trial," INSEAD Case Study N° 4956 (B). Available at ECCH.

LITMAN, J. (1999): "Electronic commerce and free speech," *Ethics and Information Technology*, 1, pp. 213-225.

O'REILLY & ASSOC.; KUNG, H. T. (1997): *The Internet and Society*, Cambrige (Harvard University Press).

TAYLOR, T. (2000): "The Internet: The new free speech battleground". Available at *http://www.cosc.georgetown.edu/~denning/cosc450/papers/taylor.html*.

Chapter 12

A Sketch of Consumer Ethics with Particular Emphasis on Virtual Options

MICHAEL NEUNER

I. Being a Consumer Entails Rights and Duties

Questions of business ethics have thus far mostly been focussed on the e-thical behaviour of the supplier. The role of the consumers is not treated with comparable concern. The question of their ethical behaviour arises from a background of pronounced signs of deterioration of the balance of welfare[1]. There are signs that the net welfare has not increased for some years now. Consumers definitely have some part in this devaluation process.

It is only with the more recent sustainability debate that normative consumer relevant questions have been made into issues. However, the full integra-

1 Cf. H. E. DALY, J. B. COBB: *For the Common Good*, Boston (Beacon Press) 1994. Calculations concerning the German balance of welfare can be found in G. SCHERHORN: *Das Ganze der Güter*, München (Beck) 1997, pp. 190–191.

tion of such questions into the field of business ethics does not appear to have fully manifested. Often the ethical foundation of the reflections is unclear. Hints of a justice based architecture remain vague, since the justice concept the considerations are founded on, is frequently not plainly expressed. Conceptions that relate to the "principle of hope" (Bloch) continue in being not obligatory or even utopian.

In the search for increased conceptual clarity a responsibility based consumer ethics could be of use[2]. As a middle range principle to be surveyed, equipped with the practical power of a "regulative principle"[3] and being relieved of the immoderate claims of "hypermoral"[4] aspirations, the advantage of it lies, among other things, with regard to plausibility, in its ability to indicate a practical, ethical attitude, which has its colloquial meaning of "responsible"[5]. The motivation in responsible consumer behaviour also exclusively originates from the satisfaction of individual needs. Here however, the goal is tempered via norms, and whose origins lie in the possibility of the autonomous will of the consumer[6].

Because responsible consumer behaviour connects new action with the failure of the old[7], consumers who submit *voluntarily* to the principle of responsibility would not only have rights, but also duties to fulfil. As is shown in the following, the realm of possibility opened up by the e-economy can be of help here.

The seed of consumer rights was sown in 1962 in an address to congress given by the president at the time, John F. Kennedy. It embraces:

---

2 Certainly it is not a matter of playing the two principles of "justice" and "responsibility" against each other.

3 I. KANT: *The Critique of Pure Reason*, Chicago (Encyclopaedia Britannica) [1781] 1990; see M. NEUNER: *Verantwortliches Konsumentenverhalten*, Berlin (Duncker & Humblot) 2001, pp. 172–177.

4 A. GEHLEN: *Moral und Hypermoral*, Wiesbaden (Aula) 1986, pp. 141–163.

5 At the latest since the critical and in its practical meaning and consequence only approximately grasped discourse of Jonas, the responsibility term has been moved into the centre of the discussion, see H. JONAS: *Das Prinzip Verantwortung*, Frankfurt a.M. (Suhrkamp) 1984.

6 A sketch of a theory of responsible consumer behaviour was proposed in M. NEUNER: *Verantwortliches Konsumentenverhalten*, loc. cit.

7 K.-M. MEYER-ABICH: *Aufstand für die Natur*, München (Hanser) 1990, p. 24.

- The "Right To Safety", which is meant to assure that health risks due to faulty or dangerous products are prevented.
- The "Right To Be Informed" roots out deception and misrepresentation on behalf of the supplier, and demands the making available of valid and reliable information as a support to consumer decisions.
- The "Right To Choose" indicates the "possibility of exiting". Consumers should have the right to withdraw from a business relationship when not satisfied.
- The "Right To Be Heard" strengthens the consumer's ability to communicate his preferences to good effect. It supports the "voice option"[8].

These basic rights of consumers, which to a great extent – also by law – have been settled, have been expanded often over time, along the lines of having a right to an environment which maintains and enhances the quality of life[9]. What is overlooked though is the indication that being a consumer implies duties. They come from negative external circumstances which one must increasingly assume are the rule, rather than the exception[10]. It has become clear that nearly half of ecological problems can be traced back to the consumer[11]. This public effect of consuming has led to an expansion of the individual sphere of responsibility into the public area. Unlike before, the legitimacy of individual consumption can no longer be established via the claim of satisfaction of needs. The question of satisfaction of human needs has as it were lost its innocence.

The ethical duties arising from the negative external effects of consuming are not legally binding. They cannot be enforced by the state, and could only

8 Cf. A. O. HIRSCHMAN: *Exit, Voice, and Loyalty*, Cambridge, Mass. (Harvard University Press) 1970.

9 K.-M. MEYER-ABICH: *Aufstand für die Natur*, loc. cit., p. 24.

10 R. U. AYRES, A. V. KNEESE: "Production, Consumption, and Externalities", *The American Economic Review*, 59 (1969), p. 282; U. KNOBLOCH: *Theorie und Ethik des Konsums,* Bern (Haupt) 1994, p. 147.

11 Meyer-Abich estimates the portion of consumer originated ecological damage at over 60 percent (K.-M. MEYER-ABICH: *Aufstand für die Natur*, loc. cit., p. 25). Beier holds the extreme view that generally all ecological damage can be traced back to the consumer (U. BEIER: *Der fehlgeleitete Konsum*, Frankfurt a.M. [Fischer] 1993, p. 7).

be so if the state were a dictatorship which had taken away the freedom of consumption; they are therefore additional duties, which morally urge and which are fulfilled, only voluntarily, via the insight and confession of consumers[12].

In the context of a responsibility based consumer ethics, duties can be derived from a Hans Jonas' inspired imperative. This imperative could charge one with the following: *As much as possible, conduct yourself as a consumer in such a way as to remain in harmony with the concerns of nature, and with the needs and interests of your social reality, both near and far from home and time, and last but not least, stay in harmony with your own, not only immediate and material needs.*

That having been said, some primary duties can be formulated, from which corresponding norms result[13].

- Responsibility for taking care of the natural "Mitwelt".[14] Intervention in nature must be seen as a *conditio humana* which is universal valid. The norm of "ecological sustainability" refers to the mode of nature acquisition, which operates against a background of destruction, cultivation and preservation.
- Responsibility to attend to the consequences of consumption on the social "Mitwelt", which every consumer is a part of. The norm of "social acceptability" means the tolerability of actions in their direct, surveyable effects on humanity.
- Thirdly consumers carry a responsibility for themselves which can not be delegated. This responsibility is bound up with the success of the individual's life. The norm of "self-compatibility" exists in reference to appropriate product quantity and quality. The appropriate quantity

---

12 These duties are "ethical" or "imperfect" duties in Kant's meaning; cf. I. KANT: *Fundamental Principles of the Metaphysic of Ethics*, London (Longmans, Green & Co.) [1785] 1940.

13 See M. NEUNER: *Verantwortliches Konsumentenverhalten*, loc. cit., pp. 44–49, for a detailed discussion.

14 While the environmental term has strong anthropocentrical, although not forcing anthropocratical connotations, the meaning of Goethe's term "Mitwelt" more clearly indicates a human being's togetherness with other persons. See for more detail G. ALTNER: "Umwelt, Mitwelt, Nachwelt", in: M. JÄNICKE, U. E. SIMONIS, G. WEIGMANN (Eds.): *Wissen für die Umwelt*, Berlin (de Gruyter) 1985, p. 279.

can only be determined by the individual. This is reached when the felt urgency of product related wants corresponds with the value ranking, which an individual allocates it in the preference order after unbiased reflection[15]. With the theory of two levels of intention it can be explained why this comparison can occasionally be necessary[16].

In the context of the possibilities in the e-economy these three abstract primary duties can be set in action by making them more concrete:

- "The duty to know": In responsible consumer behaviour the procurement of knowledge concerning the preconditions and consequences of a market decision becomes a guiding duty[17]. Such knowledge would include for example the circumstances and conditions under which consumer goods were produced. Consumers have to acquire this information themselves through market inquiry.
- "The duty to articulate responsibility related preferences": Where the preferences of consumers have been violated, there arises the ethical duty to reveal those preferences. Consumers who want to act responsibly should signal, by "exit" or "voicing" it, that their preferences have been violated and that they are not prepared to put up with it.
- "The duty to be powerful": The effectiveness of responsible consumer behaviour increases when coordination of action is attained. Through the combined conveying of preferences in the space of collective actions, it is possible to generate a potential of countervailing power. Powerful consumers can bring shared interpretations of situations to the attention of suppliers and can make plain the objectives and urgency of their preferences.

---

15 For the distinction between "urgency" and "ranking" of wants cf. W. KORFF: "Ethische Entscheidungskonflikte", in: A. HERTZ (Ed.): *Handbuch der christlichen Ethik*, Freiburg i.B. (Herder) 1982, pp. 79–80.

16 See H. FRANKFURT: "Freedom of the Will and the Concept of a Person", *The Journal of Philosophy*, 68 (1971), pp. 5–25; J. C. HARSANYI: "Morality and the Theory of Rational Behaviour", in: A. SEN, B. WILLIAMS (Eds.): *Utilitarianism and beyond*, Cambridge (Cambridge University Press) 1982, pp. 39–62; R. C. JEFFREY: "Preferences among Preferences", *The Journal of Philosophy*, 71 (1974), pp. 377–391; A. SEN: "Rational Fools", *Philosophy and Public Affairs*, 6 (1977), pp. 317–344.

17 H. JONAS: *Das Prinzip Verantwortung*, loc. cit., pp. 64–68.

Many empirical findings reveal that the norms of responsible consumer behaviour are not only a matter of theoretical reflections of a scholastic consumer ethics[18]. Above all a concern for the environment has developed into an everyday habitude on a wide basis, irrespective of the position in society. Consumers are prepared to act responsibly – not all of them and not all the time, but all in all in an extend that can not be neglected.

That responsible consumer behaviour is not more widespread to a large extent is a consequence of the consumer relevant infrastructure. This infrastructure is so formed that in key areas responsible consumer behaviour is either impossible, or it so overtaxes individuals that during the practical pursuit of their ethical imperative, high and to some extent unreasonable risks of becoming victims of deception and exploitation are incurred. The observable behaviour can at least be interpreted as an "institution determined pathology": It is an aberrant behaviour of consumers, which is not traceable back to an i-nadequately developed ecological or social awareness, but to a sham consumer-relevant infrastructure. Unlike the "theory of revealed preferences"[19] postulates, without further premises one *cannot* deduce the preferences of consumers by watching their behaviour[20].

In consumer goods markets there is a whole list of causes that lead to such pathologies[21]. Widespread above all are:

– "Information Pathologies": Ecological and social intransparency of the market leads to insecurity and "investigation failure". Investigation failure describes the general inability, within a system of action, to obtain the knowledge necessary to reach a goal[22]. The clarification is made more difficult when the information has the character of cre-

18 See for more detail M. NEUNER: *Verantwortliches Konsumentenverhalten*, loc. cit., pp. 89–162.

19 Cf. P. A. SAMUELSON: "Consumption Theory in Terms of Revealed Preference", *Economica*, 15 (1948).

20 Whoever does this anyway, runs the risk of arriving at a naturalistic fallacy. Cf. G. E. MOORE: *Principia Ethica*, Stuttgart (Reclam) [1903] 1971.

21 M. NEUNER: *Verantwortliches Konsumentenverhalten*, loc. cit., pp. 327–369.

22 See H. WILENSKY: *Organizational Intelligence*, New York (Basic Books) 1967.

dence qualities[23], and when the consumer has to deal with opportunistic supplier behaviour[24].

- The "Illusion of Objective Facticity" blinds the consumer to the fact that the relevant infrastructure is a result of a cultural creation process, and that its form – at least in principle – can be shaped and moulded. Here powerlessness is feigned where it need not be present. The illusion of objective facticity is validated by closed institutions and structural exclusion, when consumers for example withhold from suppliers opportunities for dialog and participation.

With the internet as the primordial element of the e-economy the consumer relevant infrastructure is modified in a decisive way. The thesis dealt with below states that the e-economy restores the chance to work against institution determined pathologies. Firstly the internet offers the chance to reduce investigation failure and thus makes information pathologies less probable; this makes it easier for consumers to fulfil their "duty to know". Secondly, via collective action on the internet structural exclusion can be broken up and the illusion of objective facticity can be overcome.

II. Consumer Portals and Corporate Watch Sites to Prevent Investigation Failure

The internet as a new institution of the consumer relevant infrastructure can support all phases of the buying and consumption process. In the prebuying phase reflection on wants and their delimitation against needs plays a dominant role[25]. This task derives from the assumption that in the context of ethical consumption not every desire, but rather a normative reflected provo-

23 M. R. Darby, E. Karni: "Free Competition and the Optimal Amount of Fraud", *The Journal of Law and Economics*, 16 (1973), pp. 67–88.

24 Cf. regarding the opportunistic behaviour of market players O. E. Willliamson: *The Economic Institutions of Capitalism*, New York (The Free Press) 1985.

25 See G. Scherhorn: *Gesucht: der mündige Verbraucher*, Düsseldorf (Droste) 1973, pp. 18–19.

kes satisfaction. In reflecting on wants corporate watch sites and consumer portals can be of use.

Until now providing knowledge of supplier independent sources of information was essentially a matter for the consumer institutes. The importance of presenting reports through the "Stiftung Warentest"[26] or through other independent institutions lies in information which relates primarily to consumer-*technical* risks,[27] enabling the evaluation of e.g., functional or financial risks. Consumer portals and corporate watch sites can beyond that give important hints that are concerned with consumer-*ethical* risks[28], which might possibly be connected with a consumer decision.

At consumer portals consumers provide information about their experiences with and knowledge about products and services. The biggest German operator has posted at this time about 2.6 million reports. The reports are very thorough and follow a pre-existing structure. On such sites one can find out for example that a certain sneaker has been produced in a sweat shop in Asia, under inhumane conditions. Consumers can also formulate complaints, suggestions, and can also give praise and encouragement to companies. These are then collected and the operators of the portals forward the information to the appropriate areas within the intended company. The addresses of the responsible persons are often unknown to the consumers. An important restriction underlies the information source in so far as the evaluation requires that the products are branded (e.g. "Transfair").

While consumer portals primarily provide product-specific information, critical consumers will find information relevant to companies on so called corporate watch sites. One these sites – one identifies them in that, in the internet address, next to the company's name there will be an addition like "watch" (aolwatch.org) or "sucks" (gapsucks.org) – reports are given of violations perpetrated by watched companies against ecological or social stan-

26 The "Stiftung Warentest" is the most important independent non profit consumer institute in Germany. It was established in 1964 by the German government.

27 See for more detail R. A. BAUER: "Consumer behavior as risk taking", in: R. S. HANCOCK (Ed.): *Dynamic marketing for a changing world. Proceedings of the 43th Conference of the AMA*, Chicago, IL (American Marketing Association) 1960, pp. 389–398.

28 Cf. M. NEUNER: *Verantwortliches Konsumentenverhalten*, loc. cit., pp. 179–180.

dards. The politics of concern should be made transparent. Company relevant information about big German companies can be found for example on the site of the "Association of Critical Shareholders in Germany"[29].

III. Electronic Civil Disobedience: Against the Illusion of Objective Facticity

Parallel with the spreading of the net a digital protest infrastructure has developed, which discovered the net to be an identification and organization instrument for promoting political consumption. Certainly consumption was discovered as a vehicle for the transport of social policy issues long before the age of the e-economy[30]. However, the internet offers novel possibilities to efficiently and effectively bring the subpolitical dimension[31] of consumption into the limelight.

A feature of the digital protest culture is that the net – like at one time the agora – is claimed to be a public space. The new forms of resistance and protest range from clearly illegal forms of cyber terrorism, to varieties of "electronic civil disobedience". Electronic civil disobedience is a form of decentralised, electronic collective action, which adopts the tactics of non-violent, direct protests, and experiments with them on the internet. Similar to how people can block the entrances to reception areas of buildings, one can also block the entrances to reception areas in cyberspace – to portals. Electronic or virtual sit-ins were observable on several occasions in recent years. During them thousands of activists, at predetermined, preannounced times, sent floods of messages to certain internet sites, rendering them paralysed. New to net supported protest actions are above all three things:

29 *http://www.kritischeaktionaere.de/*

30 See for example the discussion regarding the social responsibility postulate of companies, which strongly emerged from the practical management field, and was then taken up and fully dealt with by management theory, cf. T. DYLLICK: *Management der Umweltbeziehungen*, Wiesbaden (Gabler) 1989, pp. 86–126.

31 For the essentials of "Subpolitik" see U. BECK: *Die Erfindung des Politischen*, Frankfurt a.M. (Suhrkamp) 1993.

1. Rather than being used as a communications medium, the web itself is used as showplace for the protest. A particular portal becomes the centre of the action. The medium is the place.
2. The changeover of sit-ins from the real to the virtual world is at the same time a changeover from a local to a global event.
3. In contrast to before the participants can take part in the protest from home or from any other location. "Voting with your feet" is being enhanced or even usurped by "voting with your (keyboard) keys".

In Germany in 2001 a virtual demonstration was organized, which was directed against a German airline. The protest was part of a campaign with the title "Deportation Class – Against the Business of Deportation". The demonstration was inspired by the conditions under which about 30,000 rejected asylum seekers are deported out of Germany every year. Again and again in the past they were subject to minor or major abuses. The asylum seekers were according to need bound and gagged, or pacified using medication. Two asylum seekers died; both were sitting on planes of the same airline. In the aftermath the airline was inundated by demands that they pull out of the deportation business. The reaction of the airline was not very conciliatory, in that they reduced the social and political problem to a questions of internal security.

The immediate goal of the protest was to induce the airline to give up the deportation business. To reach this goal, the organizers of the protest aimed at bringing the issue into the public eye. Officially it read: "The goal is to talk about the reasons behind the protest." They wanted the airline to take responsibility for the consequences of its business. To that end a momentary demonstration of power was performed. Although those responsible were at no time unable to act, they were subjected – brightly illuminated by the spotlight of the media – to the will of the demonstrators.

The protesters wanted to document the legitimacy of their demands via a massive participation of the public. This made plain that – according to the organizers – it was not only about the interests of a particular stakeholder society, but also about issues that were held in high esteem due to the overarching interests of society as a whole.

The virtual demonstration was announced by the protest group. In order to underline the public character of the protest they also registered it with an official regulatory agency. The activists informed the public using mailing lists that the internet portal of the airline would be blocked. The address of the target site was made public and it was asked that people participate. In the end

11,000 to 13,000 deportation opponents took part in the online demonstration. Measured against its goals the demonstration was a threefold success:

1. The campaign achieved publicity; the issue and the name of the airline were in the media for more than a week.
2. The board of the company negotiated to be released from the duty to take part in the forced deportation of asylum seekers.
3. The airline had to take responsibility for its act; they received countless enquiries from around the world. This got the company on the defensive and induced them in the end to concede.

Electronic civil disobedience protests are always on the border between illegality and legitimacy. This raises the question of whether electronic civil disobedience can be a legal and legitimate mode of articulating preferences. Precondition is, that the protest must be included within the range of consumer freedom.

Right away it needs to be clarified whether the internet can have the quality of an open societal space, wherein citizens, like on the street, should have the right to make their opinion known – even and especially when it is not desired. A test of legality, in the context of the constitution, must follow from special consideration of Art. 8 and 5 GG. Over and above that, aside from civil rights standards, surely norms of the German criminal law like §§ 303a, b StGB would have to be checked.

It is easy to differentiate electronic civil disobedience from clearly illegal forms of computer crime. All protest forms move within a spectrum of possibilities involving both word and deed: Whereas in electronic civil disobedience the word, the argumentation predominates, in politicised "hacking" it is the deed that prevails over the reasoned argument. Secondly electronic civil disobedience is a peaceful, non-violent protest form. The paralysing or slowing of a site for some time does not destroy or change any data. Cyber terrorism however involves damaging attacks on property and data stocks. Thirdly electronic civil disobedience enjoys wide acceptance with the public, cyber terrorism on the other hand is not a politics of mass mobilisation. It is democratically illegitimate, because there are individual persons who cause harm. A fourth point is that democratic mass protests do not have the clandestine character of cyber terrorism acts. Electronic civil disobedience is transparent in many respects: There is "transparency of persons"; everyone knows who is behind the protest. There is transparency of subject; virtual sit-ins seek clearly sketched goals, which are made known in an easily understandable form. There is transparency of the protest event; the protests are announced. They limit themselves to fixed time periods and have clear culmination points.

Looked at as a whole, it can be argued that, at least in its moderate forms, electronic civil disobedience may be seen as a legitimate manifestation of the subsidiarity principle[32] and as an expression of an active society.

The flip side of virtual protests lies firstly in the fear that they will usurp real ones: The participation of consumers can take place with the same level of apathy as filling a shopping basket. It is conceivable that activists who take part in virtual protests might no longer attend to the content of the collective actions, and might give up non virtual and perhaps more effective forms of protests, because they feel freed from responsibility by voting via internet. Secondly electronic civil disobedience can have negative external effects. In the overtaxing of net resources all other actions taking place on the internet are indirectly affected, not just the targeted website. The reduction of the bandwidth, with the consequence of longer access times, entails a demonstration outside of cyberspace, which inconveniences other people who are pursuing their affairs.

IV. The Reutilization of Goods by Consumers Through Internet Auctions

The e-economy also has, in the post sales phase, possibilities to offer responsible consumers for fulfilling their ethical duties. Internet auctions can help to utilize used goods via second hand markets. This possibility is above all meaningful from an ecological viewpoint. Until now a great many devices, only a little reduced in functioning, or even still fully functional, have ended up in the garbage. A reuse leads to a better exhaustion of the product's life cycle. This way the need for replacement is curtailed. The problem of scarce resources is then shifted into the future. This gives time to develop backstop-technologies.

---

32 For the most well known formulation of the subsidiary principle cf. POPE PIUS XI: *Encyclical Quadragesimo Anno*, Rome 1931, nos. 79–80, see *http://www.vatican.va/holy_father/pius_xi/encyclicals/documents/hf_pxi_enc_19310515_quadragesimo-anno_en.html*

Internet auctions belong, since about a year, to the set of most visited sites on the internet. In the virtual marketplace nearly everything sellable is sold. All together there are about 500 auction houses on the world wide web. The two biggest auction houses have over 10 million members worldwide at present and more are joining daily. Goods within more than 4,300 categories are on offer. A noteworthy proportion of the goods include PCs, printers, monitors and other electronic devices, and also sports equipment.

The general conditions of trade at the auction houses are transparent, the risks of customers are well taken care of. From a consumer politics point of view the rules also cannot be reprimanded. The regulation defect – for example the German foreign sales law ("Fernabsatzgesetz, FernAbsG") is limited in its use – is extensively made up for through the use of trustee accounts, extended guarantees, and through feedback forums, which work as systems of social control. The "Stiftung Warentest" has checked the trade conditions at regular intervals, and has found most of the auctions houses to be worthy of the label "good".

V. Prospects

The e-economy offers consumers novel possibilities to make their preferences more effectively known to suppliers. Corporate watch sites provide consumers with an additional, supplier independent source of market information. The current information exchange can initiate value inspired integration processes on the foundation of mutually shared norms. In the best case social cohesion develops, which can be put into position as potential countervailing power in defence against ethically unacceptable company politics. Electronic civil disobedience can, through cheating supposedly constraining circumstances, discover the illusion of objective facticity. With the breaking up of structural exclusion the factoid character of a supplier politics disconnected from consumer preferences is unmasked.

One has to take into consideration that by far not all consumers have internet access at this time. Furthermore about 25 percent of Germans reject the medium for various reasons. The more frequent users are found amongst the younger, better educated consumers. They make up the internet elite. Their decisions can have a considerable influence on the responsiveness of companies. It is not as if the responsibility lay exclusively with these "information seekers" of the 21st century, but their decisions certainly are of strategic importance.

Hirschman showed in the context of market theory, that it is enough if not all, but just some consumers signal there dissatisfaction to suppliers[33]. If all who were dissatisfied with a supplier's performance suddenly withdrew the supplier would have no chance to adapt to the preferences of the customers. Better would be an optimal mixture of "active and passive" internet users. The "active" users build up the communicative market openness. They give companies feedback. The "passive" users simply provide them with time and money. Both need suppliers to adjust their performance to customer preferences. So, the contribution of the e-economy could consist in the improvement of the workability of product markets.

33 A. O. HIRSCHMAN: *Exit, Voice, and Loyalty*, loc. cit.

Chapter 13

Building Consumer Trust in Online Markets

SONJA GRABNER-KRÄUTER

I. Introduction

Retailers find it increasingly important to represent themselves on the Internet to get more customers, increase the public's awareness of the company and its products and – last but not least – to sell more of its products. However, moving Internet users to the "purchase click" is proving to be difficult. An important reason why online consumers are reluctant to shop online is because of the fundamental lack of faith that currently exists between most businesses and consumers on the Web. "In essence, consumers simply do not *trust* most Web providers enough to engage in relationship exchanges with them" (Hoffman, Novak and Peralta 1998, p. 2). Trust is not only a short-term issue but the most significant long-term barrier for realizing the potential of e-commerce to consumers.

Because of the essential role trust plays for the development of e-commerce it is important to analyse the factors that are relevant for the emergence of trust problems in transactions between online-retailers and consumers. Buying on the Internet presents numerous risks for consumers over and above the transaction process itself being perceived as risky (Einwiller, Geissler and Will 2000; Einwiller and Will 2001). Online transactions often do not involve simultaneous exchange of goods and money – spatial and also temporal separation between exchange partners is common. Because of the fierce competition in electronic markets the online consumer is inundated with a myriad of similar offerings to choose from and overwhelmed by conflicting marketing messages. The online consumer cannot personally inspect products or services and does not know what the retailer will do with the personal information that is collected during the shopping process. There seems little assurance that the customer will get what she or he sees on the computer screen, at a certain time and in the quantity ordered. Having only limited cognitive resources available, consumers seek to reduce the uncertainty and complexity of transactions and relationships in electronic markets by applying mental shortcuts. One effective mental shortcut is trust, which can serve as mechanism to reduce the complexity of human conduct in situations where people have to cope with uncertainty (Luhmann 1989). If and to which extent trust is an adequate means to reduce uncertainty depends on the one hand on the causes of uncertainty and on the other hand on the type of the transaction or the type of the buying process. Drawing on the theory of information two types of uncertainty are described in this paper: system-dependent and transaction-specific uncertainty. Reasons for system-dependent uncertainty in electronic commerce are potential technological problems and the lack of clear legal norms. Transaction-specific uncertainty results from decisions of economic actors and is caused by an asymmetric distribution of information between the transaction partners. It is shown that trust plays a key role in buying processes where consumers especially look for experience and credence qualities of goods or services. Finally different activities and instruments are described and categorized that online retailers can use to "produce" trust.

II. Trust as a Mechanism to Reduce Complexity

To date, we have no universally accepted scholarly definition of trust. Researchers in different disciplines agree on the importance of trust in the conduct of human affairs, but there also appears to be equally widespread lack of agreement on a suitable definition of the concept (Hosmer 1995, Rousseau and Sitkin 1998, Bhattacharya and Devinney 1998, Husted 1998). Personality psychologists traditionally have viewed trust as an individual characteristic (e.g. Rotter 1971). Social psychologists define trust as an expectation about the behaviour of others in transactions, focusing on the contextual factors that enhance or inhibit the development and maintenance of trust (Lewicki and Bunker 1995). Economists and sociologists have been interested in how institutions and incentives are created to reduce the anxiety and uncertainty associated with transactions (e.g. Williamson 1993, Granovetter 1985, Zucker 1986).

Drawing on the work of Luhmann (1989) trust can be seen as a mechanism to reduce the complexity of human conduct in situations where people have to cope with uncertainty. In this perspective trust bears important functions for the consumer – it reduces information complexity and lowers the perceived risk of a transaction. Trust can be conceptualised on different levels of analysis, reflecting the array of entities, individuals, dyads, groups, networks, systems, firms and inter-firm alliances in which trust and related processes play a role (Rousseau and Sitkin 1998, p. 398). Many theorists and researchers of trust focus on interpersonal relationships. In order to analyse trust in the context of computer-mediated environments it makes sense to extend the levels of trust, because in electronic markets personal trust is a rather limited mechanism to reduce uncertainty.

A functional perspective of trust can easily be integrated into an economic framework. To analyse trust decisions in the context of market transactions it makes sense to distinguish between trust as a subjective expectation and trust as cooperative behaviour. Within an economic framework trust as cooperative behaviour is described as a risky advance concession in the expectation of a positive outcome without any explicit contractual security or control measure against opportunistic behaviour (Ripperger 1998, p. 45). Trust-embedded actions usually are based on the expectation of the trustor that the other party (the trustee) will behave trustworthy and refrain from opportunistic behaviour. Concerning trust in social or technical systems the trustor expects that the system (in this case the object of trust) will be functioning smoothly.

As trust embodies a subjective expectation it is determined by several factors. Individual characteristics of the trustor, his basic willingness to trust, his individual experience and the experience of others with the trustworthiness of another party or the safety of a system play an important role in the development of trust. Beyond that, contextual or situational factors are critical to the understanding of trust (Rousseau and Sitkin 1998, p. 400). Across disciplines there is agreement on conditions that must exist for trust to arise – trust only exists in an uncertain and risky environment, it would not be needed if actions could be undertaken with complete certainty and no risk. The following characterization of the conditions for electronic commerce transactions focuses on uncertainty as the basic transaction dimension that determines the opportunities to use trust as a mechanism to reduce complexity. If and to which extent trust is an adequate means to reduce uncertainty depends on the one hand on the causes of uncertainty and on the other hand on the type of the transaction or the type of the buying process.

III. Uncertainty as a Basic Transaction Dimension Relevant for the Importance of Trust in E-Commerce

Trust always involves an element of risk resulting from our inability to have complete knowledge about other peoples' motivations, from our inability to monitor others' behaviour and, generally, from the contingency of social reality (Misztal 1996, pp. 17). The exchange of information via the Internet can bring about several risks that either are caused by functional defects or security problems in information and communication technical systems (system-dependent uncertainty) or can be explained by the conduct of actors who are involved in the online transaction (transaction-specific uncertainty).

1. System-dependent Uncertainty

System-dependent uncertainty comprises events that are beyond the direct influence of actors and can be characterized as exogenous or environmental uncertainty. In general the concept of exogenous uncertainty refers to uncertainty of the world (Hirshleifer and Riley 1979). Exogenous uncertainty is caused by dynamic forces of the environment and the complexity of relevant environmental factors (Brielmaier and Diller 1995). In the context of electronic commerce exogenous uncertainty primarily relates to potential technological sources of errors and security gaps or to put it economically to technology-dependent risks that can not be avoided by an agreement or a contract with another actor who is involved in the transaction.

The smooth and secure processing of an online transaction depends on the functioning of the hard- and software that is used as well as on the security of the data exchange services including the cryptographic protocols that are used. Technical safety gaps can emerge either in the data channel or on the "final points" of the process or the e-commerce system. In business-to-consumer e-commerce "final points" of the e-commerce system are the desktop system of the customer, the server of the Internet retailer and possibly the servers of the involved banks and operators of the electronic marketplace. The user can directly control transactional security only within his own system but not in the systems of other actors involved in the transaction.

To cope with system-dependent uncertainty it makes sense to concentrate on the formation of institutional-based trust, in which formal mechanisms are used to provide trust that does not rest on personal characteristics or on past history of exchange (Zucker 1986). Besides traditional intermediary institutions such as banks or consumer organizations new intermediary mechanisms such as trusted third parties play an important role in e-commerce, as they can help to promote trust among trading partners, minimize misrepresentation of product and service quality and encourage consumer confidence in conducting online business transactions (e.g. Froomkin 1996). With the growing inclusion of trusted third parties in e-commerce and the increasing sophistication of the relevant technology consumers' concerns about security of credit card numbers and personal data are likely to diminish in the near future. The focus of trust will gradually shift from engendering trust in the process and the technology to engendering consumer trust in the Internet company (Einwiller, Geissler and Will 2000).

2. Transaction-specific Uncertainty

Transaction-specific uncertainty can be seen as a kind of endogenous or market uncertainty that results from decisions of economic actors and is caused by an asymmetric distribution of information between the transaction partners (Weiber and Adler 1995b). Market uncertainty exists if partners in an exchange relationship are not completely informed about the relevant conditions of the market. From the perspective of the consumer transaction-specific uncertainty primarily concerns the quality of the products and services that are offered on the Web, which depends on the sellers' ability and willingness to perform. The quality assessment in electronic markets often is more difficult than in traditional markets. In situations where buying decisions are made in a computer-mediated environment many elements of personal interaction disappear or are inapplicable (e.g. facial play, gesture, body language) that are used in the real world (Winand and Pohl 2000).

Internet consumers have different opportunities to reduce transaction-specific uncertainty to a subjectively acceptable level. To characterize these strategies thinking patterns of information economics can be applied. The assessment of the qualities of a particular purchase can be based on three different types of qualities (Darby and Karni 1973, p. 68): search qualities, experience qualities and credence qualities. Search qualities are those that can easily be ascertained in the search process prior to purchase (e.g. the price of a product or its colour or shape). Experience qualities are those that can be discovered only after purchase as the product is used (e.g. the taste of a can of tuna fish, the functionality of a word processing program or the durability of a dishwasher). Credence qualities are those that cannot be evaluated in normal use, either because the buyer does not have the adequate evaluation know-how or because the assessment would be too expensive for him. Examples for credence qualities are product attributes concerning a special origin or production process (e.g. biologically grown) or effects of a product that are difficult to prove.

Weiber and Adler (1995b) emphasize that these types of qualities have to be considered as complementary, because with each purchasing decision the different types of qualities always are more or less existent. Different positions of a product in the "information economic triangle" of search, experience and credence qualities have the effect that consumers tend to use different strategies in order to reduce uncertainty (Weiber and Adler 1995a, p. 66). There are strategies to search for information and strategies to substitute for information. Usually, in a specific transaction process consumers use the different strategies to reduce uncertainty not isolated, but integrate them into a mix of strategies. When the assessment of quality of a particular good or service can be based primarily on search qualities the adequate strategy to reduce uncertainty is to directly search for observable product attributes. In e-commerce transactions search qualities often become "quasi"-experience qualities, because they can not be determined by inspection prior to purchasing the product. Often the consumer can evaluate Web products only by way of experience. Therefore strategies to substitute for information, where the consumer uses special indicators or other mechanisms to reduce uncertainty in order to evaluate product qualities that can not be inspected prior to purchasing are very important in online buying processes.

To assess real and "quasi" experience qualities consumers can use performance-oriented information substitutes that relate to specific attributes of the transaction object. In buying processes where the product evaluation is based mainly on experience qualities the consumer can try to use adequate indicators such as brand-names or performance bonds to reduce his uncertainty about product attributes that can not be inspected prior to purchasing. Beyond that the consumer can use comprehensive information substitutes that are more general and relate to the seller and his reputation or image in the market. Comprehensive information substitutes are even more important in buying processes of goods that are dominated by credence qualities. Concerning the evaluation of credence qualities institutions that complement free markets (such as independent controlling or certification authorities) play an important role, because the online retailer can signal trustworthiness when e.g. referring to a certificate of a trusted third party.

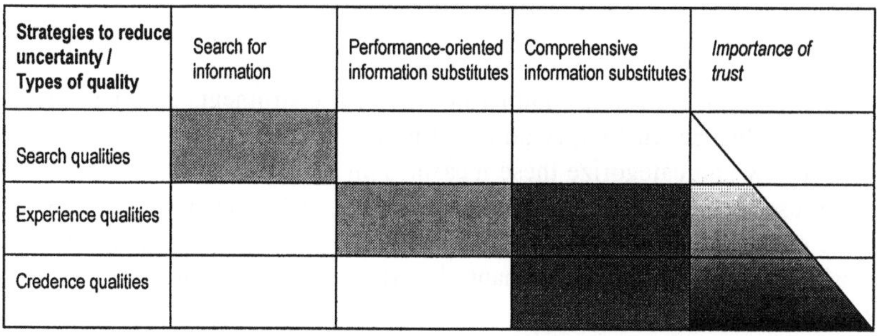

Fig. 1: Dominant strategies to reduce uncertainty

Trust either can complement or (partly) replace other strategies to reduce uncertainty in buying processes and thus can serve as a subsidiary or complementary mechanism to reduce uncertainty. Trust is more important, when transaction objects are characterized primarily by experience and/or credence qualities and less important in buying processes dominated by search qualities (see fig. 1). Especially when personalized or individualized products or services are offered the assessment of their value usually has to be based on experience and credence qualities, thus making trust an essential element in the relationship between buyer and seller. Offering personalized goods or services can be interpreted as a performance promise of the seller. The willingness of the buyer to make risky advance concession (e.g. providing his credit card number or other sensible information) will considerably depend on his assessment of the trustworthiness of the seller, but also his assessment of the functional reliability of the e-commerce system.

Concerning transaction-specific uncertainty trust is important in a double respect. On the one hand performance-oriented and comprehensive information substitutes to assess experience and credence qualities can be considered as indicators for the trustworthiness of the seller that significantly influence the expectation of the buyer. On the other hand trust serves itself as a mechanism to reduce complexity and uncertainty and therefore can at least partly replace the direct search for (more) information in buying processes.

IV. Policies to Develop and Maintain Trust in E-Commerce

Internet retailers can use numerous different instruments and measures in order to influence trust expectations of potential customers. In order to give an overview and categorize these measures an agency-theoretical framework can be used[1]. In an agency-theoretical perspective firms can apply three different categories of instruments to make transactions and cooperative relationships more efficient (Spremann 1988): information policies, guarantee policies and reputation policies.

Information policies aim at reducing information asymmetries between sellers and buyers by applying various communicative measures such as

1 Agency theory describes the structuring of economic exchange relationships between two parties, the principal and the agent (e.g. SPREMANN [1987], p. 3). Agency theorists examine how principals and agents attempt to structure the relationship to protect their own interests. The principal bears the risk that agents behave opportunistically, which is greater when the principal lacks information about agents' actions (i.e. information asymmetry). Applying agency theory to trust relationships in e-commerce, we can consider the consumer (trustor) to be the principal and the online-retailer (trustee) to be the agent.

advertising, direct marketing and public relations. Their adequacy depends on the type of buying process or the dominant types of quality of the product or service that is offered as well as on the transaction phase. It seems that information policies to develop and maintain trust are more important when the quality assessment primarily is based on experience and/or credence qualities.

In the Internet context the website mediates the relationship between the consumer and the merchant organization. It provides an essential clue for online consumers for their assessment of the efficiency and reliability of an online retailer, which is based on the quality of information on key issues such as delivery charges, order progress, and on policies on privacy, returns and redress. There are numerous recommendations how to improve the acceptance of web pages, relating e.g. to the content of the web page, the use of navigation guidance (e.g. navigation metaphors) or the design of the web page (e.g. Mevenkamp and Kerner 1999, p. 242). An online survey that aimed at determining the nature of those elements that communicate trust in e-commerce sites showed that a user-friendly and effective navigation is a necessary precondition to communicate trust (Cheskin Research/Studio Archetype/Sapient 1999). Effective navigation combined with either a well-known brand or effective, simple fulfilment are the best ways of communicating trustworthiness. Other factors that play significant roles in establishing trust are the professionalism of the Web presentation, the technological sophistication and the functionality of the site.

Guarantee policies relate to promises to limit or compensate for damages that are caused by negative events that can not be certainly avoided. Guarantee policies comprise different instruments that guarantee compensation payments in a case of damages, such as taking back guarantees, warranties and finishing touches or repairs. In agency-theoretical terminology the agent (seller) promises the principal (buyer) to compensate for damages if they occur and thus limit the decrease of benefit for the buyer (Spremann 1988, p. 620). The reliability of such promises depends on the existence or availability of adequate means for compensation in the case of damages. In the context of online transactions the buyer usually can not be sure whether or not he will recover damages, especially if seller and buyer are from different countries or if the company has no "bricks-and-mortar" presence. This insecurity partly is caused by the lack of transparency of legal norms concerning transactions in electronic markets.

Guarantee policies can be more effective for building trust in e-commerce if trusted third parties are included that focus on legal, technical and organizational factors of electronic markets and define rigorous standards for security, data protection, transparency of data use, etc. The online retailer can bind himself to meet these stringent requirements for data and delivery security, what is usually documented with an Internet-specific certificate or quality label. Such quality labels often include special guarantees. E.g., the Trusted Shops certificate includes a money-back guarantee free of charge for the consumer, provided by Gerling, one of the leading industrial insurers worldwide. Extensive tests are performed to ensure that the criteria demanded by consumer protection organisations are fulfilled *(http://www.trustedshops.de)*. Thus developing and maintaining consumer trust is easier if guarantee policies are combined with certificates of independent trusted third parties.

In an agency-theoretical perspective **reputation** is the third instrument a business firm can use to encourage trustworthiness in transactions. Through a reputation for non-opportunistic, trustworthy behaviour it is possible to reduce transaction costs. Opportunistic actions within a certain market might yield short-term benefits, but there would be a long-term cost in the sense of a lack of trust that might inhibit future acquisitions of cost-reducing and/or quality-enhancing assets (Hill 1990, cit. in Hosmer 1995, p. 386). Reputation is the result of trustworthy behaviour and plays an important part in determining the willingness of others to enter into an exchange with a given actor. Reputation serves both as a source of information that can reduce uncertainty and guide the decision of whether to trust the other party and as a potential source of sanctions. If acquiring a bad reputation has a damaging effect, the existence of shared reputations serves as an incentive for the trustee to be trustworthy and thus presents a "safety good" in a transaction relationship. The higher the reputation, the greater the loss in case of unfavourable behaviour and the more certain the trustor can be that the company will not act opportunistically. In electronic marketplaces there are new challenges to managing reputation policies, mostly because of the ease of changing identities and the extremely low costs of collecting and distributing information online (Kollock 1999).

There are two different conditions for online retailers to develop their reputation policies. Retailers, who use the Internet as an additional distribution channel have to consider the effects of the Web presentation on existing customer relationships. Multi-channel retailers can take advantage of their good reputation, references or image transfers from real-world brands. Thus retailers, who already have acquired a good reputation in traditional markets can profit from transfer effects when addressing new customers via the Internet. Compared with this, online retailers in a „newcomer-situation" have to compensate for their lack of good reputation by investing in trust developing measures and signalling activities (Schade and Schott 1993, p. 500). Newcomers in electronic markets can cooperate with partners who already have a good reputation, e.g. by participating in an electronic marketplace that is coordinated by a prestigious operator. Another Internet-specific strategy to acquire good reputation is to set up and organize a virtual community that is closely related to the company's product. Communities offer the online retailer a valuable resource for promoting user trust as well as adding value to the site and the products it sells through providing reviews, overviews, hints and tips, buying advice, etc. In virtual communities relationships between Internet users develop, as they interact in a way that is very similar to mouth-to-mouth communication and in this way create the foundation for reliable communication (Weiber and Meyer 2000, p. 282).

The situation in which online-transactions take place requires that internet companies focus on measures and policies to build and maintain consumer trust. However, trust is a complex and dynamic phenomenon that can not simply be "produced" by applying adequate instruments. Expectations and actions based on trust result from a delicate, situational interplay of different factors. The effect of the measures to develop and maintain trust in e-commerce is increased or decreased by several other – person-specific and situational – factors that can not be controlled by the online retailer. Person-specific factors comprise e.g. personality traits and behaviour patterns that interact with the individual willingness to trust. Contextual factors such as technology and legal norms related to e-commerce also play an important role for the development of trust and – with the exception of the company's website – cannot be controlled by the online retailer.

V. Conclusion

Analysing trust in the context of electronic commerce cannot deal with all aspects of this complex phenomenon, but can only touch on a subset of possible complexities. Starting from a functional perspective trust was seen as distinct but potentially coexisting mechanism for reducing the uncertainty and complexity of transactions and relationships in electronic markets. Using an "economic" model of trust the importance of trust was analysed based on considerations of economic benefits and an efficient use of the trust mechanism in e-commerce transactions was discussed. Both emotional and moral components of trust were faded out for the sake of a clear line of argumentation. Although the analysis of trust problems raises several ethical questions, moral aspects of trust were only discussed implicitly. Nevertheless, the contribution of an economic approach to the analysis of ethical problems also turns up in a functional model of trust. Moral intentions can be substituted by economic incentives that should be designed in a way that even opportunistic actors will try to behave in a socially desirable manner (Ripperger 1998, p. 68).

Because in the near future consumer trust will remain the decisive factor for success or failure of e-commerce, it is very important for Internet companies to act in a way that engenders consumers' trust. Efforts to increase the security of e-commerce systems and trustworthy behaviour of online-retailers will prove to be of advantage for both consumers and companies engaging in e-commerce.

References

BHATTACHARYA, R.; DEVINNEY, T. M.: "A formal model of trust based on outcomes", *Academy of Management Review*, 23 (1998), 3, pp. 459-474.

BRIELMAIER, A.; DILLER, H.: "Die Organisation internationaler Vertriebsaktivitäten. Problemfelder, Einflußfaktoren und Lösungsansätze aus der Sicht der Transaktionskostentheorie", in: K. P. KAAS (Ed.): *Kontrakte, Geschäftsbeziehungen, Netzwerke – Marketing und Neue Institutionenökonomik, Schmalenbachs Zeitschrift für betriebswirtschaftliche Forschung – zfbf,* Sonderheft 35 (1995), pp. 205-222.

CHESKIN RESEARCH / STUDIO ARCHETYPE / SAPIENT: "*eCommerce Trust Study*" (electronic publication 1999), URL: *http://www.studioarchetype.com/cheskin*, last access: 15 Feb. 2001.

DARBY, M. R.; KARNI, E.: "Free Competition and the Optimal Amount of Fraud", *The Journal of Law and Economics*, 16 (1973), pp. 67-88.

EINWILLER, S.; GEISSLER, U.; WILL, M.: "Engendering Trust in Internet Businesses using Elements of Corporate Branding", in: H. M. CHUNG (Ed.): *Proceedings of the 2000 Americas Conference on Information Systems*, Long Beach, CA (AMCIS) 2000, pp. 733-739.

EINWILLER, S.; WILL, M.: "The Role of Reputation to Engender Trust in Electronic Markets", in: *Proceedings of the 5th International Conference on Corporate Reputation, Identity, and Competitiveness*, Paris, May 2001.

FROOMKIN, M. A.: "*The essential role of trusted third parties in electronic commerce*" (1996), URL: *http://www.law.miami.edu/~froomkin/articles/trusted1.htm*, last access: 15 Feb. 2001.

GRANOVETTER, M. S.: "Economic action and social structure", *American Journal of Sociology*, 91 (1985), pp. 481-510.

HIRSHLEIFER, J.; RILEY, J. G.: "The analytics of uncertainty and information: An expository survey", *Journal of Economic Literature*, 17 (1979), pp. 1374-1421.

HOFFMAN, D. L.; NOVAK, T. P.; PERALTA, M.: "Building Consumer Trust Online", *Communications of the ACM*, 42 (1998), pp. 80-85.

HOSMER, L. T.: "Trust: The connecting link between organizational theory and philosophical ethics", *Academy of Management Review*, 20 (1995), 2, pp. 379-403.

HUSTED, B. W.: "The ethical limits of trust in business relations", *Business Ethics Quarterly*, 8 (1998), 2, pp. 233-248.

KOLLOCK, P.: "*The Production of Trust in Online Marktes*", 1999, URL: *http://www.sscnet.ucla.edu/soc/faculty/kollock/papers/online_trust.htm*, last access: 16 Mar. 2001.

LEWICKY, R. J.; BUNKER, B.: "Trust in relationships: A model of trust development and decline", in: B. BUNKER, J. RUBIN (Eds.): *Conflict, cooperation and justice*, Jossey-Bass, San Francisco 1995, pp. 133-173.

LUHMANN, N.: *Vertrauen. Ein Mechanismus der Reduktion sozialer Komplexität*, 3rd edition, Stuttgart (Enke) 1989.

MEVENKAMP, A.; KERNER, M.: "Akzeptanzorientierte Gestaltung von WWW-Informationsangeboten", in: W. FRITZ (Ed.): *Internet-Marketing. Perspektiven und Erfahrungen aus Deutschland und den USA*, Stuttgart (Schäffer-Poeschel) 1999, pp. 217-257.

MISZTAL, B. A.: *Trust in Modern Societies*, Cambridge (Polity Press) 1996.

RIPPERGER, T.: *Ökonomik des Vertrauens. Analyse eines Organisationsprinzips*, Tübingen (Mohr Siebeck) 1998.

ROUSSEAU, D. M.; SITKIN, S. B.: "Not so different after all: A cross-discipline view of trust", *Academy of Management Review*, 23 (1998), 3, pp. 393-404.

ROTTER, J.: "Generalized expectancies for interpersonal trust", *American Psychologist*, 26 (1971), pp. 443-452.

SCHADE, C.; SCHOTT, E.: "Instrumente des Kontraktgütermarketing", *Die Betriebswirtschaft*, 53 (1993), pp. 491-511.

SPREMANN, K.: "Agent and Principal", in: G. BAMBERG, K. SPREMANN (Eds.): *Agency Theory, Information, and Incentives*, Berlin (Springer) 1987, pp. 3-37.

SPREMANN, K.: „Reputation, Garantie, Information", *Zeitschrift für Betriebswirtschaft – ZfB*, 58 (1988), 5/6, pp. 613-629.

WEIBER, R.; ADLER, J.: "Der Einsatz von Unsicherheitsreduktionsstrategien im Kaufprozeß: Eine informationsökonomische Analyse", in: K. P. KAAS (Ed.): *Kontrakte, Geschäftsbeziehungen, Netzwerke – Marketing und Neue Institutionenökonomik, Schmalenbachs Zeitschrift für betriebswirtschaftliche Forschung – zfbf*, Sonderheft 35 (1995a), pp. 61-77.

WEIBER, R.; ADLER, J.: „Informationsökonomisch begründete Typologisierung von Kaufprozessen", *Schmalenbachs Zeitschrift für betriebswirtschaftliche Forschung – zfbf*, 47 (1995b), 1, pp. 43-65.

WEIBER, R.; MEYER, J.: "Virtual Communities", in: R. WEIBER (Ed.): *Handbuch Electronic Business. Informationstechnologien – Electronic Commerce – Geschäftsprozesse*, Wiesbaden (Gabler) 2000, pp. 277-295.

WILLIAMSON, O. E.: "Calculativeness, trust and economic organization", *Journal of Law and Economics*, 30 (1993), pp. 131-145.

WINAND, U.; POHL, W.: "Die Vertrauensproblematik in elektronischen Netzwerken", in: J. LINK (Ed.): *Wettbewerbsvorteile durch Online Marketing. Die strategischen Perspektiven elektronischer Märkte*, 2nd edition, Berlin et al. (Springer) 2000, pp. 261-277.

ZUCKER, L. G.: "Production of Trust: Institutional Sources of Economic Structure, 1840–1920", *Research in Organizational Behavior*, 8 (1986), pp. 53-111.

List of Authors

PROF. DR. HENRI-CLAUDE DE BETTIGNIES

is Professor of Asian Business at INSEAD, Fontainebleau, France, and Visiting Professor at Stanford University, Stanford, California, USA.
E-mail: hc.debettignies@insead.edu

ANASTASIA CORTES

is a doctoral candidate in the Management Department of the Pamplin College of Business, Virginia Tech, Blacksburg, Virginia, USA.
E-mail: acortes@vt.edu

DR. MICHAEL EHRET

is Assistant Professor of Business Administration, Institute of Marketing, Freie Universität Berlin, Berlin, Germany.
E-mail: michael.ehret@wiwiss.fu-berlin.de

DR. SONJA GRABNER-KRÄUTER

is Associate Professor of Marketing and International Management, University of Klagenfurt, Klagenfurt, Austria.
E-mail: Sonja.grabner@uni-klu.ac.at

DR. ANDREAS GREIS

is member of the editorial staff of the journal "forum medienethik", Tübingen, Germany.
E-mail: andreas.greis@web.de

PD DR. MICHAELA HAASE

is Associate Professor of Business Administration, Institute of Marketing, Freie Universität Berlin, Berlin, Germany.
E-mail: mhaase@wiwiss.fu-berlin.de

LIST OF AUTHORS

PROF. DR. CHRISTOPH HUBIG
is Professor of Philosophy, Institute for Philosophy, Dept. of the Theory of Science and Philosophy of Technology, University of Stuttgart, and Vice Rector for Structure/Controlling of the University of Stuttgart, Stuttgart, Germany.
E-mail: wttp@gmx.de

DR. MARK HUNTER
is a Senior Research Fellow at INSEAD, Fontainebleau, France.
E-mail: mark.hunter@insead.edu

MARTIN KALUZA M.A.
is doctorate student, Institute of Philosophy, Freie Universität Berlin, Berlin, Germany.
E-mail: mail@martinkaluza.com

DR. DIETER KLUMPP
is Managing Director of the Alcatel SEL Foundation for Communication Research and Director of the Department "Technology and Society", Alcatel SEL AG, Stuttgart.
E-mail: d.klumpp@alcatel.de

PROF. DR. DR. H.C. PETER KOSLOWSKI
is Professor of Philosophy and Philosophy of Management, Free University Amsterdam, Amsterdam, Netherlands, and Fellow, International Center for Economic Research (ICER), Turin, Italy. He is Chair, Committee on Business Ethics, German Philosophical Association.
E-mail: Peter.Koslowski@t-online.de

DR. MARC LE MENSTREL
is Assistant Professor at the University Pompeu Fabra, Barcelona, Spain.
E-mail: marc.lemenestrel@econ.upf.es

DR. MICHAEL NEUNER
is Assistant Professor of Economics at the Transatlantik-Institut, Ludwigshafen University of Applied Sciences, Ludwigshafen am Rhein, Germany.
E-mail: michael.neuner@fh-lu.de

LIST OF AUTHORS

ULRICH RIEHM

is a researcher at Karlsruhe Research Centre, Institute for Technology Assessment and Systems Analysis (ITAS), Karlsruhe, Germany.
E-mail: riehm@itas.fzk.de

DR. ROBERT VAN ES

is Lecturer in Organizational Philosophy at the University of Amsterdam, Amsterdam, Netherlands, and Consultant in Organizational Culture and Ethics.
E-mail: rob@vanSvision.nl

PROF. DR. PAUL WHYSALL

is Professor of Retailing at Nottingham Business School, Nottingham Trent University (UK).
E-mail: paul.whysall@ntu.ac.uk

ULI ZAPPE

works in the fields of philosophy, film/theatre, music and free software. He lives in the environs of Frankfurt am Main, Germany.
E-mail: uli@ritual.org

Index of Names

Page numbers in italics refer to quotations in footnotes or references

Studies in Economic Ethics and Philosophy

P. Koslowski (Ed.)
Ethics in Economics, Business, and Economic Policy
X, 178 pages. 1992
ISBN 3-540-55359-2 (out of print)

P. Koslowski and Y. Shionoya (Eds.)
The Good and the Economical: Ethical Choices in Economics and Management
X, 202 pages. 1993.
ISBN 3-540-57339-9 (out of print)

H. De Geer (Ed.)
Business Ethics in Progress?
IX, 124 pages. 1994
ISBN 3-540-57758-0

P. Koslowski (Ed.)
The Theory of Ethical Economy in the Historical School
XI, 343 pages. 1995
ISBN 3-540-59070-6

A. Argandoña (Ed.)
The Ethical Dimension of Financial Institutions and Markets
XI, 263 pages. 1995
ISBN 3-540-59209-1 (out of print)

G. K. Becker (Ed.)
Ethics in Business and Society
Chinese and Western Perspectives
VIII, 233 pages. 1996
ISBN 3-540-60773-0

P. Koslowski (Ed.)
Ethics of Capitalism and Critique of Sociobiology. Two Essays with a Comment by James M. Buchanan
IX, 142 pages. 1996
ISBN 3-540-61035-0

F. Neil Brady (Ed.)
Ethical Universals in International Business
X, 246 pages. 1996
ISBN 3-540-61588-1

P. Koslowski and A. Føllesdal (Eds.)
Restructuring the Welfare State.
Theory and Reform of Social Policy
VII, 402 pages. 1997
ISBN 3-540-62035-4 (out of print)

G. Erreygers and T. Vandevelde (Eds.)
Is Inheritance Legitimate?
Ethical and Economic Aspects of Wealth Transfer
X, 236 pages. 1997
ISBN 3-540-62725-1

P. Koslowski (Ed.)
Business Ethics in East Central Europe
XII, 151 pages. 1997
ISBN 3-540-63367-7

P. Koslowski (Ed.)
Methodology of the Social Sciences, Ethics, and Economics in the Newer Historical School.
From Max Weber and Rickert to Sombart and Rothacker
XII, 565 pages. 1997
ISBN 3-540-63458-4

A. Føllesdal and P. Koslowski (Eds.)
Democracy and the European Union
X, 309 pages. 1998
ISBN 3-540-63457-6

P. Koslowski (Ed.)
The Social Market Economy.
Theory and Ethics of the Economic Order
XII, 360 pages. 1998
ISBN 3-540-64043-6

Amitai Etzioni
Essays in Socio-Economics
XII, 182 pages. 1999
ISBN 3-540-64466-0

P. Koslowski (Ed.)
Sociobiology and Bioeconomics.
The Theory of Evolution in Biological and Economic Theory
X, 341 pages. 1999
ISBN 3-540-65380-5

Studies in Economic Ethics and Philosophy

J. Kuçuradi (Ed.)
The Ethics of the Professions:
Medicine, Business, Media, Law
X, 172 pages. 1999
ISBN 3-540-65726-6

S. K. Chakraborty and S. R. Chatterjee (Eds.)
Applied Ethics in Management.
Towards New Perspectives
X, 298 pages. 1999
ISBN 3-540-65724-X

P. Koslowski (Ed.)
The Theory of Capitalism
in the German Economic Tradition.
Historism, Ordo-Liberalism, Critical Theory,
Solidarism
XII, 577 pages. 2000.
ISBN 3-540-66674-5

P. Koslowski (Ed.)
Contemporary Economic Ethics
and Business Ethics
IX, 265pages. 2000
ISBN 3-540-66665-6

L. Sacconi
The Social Contract of the Firm.
Economics, Ethics and Organisation
XV, 229 pages. 2000
ISBN 3-540-67219-2

M. Casson and A. Godley (Eds.)
Cultural Factors in Economic Growth
VIII, 244 pages. 2001
ISBN 3-540-66293-6

Y. Shionoya and K. Yagi (Eds.)
Competition, Trust, and Cooperation
IX, 252 pages. 2001
ISBN 3-540-67870-0

B. Hodgson
Economics as Moral Science
XIV, 380 pages. 2001
ISBN 3-540-41062-7

A. Labrousse and J.-D. Weisz (Eds.)
Institutional Economics in France and Germany.
German Ordoliberalsm versus
the French Regulation School
IX, 384 pages. 2001
ISBN 3-540-67855-7

F. Vandenbroucke
Social Justice and Individual Ethics
in an Open Society.
Equality, Responsibility, and Incentives
XIII, 305 pages. 2001
ISBN 3-540-41636-6

G. Brennan, H. Kliemt and R. D. Tollison (Eds.)
Method and Morals
in Constitutional Economics.
Essays in Honor of James M. Buchanan
XVI, 571 pages. 2002
ISBN 3-540-41970-5

H. H. Nau and B. Schefold (Eds.)
The Historicity of Economics.
Continuities and Discontinuities
of Histrical Thought
in 19th and 20th Century Economics
X, 245 pages. 2002
ISBN 3-540-42765-1

J. Wieland
Standards and Audits
for Ethics Management Systems
VIII, 253 pages. 2003
ISBN 3-540-40206-3

MIX
Papier aus verantwortungsvollen Quellen
Paper from responsible sources
FSC® C105338

If you have any concerns about our products,
you can contact us on
ProductSafety@springernature.com

In case Publisher is established outside the EU,
the EU authorized representative is:
Springer Nature Customer Service Center GmbH
Europaplatz 3, 69115 Heidelberg, Germany

Printed by Libri Plureos GmbH
in Hamburg, Germany